The TV Crime Drama

TV Genres

Series Editors
Deborah Jermyn, University of Roehampton
Su Holmes, University of East Anglia (UEA)

Titles in the series include:

The Quiz Show
by Su Holmes
978 0 7486 2752 3 (hardback)
978 0 7486 2753 0 (paperback)

The Sitcom
by Brett Mills
978 0 7486 3751 5 (hardback)
978 0 7486 3752 2 (paperback)

Reality TV
by Misha Kavka
978 0 7486 37212 5 (hardback)
978 0 7486 3723 2 (paperback)

The TV Crime Drama
by Sue Turnbull
978 0 7486 4088 1 (hardback)
978 0 7486 4087 4 (paperback)

Forthcoming titles include:

Animation
by Nichola Dobson and Paul Ward

www.euppublishing.com/series/edtv

The TV Crime Drama

Sue Turnbull

EDINBURGH
University Press

Edinburgh University Press Ltd
The Tun – Holyrood Road
12 (2f) Jackson's Entry
Edinburgh EH8 8PJ
www.euppublishing.com

Typeset in Janson and Neue Helvetica by
Servis Filmsetting Ltd, Stockport, Cheshire and
printed and bound in the United States of America

A CIP record for this book is available from the British Library

ISBN 978 0 7486 4088 1 (hardback)
ISBN 978 0 7486 4087 4 (paperback)
ISBN 978 0 7486 7818 1 (webready PDF)
ISBN 978 0 7486 7820 4 (epub)

Contents

List of Figures

Acknowledgements

Heartfelt thanks to the series editors, Su Holmes (University of East Anglia (UEA)) and Deborah Jermyn (University of Roehampton), for their patience during what proved to be a turbulent time on both the work and home fronts. Their astute comments, guidance, and encouragement have been much appreciated. Special thanks also to the University of Wollongong in New South Wales (NSW) in Australia and to my colleagues for supporting and encouraging this project in its latter stages, especially Wenche Ommundsen, Vera Mackie, Mark McLelland, and the always enthusiastic Glenn Mitchell. Thanks also to Nick McGhie for last-minute technical help and to Deborah Taylor for wrangling the stills. On the home front, thanks to Richard and Will Thompson for the provision of DVDs, viewing companionship, suggestions, scholarship, and support. Sorry about *Rockford*. All errors are entirely my own.

Introduction: Promiscuous Hybrids

Writing in the arts section of *The Sydney Morning Herald* (*SMH*) in February 2011, TV columnist David Dale reported that according to the ratings figures for Australia, on the previous Sunday night (27 February) almost a third of the Australian population had watched a crime drama on television (Dale 2011). Setting aside the limitations of the ratings data as a measure of audience involvement in the contents of what is aired and/or attention to the screen, Dale proceeded to demonstrate how the free-to-air television schedule in Australia was 'packed to the rafters' with crime and punishment. Of the nineteen shows he listed that were concerned with crime and punishment, thirteen had been produced in America, four were from the United Kingdom, and only two had been produced in Australia. The shows on offer that night included a diverse range of television crime drama, from the forensic-inclined (and humorous) American series *Bones* (Fox, 2005–), loosely based on the crime novels of American forensic anthropologist turned crime writer Kathy Reichs, to the British 'cosy' mystery drama *Midsomer Murders* (ITV, 1997–), as well as the hit Australian 'true-crime' drama series, *The Underbelly Files* (Nine Network, 2008–) based on tales that are drawn from the Australian criminal underworld.

Not discussed by Dale, but also a regular part of the Australian TV schedule, were the subtitled crime dramas routinely appearing on one of two publicly owned networks, the Special Broadcasting Service (SBS), with its remit to reflect Australia's cultural diversity (Ang et al. 2008). Shows to be regularly found on SBS include *Kommissar Rex* (ORF, 1994–2004, RAI, 2008–), concerning a loveable Austrian canine sleuth, and a swag of Scandinavian shows from *The Eagle* (DR, 2004–6) to the Swedish versions of the Inspector Wallander series of crime novels by Henning Mankell (TV4, 2005–). Nor did Dale mention the range of crime dramas past and present available on the pay TV networks, including dedicated channels like Fox Crime and

Universal's 13th Street, which deliver a mix of crime drama and reality crime, or the possibility that people may be watching a crime series on DVD, or downloaded from the Internet. Free-to-air television, while still (at the time of writing) the most popular way to access television content in Australia, has many competitors. Far from *over*-estimating the amount of crime being consumed that Sunday night, it is tempting to suggest that Dale may well have *under*-estimated the consumption of these popular shows.

Dale had a theory about the popularity of the television crime drama. He attributed the attractiveness of the genre to the comfort factor, proposing that in a turbulent world everything feels beyond our control, except the remote control. We, therefore, in his opinion, turn to television for escape 'to the English midlands, the streets of Washington, the beaches of Miami, the carriages of the Orient Express . . . for reassurance that any problem can be solved in one hour' (Dale 2011). In arriving at this too-neat conclusion, Dale appears to assume that all television crime dramas follow the same structure and perform the same function for their audiences, a suggestion that this book will question as it traces the development of what has become one of the most enduring and diverse genres of television. Far from being all about reassurance, the television crime drama has often played a critical role in bringing current social issues and anxieties into the public domain, thereby unsettling what may once have been taken-for-granted assumptions about law and order. And far from the convenience of solving the problem in one hour, television crime drama may now take many hours to solve a crime without ever being able to find a solution to the social issue it represents.

In undertaking the task of outlining the parameters of this genre, I admit that I am almost as old as television crime drama itself. Indeed, I began watching TV crime long before I became an academic with a professional interest in studying the media. While I well remember watching *Dixon of Dock Green* (BBC, 1955–76) on a Saturday night from the comfort of my father's lap when living in the North East of England during the 1950s, my 'appointment' television today may include watching the latest British crime drama series on a Friday night on the ABC (that is the first established public broadcasting network in Australia with a long history of association with the BBC), or watching the Danish-Swedish crime series *The Bridge* (DR1, SV1, 2011–) on SBS or the American series *The Wire* (HBO, 2002–8) on a DVD box set or revisiting such vintage crime as *Johnny Staccato* (NBC, 1959–60) or *The Sweeney* (ITV, 1975–8).

Over the last fifty years, I have routinely tuned into television crime drama in order to be 'entertained' – an imprecise term that could encompass distraction and amusement but also a vast range of other kinds of engagement with the people, places, and problems represented. Indeed, switching on the television to watch an inevitably gloomy series such as the Swedish or British co-productions of Inspector Wallander may hardly be thought to be 'entertaining' in any conventional way. And, to be honest, sometimes I'm just not in the mood for such bleakness and will flick over to a 'lighter' kind of show, although, as this book will make clear, any crime drama may switch from comedy to something much darker and vice versa in the blink of an eye. This variation in tone, often in the space of a single episode and sometimes in the space of a scene, renders sweeping statements even about specific television series problematic, especially when this may involve a plethora of different writers and directors over an entire run.

Unlike Dale, I don't think that the genre of crime drama in all its diversity has ever operated within a predictable or narrow set of parameters, as it has developed in different times and in different production contexts, not only the United Kingdom and the United States, but all around the world. The primary focus of this book will be the Anglophone world with an emphasis on the crime drama series as it has evolved on British and American television because these are the shows with which most people who have access to the medium of television across the world will be familiar. Although, with the international circulation of such Scandinavian series as *The Killing* (Danish: *Forbrydelsen*) (DR1, 2007–) and *The Bridge* (Danish: *Broen/* Swedish: *Bron*) (DR1, SVT1, 2011–) or the series of films beginning with *The Girl with the Dragon Tattoo* (2009), also released as a six-part television series, based on the best-selling crime books of the late Stieg Larsson, this situation is clearly changing. The transnational trade in crime drama has never been more vigorous. However, I apologise in advance to readers from elsewhere (especially Australia, New Zealand, and Canada) since I know that the development of the crime drama in other regions has its own specific trajectory and history.

For the last twenty-eight years, I have been living in Australia, which imports a great deal of American and British crime dramas while often struggling to maintain a quota of 55 per cent locally produced content during what counts as 'prime-time' TV (as mandated by the Australian Communication and Media Authority and the current Australian Content Standard, which has been in place since 2005). *Homicide*, Australia's first home-grown drama series, did not appear on screens until 1964 but was greeted with much enthusiasm as people responded to the location shooting in and around the city of Melbourne.[1] In terms of style, the series was an interesting amalgam of the American and the British crime drama of the time while insisting on its Australian location, accents, and cultural context: a kind of cultural hybridity that has continued to the present day in Australian drama production more generally. One of the key stylistic influences on the first season of the Australian true-crime series *Underbelly*, which premiered on Channel Nine in 2008, was the American HBO series *The Sopranos*, which had already been a ratings success for the channel.[2]

Defining genre

In a series of scholarly books devoted to the discussion and delineation of television genres, it seems apposite to begin by discussing just how the term 'genre' may be applied to the crime drama series as it has evolved. 'Genre' is a French word meaning 'type' or 'kind', and has played an important role in the study of literature, art, and other media forms such as film and television (Neale 2001: 1). One type of film that has been subjected to a great deal of genre analysis is the Western, largely on the basis of the iconography (particular visual symbols, images, and modes of representation), although the limitations of this approach were revealed as the Western, and thinking about the Western, continued to evolve and diversify. Genres, as has often been argued, are notoriously hard to pin down, and for good reason since they are constantly mutating, as producers seek to offer their audience something agreeably familiar but simultaneously new and surprising. Genres thus offer 'horizons of expectation' (Jauss cited in Neale 1980: 20), suggesting to the viewer that what they are about to see is likely to conform to a framework with which they are already familiar but that may also exceed that expectation and surprise them, simultaneously stretching in the process the always permeable boundaries of the genre.

While a Western may be instantly recognisable because of its iconic features (for example, the landscape, the characters, the horses, and the guns), in developing a theory of genre that may apply to the medium of television, Jason Mittell (2004) has warned against a purely textual approach, suggesting that the attribution of genre does not always depend on what we see on the screen. Instead, it may be better to think of genre as a system of categorisation that has to do with a range of other factors, including the operations of the media industries, the production and policy context, the scheduling practices, the audience, the reviewers, and the critics (Mittell 2004: xii).

For example, in Australia it became commonplace during the early years of the twenty-first century to talk about 'Friday night crime' on the ABC, which regularly presented a raft of British crime drama shows from 8.30pm to 11.30pm on Fridays. The particular shows included *Silent Witness* (BBC One, 1996–), a series that focuses on crime through the lens of forensics, *New Tricks* (BBC One, 2003–) a comedy/crime drama dealing with 'cold cases' (unsolved investigations that remain open pending the discovery of evidence), and *Hustle* (BBC One, 2004–12), a show depicting a troupe of con men and women who out-con the cons. The programming practices of the Australian public broadcasting service, and the critical discourse of the television reviewers in the TV schedules, 'tell' the audience that these three quite diverse shows all belong to the same category: the crime drama. And yet, as anyone who watches them would know, the shows are quite different in terms of their content, form, style, tone, and affect, even if they were all produced in the United Kingdom by the BBC and may be grouped together under the label of 'British crime dramas' with the specific set of connotations that that label carries.

As Mittell demonstrates, there are many other ways of attributing a generic label to a TV drama, including the operations of the profession or workplace that it depicts, as in the case of the medical, legal, or courtroom drama (Mittell 2004: 8). As such, there are crime drama shows that are clearly identified in relation to the type of work involved, such as the police procedural (*The Bill*, ITV, 1984–2010), the conducting of a forensic investigation (*CSI*, CBS, 2000–), or the practising of criminal profiling (*Criminal Minds*, CBS, 2005–). It is also very common to label a crime drama according to the role of the primary investigator or hero, as is revealed by a popular publication entitled *The Best of Crime and Detective TV* produced in 1988 (Collins and Javna 1988). Here the crime shows are categorised in terms of the type of sleuth as well as the 'mode'. Generic distinctions include not only the police procedural but also the private eyes, the amateur sleuths, and the comedy crime fighters as well as brief sections devoted to such problematic categories as 'ethnic' and 'literary' detectives.

In *The Television Genre Book* (Creeber 2001), Lez Cooke discusses a sweep of crime dramas ranging from *Dixon of Dock Green* to *The Cops* (BBC Two, 1998), under the heading of 'The Police Series', noting that there may be a considerable overlap with the shows labelled as 'Action Series' that appear within the same volume (Cooke 2001: 19). And indeed there is, since it is under the latter heading that we find a description of the British crime drama *The Sweeney*, a show concerned with the operations of the elite Flying Squad (a branch of the Specialist Crime & Operations Section) within London's Metropolitan Police Service. Toby Miller defines this latter show as an action series because, he argues, the focus is on action rather than character (Miller 2001: 17) – a proposition that will be questioned later in this book when it will be argued that *The Sweeney* also offered both character development and comedy. As for the police series, Cooke suggests that what these shows have in common is a 'basic formula in which society is protected and the status quo maintained by the forces of law and order' (Cooke 2001: 19), a proposition that will also be challenged later in this book in relation to such diverse television shows as the controversial British series *Law & Order* (BBC One, 1978) and more recently, *The Wire* (HBO, 2002–8). Thus, on the one hand, we have a genre defined by what we see on the screen (the action), and, on the other, by its perceived formula.

Yet another way of ascribing genre may depend on the intended audience and the particular affect that the show may be presumed to have on them. Thus a 'teen drama' is so-called because of its imagined address to a teen audience, or a comedy show is labelled as such because of the laughter it is intended or presumed to provoke. However, as Brett Mills (2009) demonstrates in his discussion of the situation comedy (sitcom) as a genre, identifying a show as a comedy on the basis of the affect that is presumed to have on its audience becomes problematic when audiences do not find shows labelled as 'comedies' to be funny. A key example here would be the British series *The Office* (BBC Two, 2001–3), which many viewers found to be more cringe-worthy than laugh-worthy, yet the show continued to be described as a comedy and acclaimed as such.

In terms of television crime drama and its affect, we may designate the 'thriller' as a sub-genre of crime that, like a comedy, depends on an audience experience of sustained anxiety and/or excitement. David Glover describes the structure of the literary thriller, the precursor of both the film and television thriller, as a text that persistently seeks 'to raise the stakes of the narrative, heightening or exaggerating the experience of events by transforming them into a rising curve of danger, violence or shock' (Glover 2003: 137). The thriller, Glover suggests, thus often deals with international conspiracies, invasions, and wholesale corruption – as well as serial killers who may threaten entire cities or even nations (Glover 2003: 138). This definition accords well with the structure of the American television series *24* (Fox, 2001–10) in which the threat to counter-terrorist Jack Bauer's self, family, and nation is a constant theme over each 24-hour period as the action unfolds in 'real time' until the spectacular climax. A thriller is thus organised very differently from a 'mystery' in which a crime is committed (on- or off-screen) and our attention is directed towards the investigation. What is interesting here is that, in generic terms, both the thriller and the mystery are to some extent defined by their narrative structure. What they have in common is a crime. However, the point at which that crime occurs in the narrative, the particular kind of crime that it is, who commits it, and who investigates it, makes all the difference.

In the 1970s, the Russian formalist critic Tzvetan Todorov proposed a structuralist analysis of the classic detective story, suggesting that in every story of detection there are two narratives – one delineating the progress of the investigation that moves forward in time, and the other the story of the crime that has already happened (Todorov 1977). While this 'double narrative' can be identified in many stories of detection on television, especially those that employ a flashback technique to return to the crimes of the past, there are many other kinds of narrative structure apparent in television crime drama. These include the thriller, in which the crime may be still in progress, to those shows where the crime and the perpetrator are made known at an early point but 'why' the crime was committed constitutes the mystery that must be solved.

It is also quite usual to describe a crime show as British, American, or Scandinavian with the implication that shows labelled as such will have something in common based on their point of origin. Given the ongoing transnational trade in representations of crime, which began well before the arrival of the television set, it may be important to ask just how, for example, a British television crime drama may differ from an American or Scandinavian crime drama, once we get past the obvious differences in accents and scenery. Are there, for instance, fundamental differences in the structure, content, and/or style of these shows? Just to confuse the issue, is it possible to have an American-style crime drama produced in Britain? Or a British-style crime drama produced in the United States? Writing from the context of Australia, where home-grown television crime drama has developed in a dialogue with both the British and American models, the question of how original and how culturally distinctive an Australian crime drama may be has been an ongoing matter for debate in both academic and popular commentary.

To complicate matters even further, it is not unusual for a television crime drama to straddle a number of different genres, resulting in some interesting new hybrids. Thus, we may encounter a comically inflected cold-case crime drama such as *New Tricks*, or the teen crime drama *Veronica Mars* (UPN, 2004–6, The CW, 2006–7). There is even the occasional musical crime drama, such as *Blackpool* (BBC One, 2004) and the short-lived *Cop Rock* (ABC, 1990), while the much feted *The Singing Detective* (BBC One, 1986) has been routinely assigned to the category of 'quality drama', a genre that may well be defined by its perceived audience demographic rather than its content or particular form.

As Mittell suggests, in order to grasp what a particular genre may encompass, it is advisable to regard any television genre as an unstable category derived from clusters of cultural assumptions that are constantly evolving (Mittell 2004: xiv). Graeme Turner's phrase 'promiscuous hybridity' is therefore particularly apt for the genre of television crime, which has always borrowed and blurred generic categories (Turner 2001: 7). While at its core the television crime drama is concerned with crime, this theme may be developed in many different ways, drawing on an extensive repertoire of narrative possibilities that have developed over time. One strategy in delineating the emergence of a genre is therefore to take what Mittell describes as a 'genealogical approach', noting the specific cultural moments and production contexts within which the particular forms and variations of the genre in question have appeared (Mittell 2004: 30).

This is the approach adopted here, given that the television crime drama has multiple points of origin that have played, and continue to play, a key role in its evolution. As will be demonstrated, the television crime drama is a multifarious genre that continues to oscillate between competing impulses and demands.

Such competing impulses may include the desire to document crime as a social problem in order to educate and inform the public as opposed to a desire to distract and entertain: the preferred option then having implications for the 'style' of the show. Although it may be assumed that the desire to educate and the desire to entertain are antithetical impulses, it is possible for them to happily co-exist in the same show, as in the original version of *CSI* (CBS, 2000–) (see Figure 1.1), which has often been credited with (accused of) teaching its global audiences about forensic methods while also providing highly engaging popular entertainment. In this case, as in many others, while the desire to entertain is associated with a stylistically excessive, often sensational and melodramatic treatment, the desire for 'mimesis' is associated with a more sombre, social realist, documentary approach. What is particularly interesting about these competing impulses is the criterion of value that has become attached to these terms so that a

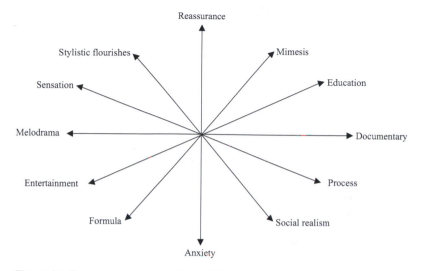

Figure I.1 The competing impulses of television crime drama.

'gritty, realist, crime drama' adopting a quasi-documentary approach in its bid for authenticity may be rated more highly than a crime drama that opts for stylistic excess and/or the reassurance of the formulaic. The desire for authenticity, however, may well come at a price. As John Cawelti points out, the further a genre strays from formulaic expectations and into the mimetic, mirroring the messy chaos of life, the more challenging and possibly more confronting it may be, with a possible result that members of the audience simply switch off (Cawelti 1976: 9–10). At which point it should be noted that it is possible to argue that the function of the formulaic is to give an aesthetically pleasing shape and form to the confusing muddle of lived experience.

To be fair to television crime drama, many different art forms are formulaic, from the three-act structure of a play, the fourteen lines of a sonnet, to the three movements of a concerto. In each case, while the form may be a given, what is of interest is the way in which the artist may surprise and excite an audience by presenting them with the new and unfamiliar in a structure that is simultaneously familiar and reassuring. In this way, the use of the formula offers the reassurance of a familiar aesthetic frame within which to contemplate that that may be too off-putting in real life. In this way, while the episodic half-hour, one-hour, or movie-length episode of a television crime drama may conform to a particular formula in terms of its familiar narrative structure, including its opening titles and end credits, what happens within that aesthetic frame may be surprising or confronting or none of the above.

One of the questions that this brief overview of the crime genre raises is why certain series have been more valued within the history of the television crime drama than others. As will become apparent, those series that have been perceived as formulaic and/or supportive of the status quo have tended to be less highly regarded by critics and commentators than those that have taken a more critical stance on issues of law and order while also 'breaking the rules' of the genre. As a result, those shows that many viewers like precisely because they are reassuring in their formulaic nature have been undervalued, while those that are more unsettling and confronting have tended to have been accorded more significance by the television industry (in terms of the awards that they have garnered), the critical reception that they have received in the press, and the academic commentary that they have attracted in a range of disciplines from cultural studies to criminology. In this way, confessing to a love of the 'cosy' British crime series *Midsomer Murders* may produce a very different response from admitting to being an ardent devotee of *The Wire*.

Truth or lies?

Partly as a result of its formulaic nature, the television crime drama has often been called to account on the basis of its depiction of crime. The challenge of finding the right balance between fact, fiction, and entertainment is clearly a tricky act to pull off in a genre considered by many commentators to play such an important role in public perceptions of law and order. For some critics, especially those who approach the genre from a criminological perspective informed by statistics about the 'real' world of crime, the television crime drama is to be condemned for its distortions. For example, criminologist Ray Surette insists that the popular media is entirely responsible for a skewed perception of crime and the criminal justice system (Surette 1998: 50). 'Whatever the media show', Surette sweepingly and erroneously states, 'is the opposite of what is true' (Surette 1998: 47). Even worse, in Surette's opinion, is the presumption that these distortions have produced a perception that the world is a dangerous place inhabited by dastardly criminals motivated by self-interest but kept in check by heroic gun-toting crime fighters bent on revenge with scant attention to police procedure or the social causes of crime (Surette 1998: 470). Surette's comments highlight the tension between a perceived obligation that the media should represent crime as it 'really' is, and the impulse to 're-imagine' crime as a form of entertainment.

Writing in 1984, David Marc went so far as to characterise the television crime drama as a 'comedy of public safety': a kind of sitcom without a laugh track in which The Law is married to Chaos. 'In each episode, Chaos steps out of line, but The Law whips her back into shape before the final commercial' (Marc 1984: 69). Note that in this construction The Law is imagined as masculine and Chaos as feminine, a gender attribution that points to the problematic issue of gender and crime that will be explored in more detail in Chapter 6. According to Marc, the attraction of this 'flat formula' apparently lay in its 'ritual affirmation of the potency of law and order' in what he describes as an 'increasingly paranoid, or perhaps merely crime-conscious society' (Marc 1984: 69). Marc, therefore, perceives the television crime drama to be too neat, too tidy, and too conservative in its vision. Except, of course, that not all crime shows conform to this formulaic pattern, neither in 1984 when Marc was writing, nor now. There were crime dramas in the past, like the British crime drama *Law & Order* (BBC, 1978) and the NBC series *Hill Street Blues* (NBC, 1981–7) in which Chaos pretty much had the upper hand and the efforts of the Law to whip 'her' into shape were singularly futile. Nor was or is The Law always gendered male and Chaos female.

And yet sweeping generalisations about the television crime drama series still abound and should be avoided, since for every claim that is made about the genre, an example can be found that contradicts it. Indeed, it is hard to make any encompassing statement about the genre as a whole, or any crime series in particular, since any long-running crime drama series may have many different writers, producers, and/ or directors, each with their own vision of how the basic formula may play out as they seek to maintain the attention of the audience. A long-running show may, therefore, go through many different iterations and stages as it evolves. For example, the first season of a show may be largely experimental as the actors, writers, and directors establish the look and style of the series. Later down the track, the show may enter a baroque stage when the desire to avoid repetition results in a form of self-parody as the ideas run out and the need for difference plays out in increasingly more bizarre and desperate ways, as was perceived to be the case for the long-running British TV series *The Bill* and as will be discussed in Chapter 2.

It is often hard to find a long-running television crime drama that is entirely consistent in its vision given the collaborative nature of television production involving multiple 'creators', all eager to experiment within the given constraints to produce something original, capture the audience's attention, and/or to put their own stylistic mark on a series – although the emergence of a number of television 'auteurs', such as filmmaker David Lynch (*Twin Peaks*, ABC, 1990–1), former journalist David Simon (*The Wire*, HBO, 2002–8), or New Zealand filmmaker Jane Campion (*Top of the Lake*, Sundance, 2013) has revealed that television drama with a long-form narrative is amenable to such stylistic consistency.

Rather than judging the television crime drama in relation to some version of 'the real', it may therefore be better to ask what it may encompass at a symbolic level and the aesthetic strategies that are employed to realise this. And so instead of condemning the genre for misrepresenting reality by pointing out that in a study of American TV crime shows conducted in 1983 murder accounted for one-quarter of the crimes committed on television while the Federal Bureau of Investigation (FBI) crime index indicated that murder accounted for only one-sixth of 1 per cent of all crime committed in America (Surette 1998: 39), we may ask instead: Why does murder feature so prominently in the television crime drama? To which the response may be that as murder is typically considered to be the most heinous of crimes, the moral stakes are higher, and the drama as a consequence is more intense.

From this perspective, it is possible to construct the television crime drama as 'an opening through which the mythic intrudes upon the everyday' (Sparks 1992: 37). For Colin Sparks, the television crime drama functions as a modern morality tale: the kind of story a society tells itself in order to offer reassurance (Sparks 1992). There are, however, television crime dramas that offer little reassurance at all, and set out to demonstrate not only that the world they represent is an unsafe place but also that we cannot rely on the forces of law and order to save us, since these may be deeply flawed, corrupt, and/or incompetent, and/or hamstrung by the politics of a hopeless administration. It is therefore possible to argue that the representation of the police in the television crime drama has consistently presented opportunities for the public to debate and question police practice, both on-screen and off-screen. As John Fiske has noted, the television police genre, like all genres, has modified its inventions in a dialectical relationship with changes in social values (Fiske 1987: 222). It also, of course, modifies its inventions in relation to changing production practices, technologies, and audience tastes. This book marks an attempt to map out some of those changes.

Mapping the field

This book is intended as an introduction to television crime drama, taking a genealogical approach to the genre and paying particular attention to aspects of the production context in which such dramas were developed. Numerous case studies are discussed in order to illustrate how and why particular shows were developed, the particular narrative form they adopted, as well as their chosen style and aesthetic. An appreciation of the origins and an understanding of the trajectory of the crime drama are essential to making sense of how the media has represented crime both in the past and currently. As the production-oriented research of academics such as John Thornton Caldwell has revealed (Caldwell 1995, 2008), how and why certain kinds of crime drama appear at particular moments and in specific places often has as much to do with the operations of the television industry itself as it does with the operations of crime in the real world. A clear example of this can be found in Chapter 4 in the account of the rapidly proliferating private eye series on early American network television.

In 'mapping the field', I admit to a preoccupation with the kinds of production narratives that have accrued around certain crime drama series. These narratives Caldwell classifies according to a set of themes, including 'war stories' or 'against all odds allegories' (Caldwell 2008: 38). In these narratives, industry professionals portray themselves as heroic individuals with the moral fortitude and strength of will to overcome all forms of opposition to get their show to air. A vivid example of this type of production narrative is to be found in Chapter 6 in the account of how the American crime series *Cagney and Lacey*, featuring two women in a buddy role, made it to the screen despite network resistance (Caldwell 2008: 38). Another kind of production narrative includes 'the genesis myth', which Caldwell associates with the apocryphal story of how the concept for the crime series *Miami Vice* started out as the two-word pitch 'MTV Cops' (Caldwell 2008: 83). And then there are the 'making it sagas' with which those who buy the DVD box set of a TV series with extras will be well familiar. In general, these kinds of extras or 'inter-texts', however, should be treated with some caution since they also constitute a form of industry self-promotion. Even when such self-reflection involves an interview with an industry spokesperson, this inevitably entails a degree of interpretation and performance on the part of the teller presenting only a partial or partisan view. Nevertheless, these 'industry narratives', which often circulate in the press even before a crime drama makes it to air, may also have considerable effects in terms of the ways in which the text is constructed and are therefore worthy of critical attention.

The reception of a television crime drama is also worthy of consideration. During the 1990s, I conducted a research study with readers of crime fiction in an endeavour to explore how and why they were devoted to the genre. In response to the very broad question, 'Why do you like crime fiction?' I received a range of answers, but most memorably 'Because it tells a STORY' (Turnbull 2002b: 243; emphasis in original). Here the respondent drew attention to the narrative drive of crime fiction, not its social or cultural relevance. The lesson to be taken from this personal anecdote is that whatever a critic or scholar may assume about the function and affect of a television crime drama, the ways in which an audience may be watching it, and the kinds of pleasure that any series may afford cannot be assumed simply from the text. Given that this current project did not engage in extensive audience research, I can only speculate and report on what other scholars have suggested about the television crime drama audience over the years. However, there are moments when I offer my own observations as an indication of how a series may have been experienced and read differently in a personal context. For example, although my American husband finds *Midsomer Murders* 'impossible to watch' in its cosy Britishness, I am routinely drawn to the show as part of my nostalgia for the English countryside, villages, home interiors (notably the curtains and cushions), and regional accents. I rarely pay attention to the crime being depicted. Drawing on my own experience, I am therefore sceptical about the kinds of claims that are made about audiences and crime fiction and invite readers to explore their own viewing experiences in a similar fashion.

Despite the possibility that people may watch a crime show for all sorts of 'other' reasons, the central preoccupation in much of the scholarly and popular literature on the genre has been that of crime and its representation, whether this be the representation of the forces of law and order and their procedures, the victims, the perpetrators, or indeed the crimes themselves. Criminologists and sociologists in particular have been quick to criticise television crime drama in terms of its alleged 'misrepresentation' of crime and the presumed effects such distortions may have (Sparks 1992; Surette 1998; Carrabine 2008). And indeed there is a considerable body of commentary on television crime drama that has explored the genre from the perspective of its relationship with crime in the real world, whether this be in relation to the representation of the policeman on the beat in the United Kingdom (Clarke 1983) or the representation of juvenile delinquency in the American crime series *Law & Order* (Rhineburger-Dunn et al. 2008). As recent evidence of this tendency, there is now a considerable academic literature on the '*CSI* effect', which addresses the question of how the judicial process may be affected by jurors being schooled in the process of forensic investigation by television crime drama and who now have an unrealistic expectation of science in the delivery of conclusive evidence, although the evidence of such an effect is far from clear (for example, Brickell 2008; Wise 2009).[3]

Other approaches to television crime drama have endeavoured to evaluate the genre in relation to the prevailing cultural climate of the era, portraying the television crime drama as a cultural barometer. In his book *From the Avengers to Miami Vice: Form and Ideology in the TV Series* David Buxton (1990) tracks the trajectory of the television crime drama, coming to the conclusion that *Miami Vice* marks the end of the road for an exhausted genre in a fallen world where it is impossible to tell the good guys from the bad. Later in the same decade, Charlotte Brunsdon argued that the proliferation of crime-based dramas on British television during the 1980s and 1990s spoke 'very directly to the concerns of a Great Britain in decline under a radical Conservative government with a strong rhetoric of law and order' (Brunsdon 1998: 223).

While there have been, over the years, the publication of many essays on a wide range of crime drama series and issues, there are also in existence a number of publications that are related to specific television crime drama series. These include the *Screen Education* issue devoted to *The Sweeney* in 1976, and more recent edited collections devoted to such series as *CSI* (Allen 2007), *The Wire* (Potter and Marshall 2009), *Dexter* (Howard 2010), and *Life on Mars* (Lacey and McElroy 2012). Such collections present the perspectives of scholars from a diversity of academic fields, each of whom approaches the series in question through the lens of their own particular discipline or interest. The British Film Institute (BFI) has also recently published a number of monographs on crime dramas as part of their TV Classics list. These include *Cracker* (Duguid 2009), *Prime Suspect* (Jermyn 2010), and the 1978 British mini-series that was entitled *Law and Order* (Brunsdon 2010). Each of these texts places the television crime drama series firmly within its production context, its historical moment, and its relationship to the genre of television crime drama as a whole, before going on to discuss its specific form, style, and narrative approach to the law and order issues that it represents. As such, these monographs are exemplary models for the student eager to pursue his or her own research on specific television crime dramas in all their historical and cultural specificity.

Strategic omissions

Many times during the writing of this book, I would be instructed by someone that I 'must' write about a specific crime drama series they loved, admired, and/or thought was important. I always took note of these suggestions, but as the project developed, I became aware that I could hardly begin to encompass the vast range of crime dramas that have appeared on British and/or American television since broadcasting began. Nor did I consider it always necessary to do so, since this is a text that attempts to outline the parameters of a genre. The spy thriller and the adventure series of the 1960s, for example, have already been well covered by James Chapman in his comprehensive study *Saints and Avengers: British Adventure Series of the 1960s* (2002), although clearly there are cross-over influences. In addressing the television crime drama, I have therefore chosen to discuss only a relatively small number of what I regard as 'key' texts that serve to illustrate some of the most significant moves that have been made in the development of the television crime drama, although why some of these texts have been perceived to be 'key' is an issue that this book will address. As such, this volume is intended as a template and a starting point with which students of the television crime drama can usefully work, mapping other shows onto the schema developed here in order to discover their own connections and to fill the always inevitable gaps and lacunae. There is so much work still to be done.

Chapter outline

Chapter 1 traces the complicated root system of the television crime drama in history, literature, and popular culture. As this history reveals, television crime dramas can usually be traced back to these sources in terms of their content, form, or style. Indeed, one of the reasons why the television crime drama is such a persistent and hardy genre is that it can draw upon such an extensive and wide-ranging pre-history to which producers and creators constantly return in the propagation of their new series. The final section of this chapter discusses a number of early British and American crime dramas in order to demonstrate the ways in which they drew upon earlier representations of crime in learning to speak 'the new language' of television drama.

Chapter 2 follows the historical trajectory of the British police procedural as this has evolved against a backdrop of changing attitudes to crime and criminology in Britain, arguing that it is possible to read the British police procedural as an index of changing social attitudes

more generally. The decision to deal with the British police procedural separately from that of the American was made largely because
this sub-genre of crime has developed differently in the two different
contexts. Such differences have to do with the context of production as
well as the cultural and social context of policing. However, it should
be noted that British audiences and American audiences were watching both British and American shows from the start and that there
has been a degree of cross-fertilisation over the years. One of the key
findings to emerge relates to the criteria that have been used to evaluate the British police procedural, in particular a social-realist approach
and a 'gritty' visual style that has become synonymous with notions of
'quality TV'.

Chapter 3 takes up the issue of quality in relation to the style and
form of the American police procedural from *Dragnet* (NBC, 1952–9)
in the 1950s to *The Wire* in the 2000s (HBO, 2002–8). Shows such as
Joseph Wambaugh's *Police Story* (NBC, 1973–8), with its focus on the
emotional lives of police officers and *Hill Street Blues* (NBC, 1981–8),
with its combination of serial and episodic narratives, are considered.
However, while *Hill Street Blues* has regularly been hailed as 'quality
television', there are a number of crime shows that have been dismissed with faint praise, including such ratings successes as *CHiPS*
(NBC, 1977–83) and *Miami Vice* (NBC, 1984–9). The possible reasons
for this neglect are explored. The chapter concludes with a comparison
between *CSI* (CBS, 2000–) and *The Wire* (HBO, 2002–8) as two series
that have been received, and judged, very differently while sharing
similar generic origins.

Chapter 4 returns to the roots of crime to identify those shows
that focus on the work of a heroic detective, professional, private, and
amateur. With his, and indeed her, origins in the hard-boiled crime
novel and radio series, the private eye first appeared on television
screens in the 1950s in a 'wave' of copycat shows that reveal the intense
competition between the American networks at this time. While the
private eye is essentially an American stereotype, the amateur sleuth
who has arguably had the most affect on the history of the crime
genre is the very British Sherlock Holmes. The extraordinary career
of Holmes on television is traced up to, and including, his spirited
reincarnation in the British series *Sherlock* (BBC One, 2010–), which
introduced the ever-resourceful sleuth to the digital era of Skype and
the mobile phone. As will be argued, prior familiarity with a detective
does not appear to be a disincentive, but rather an opportunity for
renewed acquaintance and other pleasurable experiences, including
cultural tourism. This chapter concludes with a comparison between

the on-screen careers of inspectors Morse and Wallander as exemplars of a particular type of disaffected middle-aged loner who have made the transition from crime fiction into the burgeoning transnational trade in television crime drama.

Chapter 5 considers the role of 'the specialist' in the television crime drama from their nineteenth-century roots in crime fiction through to the 1970s and the arrival of *Quincy, M.E.* on television in the United States, lecturing his university students on the vast potential of forensic science. The increasing prominence of the forensic scientist is traced through such series as *Silent Witness* (BBC One, 1996–) to arrive at the global phenomenon of *CSI* (CBS, 2000–) that, it is argued, has had a profound influence on the 'look' of many subsequent television crime drama series. The role of forensics in those series that have dealt with 'cold cases' is also discussed as are those that have taken a more 'supernatural' bent like *Medium* (NBC, 2005–9, CBS, 2009–11). This is followed by a discussion of the criminal 'profiler', in particular the memorable character of Dr Edward 'Fitz' Fitzgerald in the series *Cracker* (ITV, 1996–2006), which was one of the more politically charged series of the 1990s. The chapter concludes with a discussion of more recent 'hybrids' in this sub-genre of crime: *Luther* (BBC One, 2010–), in which the figure of the empathetic profiler and that of the police investigator are united, and *Dexter* (Showtime, 2006–) in which the central character is both a specialist in blood spatter analysis and a serial killer.

Chapter 6 takes a thematic approach to the television crime drama in terms of the politics of gender. As a genre that has often been assumed to be addressed to a 'masculine gaze', this chapter seeks to demonstrate that women have always been at the front of if not quite at the centre of the genre, although this has changed over the years. Series such as *Police Woman* (NBC, 1974–8), *Charlie's Angels* (ABC, 1976–81), and *Cagney and Lacey* (CBS, 1982–8) in the 1980s are discussed in relation to ongoing debates about women and crime. Due regard is paid to the landmark series *Prime Suspect* (ITV, 1991–2006) and the character of Jane Tennison who Charlotte Brunsdon has identified as the yardstick by which all subsequent portrayals of female detectives, on both sides of the Atlantic, have been judged (Brunsdon 2012). With this in mind, the chapter concludes with a discussion of the character of Sarah Lund in the Danish crime drama *The Killing* and the character of Saga Norén in the Swedish/Danish production *The Bridge* (DR1/SVT1, 2011) whose transnational success represents a telling moment in the trajectory of the female sleuth.

In tracing the genealogy of the television crime drama this book attempts to highlight some of the key issues and debates about the representation of crime on television. These include debates about the form and style of the crime drama series, their relationship to the 'real' world of law and order, as well as the ways in which certain kinds of shows have been privileged in the critical discourse. It is hoped that in raising the issue of 'quality', this text will also encourage a reassessment of those crime dramas that have hitherto been neglected but that have nevertheless played a significant role in the development of a genre that in the inventions of the present consistently draw upon the conventions of the past.

Notes

1. *Homicide* was produced by local independent producer, Crawfords, and ran for fourteen years on the Seven Network from 1964 to 1977.
2. As Gregg and Wilson (2010: 419) point out, impressed by the success of *The Sopranos* in a late-night slot during 2007, Channel Nine executives were keen to commission their own 'morally ambiguous' tale of gangsters in a series that sought to emulate the production values and style of the original.
3. Try entering the phrase 'CSI Effect' in an academic search engine. At the time of writing, this search produced more than 100 references.

1 The Roots of Crime

Stories of crime and punishment play a central role in the story-telling matrix of most cultures. As John Cawelti notes, Homer 'launched the subject' in *The Iliad*; murder was a favourite subject of Greek and Roman dramatists, and indeed of Shakespeare and other Renaissance dramatists, thereby suggesting that 'crime and literature have been in it together from the beginning' (Cawelti 1976: 52). Human beings, Cawelti goes on, are 'fascinated by stories of homicide, assault, thievery and roguery of all sorts' (Cawelti 1976: 52). While such stories may be fictional, they inevitably have their origins in the 'real' world of crime that is the source of their fascination. *The Newgate Calendar*, for example, which reported the tales of criminals awaiting trial in Newgate Prison in London, first appeared in the seventeenth century and continued to be published for more than two hundred years (Sussex 2010: 8). The ostensible purpose of these true-crime accounts was educational. People, including children, were encouraged to read *The Newgate Calendar*, have it read to them or, at the very least, to look at the lurid illustrations so that they may better understand that a life of crime may not turn out so well.

In opening with *The Newgate Calendar*, this chapter sets out to trace the origins of television crime drama in true crime, crime fiction, and other media, including film and radio. Before television, crime was already a popular subject for representation in many different media forms, thus establishing a matrix of narrative and stylistic possibilities that the creators of television crime drama were able to draw upon both then and now. Nor were the intentions of such representations always clear. A recent introduction to *The Newgate Calendar* suggests that this text:

> was believed to inculcate principles of right living – by fear of punishment if not by the dull and earnest morals appended to the stories of highwaymen and other felons. The editors of one version even

20

included as a frontispiece a picture of a devoted mother giving a copy to her son (who seems to be about eight years of age) while pointing out the window at a body hanging on a gibbet. (Anonymous n.d.a)

The possibility that depictions of daring highwaymen, not to mention public executions, may have been experienced as 'entertaining' appears not, however, to have crossed the minds of the moralists. Whatever people's experiences of reading them may be, *The Newgate Calendar* proved so popular that it was reprinted and updated many times over the following two centuries (Sussex 2010: 8).

In *The Invention of Murder: How the Victorians Revelled in Death and Detection and Created Modern Crime*, Judith Flanders (2011) provides considerable evidence that popular interest in true crime was rife at the start of the nineteenth century. Sensational murders, such as that of Timothy Marr and his family in 1811 (the first of two linked cases subsequently known as the Ratcliffe Highway Murders), were reported in newspapers and in an early media form known as a 'broadside'.[1] This consisted of a single sheet of paper, printed on only one side, and sold cheaply to people who were unable to afford the more expensive newspapers. Broadsides had an extensive circulation, as those who were literate would apparently read them out loud to those who were not. What is interesting for students of the television crime drama is their seriality. Like a TV series with an ongoing storyline, broadsides may appear in instalments as the story of a crime unravelled, beginning with an account of the arrest and the trial, and culminating in the publication of the perpetrator's 'sorrowful lamentation' and 'last confession' (Flanders 2011: 4). These final editions, Flanders suggests, were usually entirely fabricated since they were frequently on sale at the site of the execution while the body was still swaying on the gallows.

While the sensational Ratcliffe Highway Murders took place more than two hundred years ago, they have continued to play a role in depictions of crime both then and now. In 1927 Thomas De Quincey gave a colourful account of the crime in his essay 'On Murder Considered as One of the Fine Arts', which was first published in *Blackwood's Magazine*. In the form of a satirical address to a fictional 'Society of Connoisseurs in Murder', De Quincey pokes fun at those who are fascinated by such grisly tales: 'They profess to be curious in homicide, amateurs and dilettanti in the various modes of carnage, and, in short, Murder-Fanciers' (De Quincey 1949: 982). Nor has the tale of Timothy Marr been forgotten by television, since a recent episode of the British gothic TV series *Whitechapel* (ITV, 2009–), in which the police deal with contemporary cases that replicate historical crimes, revisited the Ratcliffe Highway Murders in two linked episodes (*Whitechapel* 03: 01–02).

Contemporary dramatisations of crime can therefore be traced back to the nineteenth century when sensational murders also found their way from the press on to the stage in theatrical adaptations of the most melodramatic kind (Flanders 2011: 99) (see Figure 1.1). One of the most frequently rehearsed cases involved the daughter of a Suffolk mole-catcher named Maria Marten who was murdered by a potential suitor, William Corder, and buried in a shallow grave near Polstead.[2] Reports of the Red Barn Murder, as it was soon labelled, were rapidly circulated by newspapers keen to give the story a more exciting and appealing twist for its readership. The first of many dramatic versions was staged in Suffolk at the Stoke-by-Nayland Fair in May 1828, while the perpetrator was still awaiting trial (Flanders 2011: 48). During the trial it was reported that there was a 'camera obscura' exhibition in the vicinity exhibiting images of Corder as the murderer (Flanders 2011: 50). Shortly afterwards, the Staffordshire Pottery produced some remarkable figures of the Red Barn, Corder, Martens, and an attractive pig in an early example of how an iconic setting and a minor character may play a role in the popular representation of crime (Flanders 2011: 173).

As a further development of what is surely an early example of a multi-platform media event motivated by fascination with the sexually charged murder of a young (white) woman, a novelisation of the case soon followed, written by 'penny-blood' author Robert Huish who would go on to write many more 'true-crime' books (Flanders 2011: 53). Penny-bloods, it may be noted, was the original name for a genre of short illustrated booklets that in the 1860s were rechristened the 'penny-dreadfuls' and in which sensational stories of murder and the daring adventures of highwaymen were described (Flanders 2011: 58). In the 1890s, dramatisations of the Red Barn Murder were still playing, although by this time melodrama had gone somewhat out of fashion and a new 'music-hall' version included a giant cabbage, an intelligent donkey called Jerry, and some dancing (Flanders 2011: 62). Nor has the Red Barn been forgotten in the twentieth century. In 1935 the first of five subsequent films about the case, *Maria Marten*, with the sub-title *The Murder in The Red Barn* (dir. Milton Rosmer) was produced and in 1992 gravel-voiced American musician Tom Waits wrote and performed a song entitled 'Murder in the Red Barn' on his *Bone Machine* album, proving once again that a good murder story may have a very long tail.[3]

Given the widespread interest in this case and others during the

Figure 1.1 *CSI* cast in season one; 2000. Credit: Photofest

nineteenth century, public moralists voiced what would become an ongoing concern about the imagined effects of such salacious material on the popular imagination, an anxiety that has hardly abated in relation to more recent depictions of crime on the screen. From the beginning, this concern had its basis in class. While the moralists tended to come from the upper echelons of society, the consumers of these popular media forms often belonged to the emerging working class as produced by the forces of industrialisation, capitalism, and empire. The middle classes, however, were not without their own stories of crime, although rather than being 'true', these were more often 'fiction'.

'Classic crime'

The emergence of crime fiction as a genre addressed to a middle-class readership during the nineteenth century is frequently identified with the publication of the short story *The Murders in the Rue Morgue* by American author Edgar Allen Poe, which first appeared in April 1841. However, as Australian historian of crime fiction Lucy Sussex has revealed, there are many other contenders for this original moment, including a novel published anonymously earlier in 1841 by, as was later revealed, the British author Catherine Crowe and entitled *Adventures of Susan Hopley: Or Circumstantial Evidence*. This case includes a murder and a mysterious disappearance solved by three female sleuths (Sussex 2010: 46). As Sussex demonstrates, the early role of women as crime writers, sleuths, and as an intended 'audience' for crime, has tended to be overlooked in the history of crime fiction as a genre.

It is evident that the rise and rise of the crime story as a literary genre during the nineteenth century went hand in hand with the emergence of a paid and organised police force, and the appearance in fiction of an independent investigator who may set him or herself up in competition – as was indeed the case in Crowe's *Adventures of Susan Hopley* and Poe's *The Murders in the Rue Morgue*. However, rather than focusing on the work of the police, crime fiction as a literary genre tended to highlight the work of gifted and not-so-gifted sleuths from Poe's amateur detective, C. Auguste Dupin, to Conan Doyle's Sherlock Holmes, who first appeared in the short story 'A Study in Scarlet', published in *Blackwood's Magazine* in 1887. While they were separated by some forty years, both Dupin and Holmes have been described as 'ratiocinative' detectives, a term that Poe himself employed to describe Dupin's methods and that merits some explication here since it has many implications for the development of television crime drama (Rachman 2008).

Wilbur S. Scott's characterisation of Monsieur C. August Dupin from his introduction to the complete works of Poe, serves to illustrate just how influential this character has been in the creation of the many detectives to follow, in print and on-screen:

> [Dupin] is not merely intellectually more agile than others; he is also eccentric; he comes . . . from an illustrious family; he is an extensive reader of rare volumes; he is subject to a 'fantastic gloom', lives in 'a time-eaten and grotesque mansion', and is one who, shunning daylight, is 'enamoured of the Night for her own sake. In short, an isolate, and a preternaturally brilliant man'. (Scott 2002: xi)

This description of Dupin in 1849 may equally well be a description of Johnny Lee Miller's version of Sherlock Holmes in the recent American series *Elementary* (CBS, 2012–). Given that the creator of Holmes, Conan Doyle, was himself influenced by Poe's detective stories, this is hardly surprising. What is surprising is how much darker the Holmes of *Elementary* is compared with other versions of Holmes on-screen, as will be discussed further in Chapter 4.

Ratiocination as a mode of investigation is usually described as involving a combination of close observation and deductive reasoning in the process of solving the crime. However, both Dupin and Holmes also exhibit dazzling displays of inferential logic: the putting together of seemingly disparate 'facts' to reveal the final truth. This combination of empirical evidence and intuition has continued to be the basis of many stories of detection on-screen and off-screen, with the television investigator often being positioned somewhere on the spectrum of empiricism versus intuition. For example, while forensic investigator Dr Gil Grissom in *CSI* (CBS, 2000–) could be described as an 'empiricist' who relies on the physical evidence, Alison Dubois in *Medium* (NBC, 2005–9, CBS, 2009–11) is an 'intuitive' whose capacity to assist the police in their investigation relies on her 'visions'.

In his discussion of the 'classical detective story' as represented by the work of Poe, Conan Doyle, and The Golden Age of detective fiction (including crime fiction by authors such as Agatha Christie, Dorothy L. Sayers, and John Dickson Carr), John Cawelti outlines the key components of the formula. The first element is the situation: An unsolved crime that must be a 'major one with the potential for complex ramifications' (Cawelti 1976: 81). The second is the 'pattern of action', including the introduction of the detective, the crime, and the clues, the process of the investigation, the announcement of the solution, the explanation of the solution, and the dénouement, noting that these do not always occur in sequence, as is evident in a television crime drama like *Columbo* that features a ratiocinative investigator (NBC, 1968–78). In the first act of each one-hour episode the audience witnesses a perpetrator commit a crime (with usually a guest star in the role of the criminal). In the second act, Detective Columbo (played by Peter Falk), appears in his guise as a shambolic buffoon in a shabby trench coat to commence his investigation through a process of close observation and interviews. In the final act, Columbo explains how the various clues he has identified have led him to the revelation of the perpetrator. The pleasure for the audience, therefore, lay not so much in finding out 'whodunnit' as it was in watching Columbo outsmart the criminal through a process of deduction and inference.[4]

As Cawelti notes, the third key component of the classical detective story is the cast of characters and the relationships that they have to one another. This includes the criminal, the victim, the detective, and those who are threatened by the crime but who are incapable of solving it (Cawelti 1976: 91). The fourth is that of the setting, which in the classical detective story Cawelti suggests is likely to be isolated in some way: Examples may include a locked room, a lonely country house, or a remote village. The isolated setting is necessary, Cawelti argues, because 'it establishes a framework for the treatment of manners and local colour in a fashion often reminiscent of the great Victorian novelists' (Cawelti 1976: 97).

Here we may point to the popular British television series *Midsomer Murders* (ITV, 1997–) that has been sold to more than 100 different territories around the world (Anonymous n.d.b). The 'isolated' setting (in both time and space) is the fictional county of Midsomer with, as has often been wryly observed, an extraordinarily high crime rate. In 2011, in an interview with the British magazine *Radio Times*, the producer Brian True-May described the long-running series as a 'last bastion of Englishness', conceding that while contemporary British society may well be diverse and cosmopolitan, Midsomer clearly was not and the show would not work as a crime drama series if it was. As a result of these comments, which were perceived as being profoundly racist, True-May was suspended. In True-May's defence, it may be argued that the appeal of *Midsomer Murders* may depend upon a nostalgia for the idealised, less ethnically diverse version of 'Great Britain' as imagined in the pages of the classical detective story at the start of the twentieth century: a place where crime may be committed but where the perpetrator would be brought to justice through the deductive logic of a clever investigator who would always arrive at the truth.

What *Midsomer Murders* offers is the pleasure of the classical formula played out against a backdrop of rural picture-postcard settings inhabited by a range of types who are instantly recognisable in their quirky Englishness. As such, *Midsomer Murders*, like *Columbo*, is formulaic rather than mimetic in its depiction of crime and relished by those who enjoy the reassurance of the familiar while being disparaged by those who prefer the representation of more 'serious' crime. As a British expatriate living in Australia, I may note that one of the great pleasures for me in watching *Midsomer Murders* has less to do with the narrative and the depiction of the crime as it has to do with landscape, real estate, and interior design. Like the viewers who wrote to Ien Ang about why they liked watching the American prime-time melodrama *Dallas*, I also watch *Midsomer Murders* for the costumes and curtains (Ang 1985), a motivation that suggests that the reasons for watching some television crime drama may have little to do with the drama of crime.

While the classic British detective story involving ratiocination has continued to play a significant role in the development of contemporary television crime drama, American crime fiction took another turn in the early years of the twentieth century, towards what has been commonly labelled the 'hard-boiled'.

From hard-boiled to noir

Even though it has been suggested that the origins of the American 'hard-boiled' tradition lie in the 'pathfinder fiction of James Fennimore Cooper and the straight shooting cowboy of the nineteenth century dime novels' (Burns 1999: 199), the appearance of the 'hard-boiled' detective is usually associated with the emergence of popular and cheap 'pulp' fiction publications such as *Black Mask* in the 1920s. It was here that Dashiell Hammett introduced the character of the Continental Op in 1923, a fat, nameless, middle-aged investigator intended to offer a 'realistic contrast' to the ratiocinative puzzle mysteries that were then in vogue on both sides of the Atlantic (Burns 1999: 200). While the Continental Op was a fictional character, his adventures were no doubt informed by Hammett's own experience as a private eye for the Pinkerton Detective Agency, which he joined in 1915.

Writing in 1946, Raymond Chandler applauded Hammett's fiction, suggesting that his more 'realistic' crime stories 'gave murder back to the kind of people that commit it for reasons, not just to provide a corpse' (Chandler 1946: 234). Of even more significance, in Chandler's opinion, was Hammett's style, since '[h]e put these people down on paper as they are, and he made them talk and think in the language they customarily used for these purposes' (Chandler 1946: 234). Irritated by those who had suggested that Hammett was merely a 'hard-boiled' chronicler of the mean streets, Chandler described the detractors as 'flustered old ladies – of both sexes (or no sex) . . . who like their murder scented with magnolia blossoms and do not care to be reminded that murder is an act of infinite cruelty' (Chandler 1946: 235–6).

What is interesting about this latter comment is the way in which it establishes the hard-boiled and its claims to realism as intrinsically masculine while feminising both the mystery story and its readers. Nor is this characterisation entirely accurate since, as Cawelti points out, Hammett's stories were hardly more realistic than the classical detective stories. 'Hammett's power as a writer', Cawelti writes, did 'not lie in his greater fidelity to the realistic details of crime and punishment but in his capacity to embody a powerful vision of life in the hard-boiled detective formula' (Cawelti 1976: 163). Within this formulaic construction, the hard-boiled private detective is a character imbued with a mixture of sentimentality and toughness, described as speaking in Hammett's characteristic 'flat, hard-edged, and laconic vernacular style' (Cawelti 1976: 166).

With regards to Hammett's approach to crime and criminality, Cawelti suggests that his hard-boiled fiction constitutes a 'bitter and ironic parable of universal corruption and irrational violence' (Cawelti 1976: 173). This mean-world scenario is much 'darker' than that envisioned by his successor, Chandler, whose protagonist, Philip Marlowe, considers the problems of contemporary society to be largely the result of American greed and, therefore, to be redeemable. In Chandler's own typification of the hard-boiled hero, he famously describes his ideal detective as a chivalric 'man of honour' who is 'neither tarnished [n]or afraid', adding that 'if there were enough like him, I think the world would be a very safe place to live in, and yet not too dull to be worth living in' (Chandler 1946: 237). Whatever the world view, either hopeless or hopeful, the figure of the hard-boiled detective and the style of both Hammett and Chandler were to have a lasting influence on the television crime drama in America. For example, we may flash-forward to the American teen crime drama series *Veronica Mars* (UPN, 2004–6; The CW, 2006–7) as a show that made cunning use of the legacy of both Hammett and Chandler in its creation of a 'hard-boiled' female teen sleuth in a series with a number of stylistic 'noir' overtones – a term that needs some explication here.

While 'hard-boiled' is the adjective used to describe a type of crime fiction, the phrase 'film noir' was first used in 1946 by French film critic Nino Frank to describe a number of psychologically complex American thrillers that had appeared in France after the Second World War (Peirse 2010: 189). Frank coined the phrase as a play on the title of the *Série-noire* paperback crime thrillers with their distinctive black covers that belonged to the hard-boiled school of fiction (Peirse 2010: 190). While the phrase 'film noir' has been applied to adaptations of both Hammett's and Chandler's work, such as Hammett's *The Maltese Falcon* starring Humphrey Bogart as Sam Spade (dir. John Huston; 1941) and Chandler's *The Big Sleep* also starring Humphrey Bogart – this time as Philip Marlowe (dir. Howard Hawks; 1946), the phrase also encompassed the adaptation of a range of novels by other authors who were not writing detective fiction. This included the 1946 film adaptation of James M. Cain's *The Postman Always Rings Twice* (dir. Tay Garnett; 1934), which exemplifies the characteristic bleakness of 'noir'. This is a story about doomed people who live doomed lives in a society that is itself a crime, as was brilliantly parodied in the 1980s' crime series *Moonlighting* (ABC, 1985–9), which also took on the politics of gender in noir (see Chapter 6). As William Luhr has suggested, the appeal of 'film noir' lies in 'its masochistic erotics of doom, [that is,] its ability to draw viewers into nightmare-like, paranoid narratives of degeneration and failure' (Luhr 2012: 6). A useful full-form of the acronym 'noir' may therefore be: Negative Outcome Is Requisite. In other words: It's only going to end in tears.

Not all films, or indeed television shows, which have been described as 'noir' are necessarily so bleak. In many cases the term 'noir' is used to designate a particular 'style' that is associated with film noir. In his much-quoted essay, 'Notes on Film Noir' (1972), Paul Schrader suggested that the roots of film noir can be found in Warner Bros.'s 1930s' gangster films, French 'poetic realism' (1930s' film movement in France), German Expressionism (a number of related creative movements beginning in Germany before the First World War), and the melodramas of director von Sternberg. For example, in film noir, as in German Expressionism, oblique and vertical lines are preferred to the horizontal, especially in the representation of the city, the majority of scenes are lit for night, and the faces of the actors are often blocked out by shadow, creating a fatalistic, hopeless mood (Schrader 1972: 57). Far from being excessive or extraneous to the action, film noir's techniques thus emphasise loss as well as nostalgia, a lack of clear priorities, and insecurities, submerged 'in mannerism and style' (Schrader 1972: 58).

While Schrader suggests how the style of film noir may be related to the expression of a world view, Alison Peirse employs the term 'noir' in her discussion of the television series *Dexter* (Showtime, 2006–) to designate a number of structural elements that she associates with noir. These include the tropes of the conflicted male protagonist and the femme fatale, the theme of violent death and detection, and the particular mode of narration that involves the use of voice-over and flashback (Peirse 2010: 191). For Peirse, 'noir', therefore, implies certain kinds of narrative tropes as well as a style. As a result, 'noir' has become a term that needs to be carefully scrutinised in order to determine just how it is being used and in relation to what specific features of whatever drama to which it is being applied.

While both the classic detective story and the hard-boiled school of American writing have played a key role in the ongoing development of the television crime drama series, particularly in the creation of the detective as hero, the evolution of the police procedural as a sub-genre has a rather different trajectory.

The police procedural

With the establishment of a professional and paid police 'force'[5] by the turn of the twentieth century in both the United States and the United Kingdom, it is interesting to note just how soon the theme of crime and detection began to appear within the new medium of film. *The Great Train Robbery*, a twelve-minute film produced in 1903 for Thomas Edison's film company and directed by Edwin S. Porter, has been described as 'the first blockbuster crime drama', featuring as it does the hold-up of a passenger train, the robbery of those on board, and the pursuit and then the capture of the perpetrators.[6] In 1905, Edison released two other films dealing with law and order issues. The first, *Life of an American Policeman* (also directed by Porter) may, at a stretch, be described as an early police procedural, while the second, *Police Chasing Scorching Auto*, although only about three minutes at length, could be labelled an action drama. Running for only fourteen minutes, *Life of an American Policeman* contains a number of vignettes representing a day in the life of an ordinary police officer that are worth describing in some detail as they also anticipate many of the subsequent moves of the television police procedural. As Charles Musser has suggested, this is a film that exhibits 'explicit social concern', presenting a 'complex, sometimes contradictory, and finally conservative vision of the world' (Musser 1991: 10).

The film opens with a charming domestic tableau depicting the eponymous policeman eating breakfast at home with his wife and three children. The toddler has commandeered the policeman's hat and struts around the table brandishing a police baton, until his father scoops him up and hands the child over to his wife before heading off for a day of public service that includes helping lost children and rescuing a woman who attempts suicide by jumping into the Hudson River (flowing through eastern New York State). This proto-typical police procedural thus depicts both the domestic and the routine rather than any major crime, and, as such, foreshadows those television crime dramas that are as much concerned with the private lives of members of the police service as their professional careers. The much briefer, *Police Chasing Scorching Auto*, begins with a speeding car full of revellers pursued by two policemen on bicycles and another two on horseback. To be accurate, the car is hardly 'scorching' by modern standards, given that the bicycles and the horses rapidly close in on the offenders in a sequence remarkable largely for the camera work. In this early example of a long tracking shot, the camera is mounted on another vehicle and follows the action from behind as 'we' pursue the bikes pursuing the renegade auto. It's a remarkable example of the early use of point of view to engage the viewer in the action.

Only a few years later, such thrilling chases were already being parodied in a number of silent films produced by Mack Sennett for his Keystone Film Company in Edendale, California. The Keystone Cops were a troupe of (initially) seven fictional incompetent policemen who first appeared in the film *Hoffmeyer's Legacy* in 1912, and who would go on to appear in a number of later films, and subsequent revivals, while achieving iconic status as a lasting representation of police stupidity. This comic interlude is important, since it demonstrates the complexity of the image of the police in popular culture in the early years of the twentieth century, particularly during the 1930s when many forms of popular culture including film, pulp fiction, theatre, and magazines were critical of the capitalist cultural hierarchies that had resulted in the economic downturn (Battles 2010: 25).

The most remarkable hero of the 1930s' crime film, however, was not the detective but the gangster who emerged at this time as arguably the first 'ethnic' hero in American popular culture (Denning cited in Battles 2010: 26). This self-made man, played by actors such as Edward G. Robinson or James Cagney, 'epitomized style, glamour and individual success in a culture that increasingly demanded conformity to corporate institutions' (Battles 2010: 26). Even more significant was the fact that the police were shown to be largely ineffective in curbing the gangster's activities in ways that pre-date such television series as *The Sopranos* (HBO, 1999–2007) and more especially *Boardwalk Empire* (HBO, 2010–) with its return to the Prohibition era of the 1920s and 1930s. The police and the authorities, however, were less than impressed by the success of the gangster on film and it is against this historical backdrop that Kathleen Battles (2010) traces the emergence of the radio docudrama as a type of media public relations tool intended to reassert the authority of the police.

According to Battles, the medium of radio functioned in the first half of the twentieth century as the most popular and pervasive form of entertainment in the home, *and* as a vital medium of communication for the police in an era of increased mobility, largely as a result of the automobile. Radio functioned both as a network of communication, linking the police officers on the beat in their new radio-equipped cars, and as a broadcast network linking listeners. The radio crime drama was thus closely related to the emergent practices of policing. As a result, in Battles' opinion, the radio crime drama became a key site of struggle over the meaning of policing and the control of discourses surrounding policing, citizenship, and criminality (2010: 6). In this instance, the police were largely successful in their attempts to control their representation on-air during an era of police reform that saw the role of the 'force' change from one of social maintenance to that of criminal apprehension (Battles: 2010: 7). And yet one of the most telling moments in Battles' history reveals that in the management of their public image, the police did not always have it their own way.

In 1935, the head of the Federal Bureau of Investigation (FBI), J. Edgar Hoover – the mastermind behind President Franklin D. Roosevelt's 'war on crime' – was keen to have the radio drama *G-Men* reflect favourably on the operations of his investigators (Battles 2010: 38). With stories drawn from the files of the FBI, Hoover wanted to use the show as a form of propaganda and a public relations tool. This ambition, however, brought him into conflict with another consummate showman, radio producer Phillips H. Lord, who was determined to make *G-Men* as entertaining as possible in the interests of the listeners as well as the commercial sponsors (Battles 2010: 46). Given that *G-Men* was based on already solved police cases, the show had a potential disadvantage in maintaining audience engagement in the narrative. So while Hoover wanted the radio drama shows to delineate the careful, thorough, scientific, and often tedious work of the FBI agents, Lord wanted to subordinate the tedium of the procedure to the excitement of the chase (Battles 2010: 49). In a victory for Lord, the audience, and the show's sponsor (Colgate-Palmolive), the overly procedural and didactic *G-Men* was cancelled after only thirteen episodes and Lord given free rein to make his new replacement show, *Gang Busters*, as exciting as possible.

Gang Busters was an immediate success and continued on radio for almost twenty years before transitioning to television in 1951 alongside its rival *Dragnet*, providing early evidence that a realistic approach to the crime drama need not be a deterrent to audience engagement if handled skilfully. Like *Police Headquarters* and *Calling all Cars*, *Gang Busters* brought the representation of crime and policing into the living rooms of urban, suburban, and rural homes long before the arrival of the television crime series. However, while radio may have been the most important domestic medium of entertainment and the most important technology in the management of crime in the first half of the twentieth century, the arrival of television marks both a shift in the entertainment landscape as well an era of increased 'visual' surveillance. As such, the early television series *Dragnet* is of particular interest because of its simultaneous existence on a number of different media including radio, film, and television, not forgetting the popular press and its commentary.

Figure 1.2 *Dragnet*: scene from the 'The Big Cast', starring Lee Marvin in a guest role; 1952. Credit: Photofest

Dragnet

Dragnet star Jack Webb's career as an actor began with a short-lived, half-hour comedy show on ABC radio in 1946 followed by his role as a fictional private investigator (PI) in the series *Pat Novak for Hire* (1946–7). In 1948, Webb played the role of a crime lab specialist, a prototypical forensic investigator, in a film directed by Alfred Werker and an uncredited Anthony Mann. *He Walked by Night* is a police procedural that favoured a semi-documentary approach with stylish noir overtones. Like *G-Men* and *Gang Busters*, the film was based on a real case and employed the services of a policeman as its technical advisor. The opening title card – 'The record is set down here factually . . . as it happened. Only the names are changed . . . to protect the innocent' – was later adapted by Webb for his own police procedural, *Dragnet*, which began on NBC radio in 1949 before moving to television in 1951. *Dragnet* was broadcast on both media until 1954, when Webb also made a feature film of the same name, thereby rendering the show a cross-media phenomenon. After the demise of the radio version, the television show *Dragnet* carried on for another five years.

Subsequently revived by Webb for a brief period from 1967 to 1970, the later *Dragnet* failed to achieve anything like the significance of its earlier incarnation, despite the addition of colour. This may have been because, as Mittell suggests, Webb's Manichean, black and white vision of the universe and the role of the police no longer had much appeal in the counter-culture era of the sixties (Mittell 2004: 148).

Each half-hour episode of *Dragnet* was bookended by its opening and closing credits, accompanied by an immediately recognisable musical theme. Every episode would begin with the emphatic 'Dum de dum dum' and the image of Sergeant Joe Friday's LAPD (Los Angeles Police Department) Badge 714, followed by a documentary-style insert of the city of Los Angeles with a voice-over commentary by Webb. This voice-over not only evoked the style of documentary narration but also recalled the laconic voice of the hard-boiled detective in an early instance of creative genre hybridity. Webb would then appear as Friday, alongside whichever partner with whom he may be working at the time on whatever detail they may have been assigned ('We were on the Homicide watch'). The next half hour would follow the routine investigation of a case, inevitably resolved in some way, with the outcome being announced on-screen at the end. While this was the 'classic' formula, watching a sequence of episodes from *Dragnet* reveals considerable variation in the tone of the cases portrayed.

One of the most interesting episodes from the first series, 'The Big Cast' (1952), features Lee Marvin as a serial killer named Henry Ross who is arrested by Friday and his partner Ed Jacobs following a clumsy scuffle in a hotel room. Following a brief interrogation, Ross coolly confesses to a series of murders, revealing himself to be a man with no empathy and no conscience; he kills simply for convenience. Murder to him is just a 'little thing', Ross tells his detective audience, and criticises the writers of detective stories and murder for their embellishment of the crime. This is an oddly self-reflexive moment for the television crime drama and argues against any easy dismissal of *Dragnet* as a formulaic and unoriginal show. It also anticipates, in Marvin's chilling performance, a fascination with the serial killer who was to dominate popular culture and television crime in the 1990s.

Shot on film (Webb's medium of choice despite the contemporary consensus that 'quality' television should be live), the visual style, and indeed the overall bleak tone, is that of film noir. Webb's decision to use telefilm also enabled him to portray the 'authentic' Los Angeles, usually in an opening exterior shot of the city and its inhabitants in montage sequences that became increasingly more elaborate (Mittell 2004: 143). In his endeavours to produce a half hour of television that looked like a cinematic film, Webb's directorial style in this episode includes the use of long shots and medium shots but also overhead shots looking down on the three men at various points during the interrogation. There are also extreme close-ups of all three, in particular Marvin's eyes, including a startling shot in which one eye fills the entire screen. As Mittell points out, Webb was well aware that he was shooting not for a large film screen, but for the small screen in the corner of the living room that could have only limited effects from the depiction of a cinematic image. The intermittent use of close-ups is therefore both prescient and stylistically impressive. The overall effect of the episode that encapsulates the nihilism of noir is deeply unsettling and hardly reassuring despite the arrest of the killer.

Another episode, 'The Big Show', from series two, illustrates a different aspect of Webb's directorial style: the use of line editing (the camera cuts to each speaker as his or her dialogue begins, thus eliminating reaction shots). Given that, at this point, Webb was directing the show both for radio and television, he made extensive use of a teleprompter to save time, instructing his cast to simply read their lines in a flat monotone. Looking at this episode now, what is remarkable is that the radio performers Webb often employed for both the radio and television versions of the show really do look like the kind of 'ordinary' people one would meet on the street or encounter at a bus depot rather than television actors chosen for their televisual appeal.

Innovative in style and complex in theme, *Dragnet* is a television crime drama that deserves, as Jason Mittell persuasively argues, much more credit and consideration than it has been accorded in the recent past. At the time, however, Webb's innovations in the television police procedural were well received by the audience despite what David Marc describes as their formulaic 'flatness', thus denying the possibility that the repetition of this formula may also be an aspect of the show's appeal and artistic merit (Marc 1984: 73). While the formula, or at least the structure, of a television show may indeed stay the same, every week a new variation may be played out within it. To imagine that experimentation with form is only a feature of a later, more evolved, television landscape is, therefore, to ignore the level of experimentation that was an essential feature of the early years of television.

Dixon of Dock Green

Like *Dragnet*, the early British police procedural can also trace its origin to both radio and cinema. The character of policeman George Dixon first appeared in the 1949 Ealing film *The Blue Lamp* (dir. Basil Dearden) where he was killed some forty minutes into the narrative by a 'juvenile delinquent' played by a young Dirk Bogarde. However, in Susan Sydney-Smith's opinion, the most relevant starting point for the television crime drama as it developed in the United Kingdom is not the feature-length crime film, but rather the public service films and radio documentaries produced by the BBC in the period from the First World War through to the Second and its immediate aftermath (Sydney-Smith 2002: 20).

Unlike America, where the television landscape was dominated in what Jeremy Butler describes as the 'network era' by the three major commercial networks – ABC, CBS, and NBC (Butler 2012: 4) – in Britain a public service model and ethos initially prevailed, with the BBC extending its dominance of broadcasting from radio to television in the time before and after the Second World War (Creeber 2003: 22). After many years of heated debate, the United Kingdom's first commercial television service, Independent Television (ITV), was established under the terms of the 1954 Television Act, commencing broadcast in September 1955 (Medhurst 2006: 119). Funded by advertising rather than by revenue generated through the purchasing of TV licences, the new commercial TV service was nevertheless bound by many of the same public service requirements as the BBC, including the need to produce a certain number of hours of locally produced programming, documentaries, news, and current affairs (Medhurst 2006: 120). Despite these strictures, the new commercial broadcaster was perceived as a rival to the BBC, offering audiences more of what they wanted in terms of popular entertainment. As Su Holmes has revealed, the emergence of ITV thus prompted considerable political, institutional, and cultural debate about the status of 'popular' television, with the BBC forced to consider how it may respond to the competition (Holmes 2008: 23). As it is, even before the emergence of ITV in 1955, the BBC, with its obligation to inform, educate, and entertain, had already begun to develop shows around the drama of crime, although interestingly these were initially created not within a unit devoted to drama or light entertainment, but in documentary.

A key figure in Sydney-Smith's account of the emergence of the TV crime drama on the BBC is Robert Barr, a former journalist and crime reporter who, as the unofficial leader of the BBC Documentary Unit from 1947 to 1953, was responsible for a series of prototypical television crime shows. These included *War on Crime* (1950), *I Made News* (1951), and *Pilgrim Street* (1952). The latter, written by Jan Read who had co-written *The Blue Lamp* with Ted Willis and who would go on to write *Dixon of Dock Green*, was reportedly the first-ever television series to feature the 'ordinary uniformed copper' and as such is identified as an immediate predecessor to *Dixon of Dock Green* (Sydney-Smith 2002: 20).

As the leading figure in the Drama-Documentary Unit of the BBC, Robert Barr's Fleet Street connections enabled him to persuade Robert Fabian, then head of the elite Flying Squad (a branch of the Specialist Crime & Operations Section) within London's Metropolitan Police Service, to appear in Barr's semi-documentary series *I Made News*, a weekly show based on the story of a person who had figured in the headlines that week. Fabian subsequently became the eponymous real-life hero of the spin-off series, *Fabian of the Yard* (1954–5), as played by actor Bruce Seton. While each episode dramatised a case drawn from Fabian's own files, at the conclusion actor Seton would morph into the real-life detective inspector Fabian speaking directly to camera while offering ocular evidence that what we had just witnessed was 'true': evidence that included not only Fabian's confirming presence, but also his account of the outcome of the case, occasionally supported by some form of memorabilia.

According to Sydney-Smith, *Fabian of the Yard* is an exemplary instance of what she defines as the Scotland Yard sub-genre of crime drama that was to prove extremely popular in both Britain and America where *Fabian* was shown on the CBS network and re-christened *Police Car*. Shot on film both in a studio and on location around post-war London, scenes were often accompanied by a voice-over commentary offering reassurance about the excellence of the British police force as well as an intermittent travelogue. Thus, in the second episode of the series, 'Bombs in Picadilly', we are afforded a quick tour of the Tower of London 'started by William the Conqueror in 1078', before watching Bruce Seton as Fabian giving 'merry chase' to a bomber through the back streets of Chelsea, not far, we are informed by our voice-over tour-guide, from 'the former studio of James Whistler, famous American painter'. This latter comment reveals that the producers were well aware of the American audience for the show on CBS, a point that serves to unsettle the conventional wisdom that the BBC of the time was insular, parochial, and uninterested in an export market.

In this episode, Fabian enlists the help of a female police officer called Wetherby whom he sends undercover as a 'cheap Edgware Road type' on a mission to get up close and personal with the dangerous bomber. In the course of a two-minute montage accompanied by upbeat music on the soundtrack, PC Wetherby is transformed from a buttoned-down officer with a severe bun into a Lauren Bacall looka-like, complete with a seductive curtain of hair and a split skirt that she casually pulls aside in order to check the seam in her stocking for the benefit of a camera carefully positioned to catch the best shot of her elegant knee and shapely thigh. Pause for a quick intake of breath, and we get back to the business of catching the bombers who are threatening mayhem in their paradoxical campaign for world peace.

As an early form of the television crime drama, *Fabian of the Yard* thus encapsulates many of the competing impulses of the genre as it has variously developed over the years. In terms of style, the episode oscillates between film noir in the carefully framed and lit studio shots to the realism of documentary in the filmed inserts of post-war London. The tone also shifts from the didactic to the playful makeover of PC Wetherby, which offers voyeuristic pleasure to an imagined heterosexual male spectator while also providing potential cosmetic interests for a female viewer. *Fabian of the Yard* thus reveals a tension between the impulse of the television crime drama to document the reality of crime versus an impulse to entertain. For Sydney-Smith, *Fabian of the Yard* also marks the start of a bifurcation in the British police procedural between those series that would focus on the work of the high-profile detective, and those focusing on the work of the uniformed police. In terms of the latter, the early police procedural *Pilgrim Street* (1954) merits consideration as an immediate forerunner to *Dixon of Dock Green* (1955–76).

Conceived by Robert Barr and Jan Read, *Pilgrim Street* dealt with 'ordinary everyday crime' rather than the heroic cases of Scotland Yard detectives (Sydney-Smith 2002: 80). Like *Fabian of the Yard, Pilgrim Street* was also a curious hybrid. Claiming authenticity as 'a series of six documentary stories about a London police station', the 'manor' portrayed in *Pilgrim Street* was entirely fictitious (Sydney-Smith 2002: 81). It is also salutary to note that, in its depiction of the routine work of policing – 'missing children; lost visitors from abroad; a girl who has taken a fall down some steps; and a bag catcher' – an average day in the life of the Pilgrim Street police station recalls that of Edwin S. Porter's 1905 film *Day in The Life of an American Policeman*, without the opening scenes of domestic bliss.

Attention to the home life of the London policeman would have to wait until the arrival of *Dixon of Dock Green* in 1955, a series produced not within the Documentary Unit of the BBC, but within the new Light Entertainment Department at that 'watershed' moment when the BBC was faced with competition from its new commercial rival, ITV. *Dixon* thus emerged at a critical moment, when the BBC was struggling to come to terms with what 'entertainment' may mean for the national broadcaster. At this juncture, the BBC was required to consider what their audience may actually 'want' (rather than what the audience may 'need' in terms of cultural enlightenment) given that television was first and foremost a domestic medium received in the home by families with diverging interests and attention spans.

The first half-hour episode of *Dixon* was broadcast on Saturday, 3 January 1955 at 8.15pm (Sydney-Smith 2002: 104). The second season, in 1956, was subsequently scheduled on a Saturday night at 10.00pm before being relocated to 7.30pm for the third, fourth, fifth, and the start of the sixth seasons. It was not until the seventeenth episode of the latter season in 1960 that *Dixon* settled into what was to become its familiar 6.30pm slot on a Saturday night, where it remained for most of its subsequent twenty-one years. In this early evening time position, *Dixon* was the kind of show that everybody in the family could watch gathered around their invariably small television screen on which the quality of the image might vary considerably depending on the strength of the signal. Although the production values may have been poor, watching pictures that moved in the comfort of one's own home was still, in the 1950s, a novelty when compared with the activities of listening to the radio or going to the cinema. Dixon rapidly became an early form of appointment television, as I well remember from my own viewing experience.

First came the theme music, initially Jack Warner himself whis-tling 'Maybe It's because I'm a Londoner', before the mournful 'An Ordinary Copper' became routine. George Dixon himself would then appear out of the gloom to stand under the 'blue' lamp that was in fact white on our monochrome screens. 'Evenin' all' he would announce (typically, but not always),[7] as he tipped his helmet in respect and proceeded to outline the 'issue' of the week. And so the episode would unfold, until Dixon reappeared at the end of the show with a closing homily and a formal good night, this direct address to camera gesturing towards the documentary roots of the television crime drama as well as ensuring that any didactic message on law and order matters was not overlooked. The tight format of this half-hour show, bookended as it was by opening and closing monologues that were pronounced by a familiar figure, thus offered a comforting aesthetic framework through which to contemplate the uncomfortable threat of crime.

At this point I'd like to introduce a more personal note here in order to unsettle assumptions about how the show was watched and received at the time. Despite what has been written about the relative stability of post-war Britain and the role of *Dixon of Dock Green* in reasserting this, I remember the experience of watching *Dixon* rather differently. As a child in the 1950s, allowed to watch *Dixon* on a Saturday night, I remember this time as a period of both regional and national anxiety.

Living in the North of England near shipyards and coal mines that had been heavily bombed during the war, I was concerned about where the next attack may come from and whether or not this may be nuclear. I was also worried about more local crime, given that my parents' home had been burgled twice, the second time while we were upstairs asleep in bed. George Dixon may have been keeping them safe in London, but it didn't seem safe at all where I lived.

Furthermore, while I certainly remember George Dixon as a solid, patriarchal figure who spent a lot of time in the police station, what I remember most vividly are the scenes of domesticity, given that episodes routinely included a domestic sub-plot involving challenges to Dixon's authority from his wife, daughter, and eventual son-in-law, detective Andy Crawford. So even though Sydney-Smith (2002: 10) suggests that the marriage of Dixon's daughter to detective Andy Crawford served to 're-position the feminine at the heart of the domestic sphere', I remember the domestic sphere as represented in *Dixon* as being one of ongoing tension and drama. Like Lucille Ball's Lucy Ricardo in the Desilu sitcom *I Love Lucy* of the same era, the women in the home always seemed to be either fighting to get out or resentful of their lot for having stayed. Nothing was settled in the 1950s, either at home or on television.

I offer these personal recollections in order to demonstrate that the experience of watching a television crime drama at a specific moment in time and in a particular social and historical context may be impor- tant in the consideration of a genre history. This is not to deny the importance of the text, but rather to warn against the assumption that the salience of a television series can simply be assumed from a revisionist analysis of the text or what has been written about it. Thus, although it may well be true that *Dixon of Dock Green* represented a 'conservative attitude to crime', viewing crime as the product of individual failing rather than as a product of social conditions, this was not necessarily what it conveyed to me at the time. Indeed, the fact that every week Dixon had another problem to deal with both at home and in the police station simply underlined the fact that such problems were both endemic and insoluble in the long term. While the half-hour series format certainly offered closure at the end of every episode, this was only ever temporary and viewers knew, indeed they were assured by the routines of television scheduling, that another problem would emerge at the same time, in the same place the following week. Rather than offering comfort, the routine scheduling of television crime made sure that viewers' anxiety could never be completely allayed.

For the police force that he came to represent, Dixon was a figure of reverence, a symbol of how the police wanted to be thought of by the general public, which is not the same as how things may have been in reality. One of the principal criticisms that has been made of *Dixon of Dock Green* over the years is that as a drama series it betrayed its documentary roots, becoming too cosy and, connected to this, too distant from the social realities of crime and policing in post-war Britain, realities that subsequent TV series, like *Z-Cars* (ITV, 1962–78), were more willing to address. Despite this dismissal, the fact that one of George Dixon's closing monologues was recycled for the final scene of *Ashes to Ashes* in 2010, suggests that the legacy of *Dixon* has not been forgotten.[8]

Moving on

When Jack Warner died in 1981, his coffin, topped by a wreath in the shape of a blue lamp, was borne by officers from the real Paddington Green station in London where the writers had conducted their 'original research' for the series (Sydney-Smith 2002: 105). When Jack Webb died one year later in 1982, he was accorded a funeral with full police honours and buried with a replica of the LAPD Badge bearing the rank of sergeant and the number 714 that he had long worn in character as policeman Joe Friday. The mayor of Los Angeles even ordered flags to be lowered to half-staff in honour of Webb's (or possibly Friday's) passing.[9] The respect shown these actors and the iconic policemen whom they had come to embody, underlines their significance in tracing the emergence of the television crime drama in both America and Britain as well as the significance that the police themselves may invest in representations of their work.

In her excellent overview of the early British police series, Sydney-Smith warns against eliding the development of the American crime drama with that of the British crime drama (2002: 8). While this point is well taken and the two will be treated separately in subsequent chapters, it is salutary to note that as early police procedurals, *Dixon of Dock Green* and *Dragnet* have much in common: Both were revered by the police force they represented and as a possible result of this alignment have been highly criticised for their alleged conservatism; both owe a debt to a feature film; both owe a debt to radio, either in the form of documentary (*Dixon*) or drama (*Dragnet*); and both have been endlessly parodied and cited. Most importantly for the argument here, both played a foundational role in establishing the crime drama series as a form of television entertainment and as a routine feature of the viewing schedule in their respective countries.

The 1950s, however, is the moment when the television crime

drama on both sides of the Atlantic begins to diverge. While the police procedural, with its focus on an ensemble cast and the routine of policing, continued as one specific thread, the Scotland Yard sub-genre of heroic policeman helped pave the way for the 'celebrity' police detective. In the United States the semi-documentary impulse of *Dragnet* and its attention to the procedures of policing would inspire shows such as *Highway Patrol*, which would in turn inspire British television producer Troy Kennedy Martin in the creation of *Z-Cars*. Increasing attention to the emotional lives of the police (that had been largely ignored in *Dragnet*) would come to the fore in the anthology series by real-life policeman Joseph Wambaugh entitled *Police Story* (NBC, 1973–8). Meanwhile, the ongoing influence of the classical mystery story and the hard-boiled detective would become manifest in many other crime dramas involving the police, private eyes, gifted amateurs, and specialist investigators.

There is, however, a problem with this genealogical approach to the television crime drama in that it assumes a chronological and forward progression in terms of format, style, or even attitudes to criminality and policing. Although it may well be true that the aesthetics of the crime drama may change, often as a result of changing technology, and that attitudes to law and order issues may change as well, the trajectory of the television crime drama is one of loops, spirals, and returns. Thus, the American franchise *CSI* echoes *Dragnet* in 2001 while *Life on Mars* (BBC One, 2006–7) and *Ashes to Ashes* (BBC One, 2008–10) return to *The Sweeney* and eventually *Dixon of Dock Green*. Meanwhile, in its attention to police corruption and the failure of the criminal justice system the four-part British series *Law and Order* in 1978 anticipates the similarly critical HBO series *The Wire* (HBO, 2002–8) (Brunsdon 2010: 2). The past of the television crime drama is also its present and will invariably play a role in its future.

While this account of the emergence of the television crime drama from the primordial soup of crime – a soup that includes true crime, melodramatic plays, the detective story, the hard-boiled thriller, film noir, the semi-documentary feature film, the radio crime show, and the routine representations of crime in the news – is by no means exhaustive, it serves to indicate the complexity of the origins of the television crime drama. The ways in which the crime drama developed in both the United States and the United Kingdom, however, is a product of many other forces that include the particular and very different television production environments, as well as different social attitudes to law and order issues, as will be revealed in the following discussion of the British police procedural.

Notes

1. 'On the night of 7 December 1811 a twenty-four-year-old hosier named Timothy Marr, his wife, their baby and a fourteen-year-old apprentice were all found brutally murdered in their shop on the Ratcliffe Highway in the East End of London' (Flanders 2011: 1).
2. Polstead is now the home of Baroness Rendell of Baburgh, better known as the British crime writer Ruth Rendell.
3. One stanza reads: 'There's always some killin'/You got to do around the farm/A murder in the red barn/Murder in the red barn.' Tom Waits's song 'Murder in the Red Barn' is on the album *Bone Machine* released in 1992 by Island Records.
4. The first episode of *Columbo* in 1968 (following two pilots) was written by Steve Bochco (who would go on to create the police procedural *Hill Street Blues*), and was directed by Steven Spielberg, who would also go on to further work in Hollywood.
5. The police force is now more usually identified as a police 'service'. The use of the term 'force' or 'service' appears to vary according to jurisdiction and historical context.
6. This is from the commentary on the DVD box set *Edison: The Invention of the Movies*, produced by the Museum of Modern Art (MoMA) in conjunction with the Library of Congress, 2005.
7. Susan Sydney-Smith suggests that there was considerable variation in Dixon's salutations to the audience (2002: 109).
8. The resonance of Dixon's appearance at the end of *Ashes to Ashes* is noted by Simon Brew on the fan website, *Den of Geek* (Brew n.d.).
9. Webb was interred in the Forest Lawn, Hollywood Hills Cemetery in Los Angeles, and was given a funeral with full police honours. On Webb's death, chief Daryl Gates announced that badge number 714, which was used by Joe Friday in *Dragnet*, would be retired. Mayor Tom Bradley of Los Angeles ordered all flags to be lowered to half-staff in Webb's honour for a day, and Webb was buried with a replica LAPD Badge that bore the rank of sergeant and the number 714 (Anonymous n.d.c.).

2 'Gritty Realism': The British Police Procedural

Although *Dixon of Dock Green* continued for twenty-one years, finally ending in 1975, at a point when Jack Warner was himself eighty years of age and long overdue for retirement, the police procedural as a genre had already begun to evolve in terms of both form and content. Series such as *Z-Cars* in the 1960s, *The Sweeney* in the 1970s, and *The Bill*, which began in 1984 and continued until 2008, represent significant moments in the history of the genre in Britain, not only because of the different ways in which the police and police work were portrayed, but also because of changes to the form, style, and aesthetics of television crime drama. While some of these changes can be attributed to advances in technologies of production, for example, the shift from 'live' performance in the studio to the use of film and video enabling more location shooting, others may be the result of perceived changes in audience taste as well as changing public perceptions of crime and policing in different cultural contexts. As Charlotte Brunsdon has suggested, in seeking to dramatise these social changes, television crime constitutes a 'privileged site for the staging of the trauma of the breakup of postwar settlement in Britain' (Brunsdon 1998: 223).

This chapter attempts to tease out some of these developments in form and style against the backdrop of British social history and the technologies of production available to the television industry in the United Kingdom. *The Bill*, in particular, offers a useful case study in the evolution of the genre, given that over the twenty-six years of its time on air, this police procedural underwent a variety of makeovers in a bid to keep pace with changing social attitudes and different audience tastes as well as a rapidly changing broadcast environment. This included the deregulation of British television in the 1990s (Lacey and McElroy 2012: 3), and increased competition from satellite, cable, and other TV platforms in the new millennium.

Of particular interest in this account is the question of what has been valued within the British context of production and reception, and how this compares to the American notion of 'quality' television that will be considered in more detail in Chapter 3. It would appear that, in Britain, those series that have adopted what is routinely described as a 'gritty' social-realist approach to their subject matter are regularly perceived to be of better quality and greater value than other types of crime series. Such criteria are readily apparent in the diverging critical reception of the long-running series *The Bill*, which encompassed a number of stylistic and formal approaches to the police procedural during its twenty-nine years on air. While a social-realist approach can be traced to the documentary origins of the early television crime drama as outlined below, it should be noted that a social-realist approach and a 'gritty' look requires as much, if not more, artistic manipulation as any other 'look' on television.

Looking North

In tracing the development of the British police drama through the 1950s and 1960s, Susan Sydney-Smith draws attention to a series of stand-alone television story-documentaries that were written by Colin Morris (a Liverpudlian)[1] and were directed by Gilchrist Calder, entitled *Tearaway* (1956), *Who, Me?* (1959), and *Jacks and Knaves* (1961) (that had four parts). Each of these dramas was set in the vicinity of Liverpool and signals a reorientation of the television crime drama away from the world of the London-based policeman and detectives, such as Dixon and Fabian of the Yard, towards an interest in what was occurring in the regions to the north (Sydney-Smith 2002: 120). This reorientation should also be considered in relation to a more pervasive shift in British culture as exemplified by the work of 'angry young men' dramatists such as John Osborne (*Look Back in Anger*, 1956) and novelists such as John Braine (*Room at the Top*, 1957) and Alan Sillitoe (*Saturday Night and Sunday Morning*, 1958), the adaptation of whose books also contributed to a 'new wave' of British cinema that dealt with working-class life in bleak Northern settings (Laing 1990: 127).

In his account of British television drama, Lez Cooke points to the British soap opera *Coronation Street* (Granada, 1960–) as the first television show to 'break ranks' and embrace the 'new mode of social realism' or 'kitchen sink' drama in its 'iconography, character types and storylines' (Cooke 2003: 33). With its working-class characters, provincial location in the industrialised North, 'ordinary' settings including the public house, the street, and the kitchen – all shot in such a way as to suggest an unmediated reality, not to mention its often cantankerous and comic characters, *Coronation Street* helped pave the way for a similar social-realist move in the television crime drama. According to Sydney-Smith, one of the more significant aspects of the new Northern-based police dramas was the introduction of humour in the portrayal of quirky Northern characters (Sydney-Smith 2002: 128).

It has been suggested that another reason that these Northern-based crime series were remarkable is that instead of attributing crime to individual acts of moral failure, their focus was on the underlying social causes of crime in a region experiencing significant cultural change as a result of post-industrialisation (Sydney-Smith 2002: 129). While some members of the public were not impressed by these innovations, *Jacks and Knaves* subsequently won The British Television and Screenwriter's Guild Award in 1961 for best dramatic series (Sydney-Smith 2002: 141). The reaction of the police to these new series was even more complicated: While some thought that the programmes were excellent, others considered that they showed the police in an 'unfortunate light', as 'fools lacking in discipline' (Sydney-Smith 2002: 142).

This was the context for the emergence in 1965 of the successful television crime drama *Z-Cars*, which brought together the earlier tradition of the BBC Documentary Department in its goal of presenting a 'realistic' portrayal of policing (based on the cases of a real policeman) with a turn to melodrama and humorous interludes featuring quirky Northern types (Sydney-Smith 2002: 153). *Z-Cars* arguably positioned itself somewhere between the imperatives of social realism and entertainment with a distinct emphasis on the latter. It is no coincidence, as Laing (1990: 126) makes clear, that this move coincided with the arrival of Hugh Carleton Greene as the director general of the BBC, determined to let in 'a breath of fresh air' to what was perceived as its rather staid and stuffy establishment. Carleton Greene was responsible not only for the introduction of *Z-Cars*, but also for such iconic and entertaining shows as the political satire series *That Was The Week That Was* (BBC, 1962–3), the sitcom *Steptoe and Son* (BBC, 1962–74), the medical drama *Dr Finlay's Casebook* (BBC, 1962–71), and the crime series *Maigret* (BBC, 1960–3), based on the novels of the prolific Belgian author Georges Simenon.

Z-Cars, according to one of its apocryphal stories of origin, began with a case of mumps (Sydney-Smith 2002: 159). Confined to bed, writer Troy Kennedy Martin passed his time monitoring the police broadcasts on his radio. And so when the head of the Documentary Department, Elwyn-Jones, sent Kennedy Martin to Liverpool to explore the possibilities of creating a new crime series based on the concept of mobile car patrols, *Z-Cars* was the result. In other accounts, Kennedy Martin often attributed the origins of *Z-Cars* to the inspiration provided by the American series *Highway Patrol* (1955–9) starring Broderick Crawford as policeman Dan Mathews, which had also been shown in Britain during the 1950s (Laing 1990: 127). This attribution suggests that while it may be true that the development of the British and American police drama series are best treated separately, in effect a degree of cross-fertilisation quite possibly occurred, not only in terms of format and content, but also in terms of style and aesthetics.

With its roots in the earlier documentary approach to the television crime drama series, three of the first thirteen scripts of *Z-Cars* were based on the cases of a real-life policeman, DCI Prendergast. This affiliation with the real world of crime, however, did not save the series from the criticism of senior members of the constabulary who were once again extremely hostile to the depiction of police officers as ordinary men with more in common with the working classes that they policed than their middle-class managers (Laing 1990: 125). Hence a debate about the 'accuracy' of the series in terms of its portrayal of the police ensued in the press.

For Sydney-Smith, one of the key points to be made about *Z-Cars* is that it focused on the police as a unit or force, rather than on the work of a heroic individual (such as Fabian or Dixon). Furthermore, the structure of *Z-Cars* as a thirteen-episode series mimicked the American practice of dividing the television year into two seasons, thus revealing an ongoing interplay between American and British television production, specifically at the level of format (Sydney-Smith 2002: 164). This episodic structure necessitated a collaborative effort on the part of the writers allocated to different episodes with Troy Kennedy Martin as the most prolific contributor to the first series (eight episodes) including the first, 'Friday Night'.

Z-Cars subsequently ran for five seasons before the first version of the show ceased production in December 1965 (Laing 1990: 125). The series was revived in 1967 in a different, soap-opera format, which involved twice-weekly, twenty-five minute episodes, before returning to a weekly fifty-minute episodic format in 1971 – the structure it retained until its demise in 1978. Although early viewing figures were disappointing, these rapidly improved, with peak audience figures during early 1963 averaging 16.65 million viewers, many of whom were watching repeats, *Z-Cars* being one of the first TV shows in Britain prior to the introduction of the time-shifting video recorder to offer this opportunity (ibid.).

As described by Sydney-Smith, each episode of *Z-Cars* opened and

closed with a stirring North Country marching tune played on the
bagpipes as the graphics marked out a triangle, indicating the route
of the two patrol cars with their call signs 'Z Victor 1' and 'Z Victor
2'. The name of the series, Z-Cars, thus derives from the radio call
sign of the mobile units concerned rather than, as has often been
assumed, the make of the cars employed by the mobile units: the Ford
Zephyr. While early episodes were transmitted live from a studio,
the producers also made use of inserts filmed in the Ealing Studios at
Ealing Green in West London. Most episodes were also 'telerecorded'
(kinescoped), which involved pointing a 16mm camera at a television
screen with the result that some of these early episodes, including the
very first one, have survived (see Anonymous n.d.d).

As the series developed, Z-Cars quickly established its own televisual
aesthetic that involved a fast-cutting style with 'up to six cameras
and fifteen sets per episode' (Laing 1990: 128). Any episode may also
include the use of montage devices borrowed from the style of documentary film, and studio sequences involving the use of back projection with the police cars mounted on rollers, thus enabling the camera
to shoot through the windscreen and to capture the conversations of
the Z-Victor teams as they patrolled their beat. As Laing notes, this
meant that the average Z-Cars' camera shot lasted for only twelve
seconds (ibid.).

According to Lez Cooke (2001: 22), the narrative pace of these
early episodes was indeed fast. In a move that would anticipate many
of the crime drama series to come, Kennedy Martin's strategy was to
interweave a number of different storylines into one episode, 'thereby
increasing the complexity of the narrative structure and maximising
audience interest and involvement with a range of different characters
and stories' (ibid.). The series was, however, character driven rather
than plot driven with particular attention paid to the 'reality of people's lives': both the police and the citizenry with whom they interacted
(ibid.). This was especially true of the paired policemen whose often
testy working relationship provided an ongoing dynamic for the show.

In terms of the representation of crime and policing, according to
Sydney-Smith, Z-Cars also played out a tension between competing
political impulses at the BBC. On the one hand, there was the established tradition of the rather conservative story-documentary series,
celebrating the heroic efforts of the noble police such as Fabian or
Dixon. On the other was the desire on the part of a new wave of television writers and directors such as Kennedy Martin, John McGrath,
and Ken Loach to critically investigate the role of the police from
a social-realist perspective: a perspective with which Loach would

become firmly identified, as a director of both television and film, in subsequent years. According to Charlotte Brunsdon, who cites John McGrath on the issue, *Z-Cars* was less about policing and more about documenting the lives of ordinary people in a self-conscious 'state of the nation' project (Brunsdon 2010: 18). For his part, Kennedy Martin was keen to break with the 'naturalism' of television. In this case, naturalism may best be described as the 'illusion of reality' associated with the semi-documentary style of the earlier police series, a style that Kennedy Martin vigorously attacked in his manifesto 'Nats Go Home' (1964), where he called for a new grammar of television with an emphasis on the images and the mise en scène rather than on the dialogue.

Despite its occasional use of filmed inserts, and with more than 250 edits designed to keep each episode 'action-packed and fast-moving' (Cooke 2003: 58), *Z-Cars* was not the fulfilment of Kennedy Martin's dreams for television. This would have to wait until the development of new technologies of television production in the 1970s and 1980s. However, *Z-Cars* did have considerable effects in terms of the public imagination largely because of what Lez Cooke describes as its 'more realistic portrayal of the police', which would set the benchmark for realism in fictional representation of the police for many years to come (Cooke 2003: 58). As a consequence, Kennedy Martin was hailed as 'a pioneer in portraying the police as less than perfect in the British TV drama'.

While Kennedy Martin left the series at the end of the first season because he considered *Z-Cars* to have lost its radical potential, many of the writers and directors who had worked on that first series carried on (Sydney-Smith 2002: 177). These included Northern writer Alan Plater and director Ken Loach. Plater would go on to write eighteen episodes of *Z-Cars*, including the finale, before moving on to the sequel *Softly Softly* (BBC, 1966–9) and a long screen-writing career including such later literary-based series as *Dalziel and Pascoe* (BBC One, 1966–2007) and the Inspector Morse spin-off show *Lewis* (ITV, 2006–) (Coveney 2010). Ken Loach would direct the landmark television docudrama *Cathy Come Home* in 1966 before directing his first feature film *Kes* in 1969, both of which were produced by Tony Garnett who would later play a very significant role in the development of the television crime drama as described below.

While the original 'live' series of *Z-Cars* ended in 1965, the show was revived in March 1967 and continued until September 1978. Meanwhile, inspector Barlow as played by Stratford Johns was given his own series, *Softly Softly*, and migrated South in a return to the sub-genre of the police drama constructed around the figure of a senior detective as hero. This move would appear to confirm Lez Cooke's proposition that in the 1970s the television crime drama in both the United Kingdom and the United States turned away from the police force as an ensemble to a focus on the heroic maverick cop (Cooke 2001: 22). Cooke, therefore, draws a parallel between the emergence of *The Sweeney* on ITV in 1975 with American series such as *Kojak* (1974–8) and *Starsky and Hutch* (1976–8), both of which were also broadcast on the BBC during the 1970s.

The Sweeney

While Cooke is keen to draw a distinction between the 'fashionable and charismatic' American detectives as compared with the 'new', more 'ruthless', breed of police detective as represented by *The Sweeney*, he argues that what all of these new detectives had in common was a 'self-righteous belief in the validity of their own methods even if those methods involved a degree of violence and a bending of the rules' (Cooke 2001: 22). According to Colin Sparks, these extra-legal moves frequently put the cops on the street in direct conflict with their superiors back in the office (Sparks 1992: 134). In the United Kingdom, the result was the depiction of a very particular kind of British class antagonism as the working-class officers refused to recognise the legitimacy of bureaucratic imperatives forced upon them by their middle-class superiors back in the squadroom when faced with the urgent imperatives of violent crime (ibid.). For policemen such as detective inspector Jack Regan (John Thaw) of the Flying Squad and sergeant George Carter, when it was a case of bringing offenders to justice the ends justified the means whatever the rules of engagement might be (see Figure 2.1). Ironically, it was the rules that ended Regan's career in a final episode that culminates in a bitter tirade against the bureaucracy that had constrained and doubted him (Cooke 2001: 22).

While *The Sweeney* is routinely characterised as an action-packed crime drama full of car chases, squealing tyres, and punch-ups, a closer look at the series as a whole (re-released on DVD) tends to confound this totalising view, suggesting that for students of television it is always advisable to go back to the text if and when possible. For example, in the first episode of the first season, 'Ringer', we meet Regan as he examines his hung-over face in a bathroom mirror. Dressed in an attractive floral nightgown, he hunts for his trousers in an untidy living room suggestive of a night of heavy drinking. We follow him into the bedroom where he wakes an attractive woman to

Figure 2.1 *The Sweeney*: Jack Regan (John Thaw) and George Carter (Dennis Waterman) in the first episode, 'Ringer'; 1975. Credit: FremantleMedia

ask her if he can borrow her car. The fact that this vehicle, a trendy mini, is stolen while Regan is making a call to the office from a telephone box adds to the farcical elements that are threaded through an episode that builds to an all-in brawl involving members of the Flying Squad and a gang of armed villains.[2] This mayhem is brought to a halt when the charismatic criminal at the centre of the plot, played by Brian Blessed (whom most of the audience would probably recognise as the actor who had so memorably played PC Fancy Smith from *Z-Cars*), is shot and killed: his body artfully arranged for the benefit of a camera looking down from above. It's a telling moment in terms of the consequence of a life of crime.

A striking aspect of this episode is the attention to language as a means of determining character and class. In a voice-over commentary to 'Ringer' on the 2007 DVD release, Trevor Preston describes himself as the only working-class writer on a series created by, and for the most part performed and produced by, middle-class people. Preston, therefore, insists on the authenticity of the 'street' language he employed in the script but laments the fact that this meant that the series did not make it on to American television because of a perception that the dialects would be too impenetrable. 'It could have been a cult', he laments several times in the voice-over commentary.

As is also revealed in this voice-over commentary, which includes actors Dennis Waterman and Garfield Morgan (detective chief inspector Haskins), the transmission order of episodes in the first season was not determined until production was well advanced. 'Ringer' (that is cockney street slang for a car thief) was selected because it contained an expository scene between the commander of the unit and Haskins, Regan's new boss, during which the commander describes Regan as a man with whom Haskins had best be 'straight'. Regan, in other words, is not a corrupt police officer, a point that would have been of particular significance for a viewing audience well aware of allegations of corruption in the real Flying Squad at the time (Hurd 1976: 48). Regan's 'straightness' is important given that Regan and Carter are working-class men who look and sound more like the criminals they are out to catch than their middle-class superiors. Regan is thus established as a maverick cop who frequently bucks the system to the frustration of his commanding officers but who is an essentially honest and good man. However, the elite unit of the Metropolitan Police Service to which he belongs, the Flying Squad, is portrayed in a rather more complex way, as is revealed by Troy Kennedy Martin's comments on the voice-over commentary to the episode 'Thin Ice'.

Having been invited to write for the series by his brother Ian who created it, Troy suggests that he himself knew the Flying Squad to be riddled with corruption. This was hardly a secret: Police corruption had been front page news since 1969 when *The Times* newspaper reported its own investigation into corruption in the Metropolitan Police Service (Brunsdon 2010: 21). In 1972, Robert Mark was appointed commissioner of the Metropolitan Police with a mandate to 'stop the rot' and, to this end, a specialist department known as A10 was established, the role of which was to investigate any such charges (Brunsdon 2010: 22). In July 1977, by which time *The Sweeney* was three seasons old, the commander of the Flying Squad, detective chief superintendent Kenneth Drury, was convicted of five counts of corruption and jailed for eight years (Walker 2004). An internal investigation, entitled Operation Countryman, was then launched and a further twelve officers were convicted of corruption and many others resigned (Walker 2004).

As far as Kennedy Martin was concerned, the only way he could reconcile himself to writing about a police unit already known to be corrupt was to write his assigned episodes as comedies. Thus the third episode in the first season, 'Thin Ice', is in Kennedy Martin's own terms a 'shaggy dog' story featuring the well-known comic actor Alfred Marks in the lead as the hapless villain. As Kennedy Martin, producer Ted Childs, and director Tom Clegg reveal in their voice-over commentary to this episode, because the show had no script editor in this first season, no uniform 'tone' or style was imposed on the writers with the consequence that there was considerable variation in the scripts. Cohesion and continuity for the series was perceived to be more a product of the ongoing characters and the fifty-minute format than a consequence of any overall strategy.

Kennedy Martin's contributions to season three, which was broadcast in the second half of 1976, once again present the Flying Squad and the British establishment in a less than flattering light. The episode 'Visiting Fireman' (03: 03) contains not only moments of comedy (Regan and Carter perform a drunken vaudeville act in a Turkish Club for the amusement of their visiting Turkish colleague) but also the suggestion that the British Secret Intelligence Service (SIS) is involved in covering up a clandestine plutonium trade with the Middle East. At one point Regan suspects that he himself is being shadowed by a member of the internal investigation unit, A 10, although given the comic undercurrent of the episode, this turns out to be an unfortunate neighbour whose car Regan reprehensibly rams. It is a comedy of errors from start to finish in which no one looks good, especially the Flying Squad.

Another episode in this season, 'Bad Apple' (03: 06), written by Roger Marshall, also addresses corruption within the Metropolitan Police Service. It may be noted that the title of this episode recalls an early episode of *Dixon of Dock Green*, entitled 'The Rotten Apple' (02: 10), which carried the reassuring moral that one bad apple in the barrel (one corrupt police officer on the force) does not necessarily make bad the whole barrel of apples (all of the police officers). The 'bad apple' in *The Sweeney* episode, however, does indeed involve more than a single police officer in the Metropolitan unit under investigation. While Regan goes undercover at a local bar, Carter presents himself at the local police station and buddies up to the suspected officers in an episode that concludes with a disheartened senior policeman being confronted with the reality of rampant corruption in his squad.

I have drawn attention to these particular episodes in order to challenge what would appear to have become the conventional wisdom about *The Sweeney*: that it was a series that featured violence instead of detection and action rather than character. Looking back at the series in 2004, in the context of a BBC News' feature article recalling the history of the Flying Squad, Andrew Walker characterised *The Sweeney* as follows:

The show's rough-edged, fast-paced style won millions of fans, enthralled by car chases with Ford Granadas and Mark II Jags, seedy criminals' wives, and John Thaw's world-weary Detective Inspector Jack Regan with his trademark admonition: 'Shut it!' (Walker 2004)

In fact *The Sweeney* was a much more complex series than either of these descriptions would suggest, not only in its treatment of law and order issues, but also in its treatments of character, including the many women who feature in minor, but remarkably vivid and strong, roles – not always as 'seedy criminals' wives'. This complexity is highlighted in the special issue of *Screen Education* published in 1976 that was devoted to *The Sweeney*, when the show was halfway through its third series. At this time, when *The Sweeney* was at the height of its popularity, there had been two novelisations, the first of two feature films was in production (*Sweeney!* 1977; *Sweeney 2* 1978) and there had been the publication of a children's book, including stories, comic strips, a board game, and factual material on the stars as well as the Flying Squad (Drummond 1976: 15).

The essays collected in the *Screen Education* issue tackle the show from a variety of angles, addressing the structural and narrative constraints of the show (Drummond 1976), the portrayal of the police (Dennington and Tulloch 1976), and the contradictions and coherence of the show as a whole as it navigated what Geoff Hurd identified as a series of tensions around such issues as the exercise of authority within a bureaucracy (Hurd 1976: 50).

While acknowledging that, in the final analysis, the series may well be 'pro-police', Ed Buscombe points out in his closing remarks that *The Sweeney* did not portray the police as monolithic. Instead they were revealed as all too human with Regan, in his working-class affiliation, always on the side of the underdog and anti-authoritarian in his dealings with bureaucracy (Buscombe 1976: 68). Finally, Buscombe (1976: 69) notes, *The Sweeney* is 'of the people' because it is 'very much an ITV rather than a BBC production', suggesting that the face of the police on the commercial network was very different from that on its more 'genteel' counterpart, the BBC, a comment that reveals the ongoing and somewhat erroneous conceptualisation of the BBC as both 'stuffy' and out of touch. Made by the independent British film and television production house, Euston Films, which was itself a subsidiary of the larger production house, Thames Television (part-owned by EMI Group Ltd), those who worked on *The Sweeney* were employed on a freelance basis and firmly located in a system of what Paterson describes as 'commodity production' (Paterson 1976: 7). *The*

Sweeney is thus perceived as a very different type of series from those produced in-house at the BBC. Within this structure, Paterson notes, the producer, Ted Childs, was the dominant figure, editing the script and also intervening on set when needed (8).

While there is much debate about the generic origins and the aesthetics of *The Sweeney* in this *Screen Education* issue, Childs and Kennedy Martin offer their own account of the conception of the series and how it should look in the commentary to 'Ringer'. According to Childs and Kennedy Martin, after a great deal of Italian red wine and a pizza, the three went to see the movie *The French Connection* (dir. William Friedkin, 1971). This film, which is set in New York City and is based on a 'true' case of drug smuggling, had garnered an R rating according to the Motion Picture Association of America's film-rating system as a result of its violence, which meant that those under 17 would only be permitted access to the cinema if accompanied by a parent or guardian. With its seedy urban backdrop this, Childs and Martin agreed, was the look and the tone that they wanted to achieve, on a budget of £35,000 per episode.

Obtaining this *French Connection* look proved a little easier with the introduction of the latest Arriflex 16mm cameras and new Eastman film stock that provided the sought-after image quality. However, in order to make television that looked and sounded like a feature film, it was also necessary for the crime drama series to move out of the studio and to be shot on location. This move had the ancillary advantage of lowering the costs of production. According to Kennedy Martin and Childs,[3] the outsourcing of *The Sweeney* by Thames Television to Euston Films was prescient in its use of a crew where the members were paid by the hour rather than as ongoing employees of a television network since this eventually became the dominant model for television production on all networks. However, this outsourcing was not always easy to manage, given that there were at least three unions involved during a period of increased union activity. Nevertheless, working on the series was apparently a highly enjoyable and largely democratic affair, with everyone, cast and crew, congregating in the local pub (The Red Cow) in Hammersmith on a Friday afternoon (Commentary 'Thin Ice', Network 2002).

While the first episode of *The Sweeney* may have begun in playful mode with Regan in a borrowed chintzy dressing gown, the last ended in bitterness. Wrongly accused of corruption, Regan leaves the Flying Squad offices in high dudgeon, furious that his integrity has been questioned. Considered in its entirety, *The Sweeney* therefore ends on a note of disillusionment with the body representative of law, and the

Flying Squad, accused of letting down its loyal officers because of its own moral failure to distinguish the good from the bad. This conclusion is even more interesting if we consider this final episode, broadcast on 28 December 1978, not only in relation to the 'real life' of the Flying Squad as it had unfolded in the newspapers over the 1970s, but also as a response to a very different television crime drama that had screened in April of that year.

Law and Order British style

The original *Law and Order* (not the more recent American version), written and produced by Tony Garnett for BBC Two with a script by G. F. Newman and directed by Les Blair, followed the career of London villain, Jack Lynn, through the criminal justice system. Following in the tradition of what Brunsdon has identified as the more experimental thread of British television drama, each episode offered a different narrative perspective including that of 'The Detective', 'The Villain', 'The Brief', and 'The Prisoner'. As such, *Law and Order* occupies a space within the history of the TV crime drama somewhere between the aspirations of television as an art form and television as a medium of popular entertainment (Brunsdon 2010: 4). It was also a highly political intervention in the ongoing debate about law and order during the decade. Although the series was not based on any one case, it echoed a number of different incidents involving real-life criminals that had been reported in the press over the preceding years. More importantly, the series set out with a very clear agenda to show 'how far the workings of the criminal justice system were from most people's ideas of justice and the law' (Brunsdon 2010: 6).

This it did rather too effectively, provoking reactions from the police federation, magistrates' associations, and prison officers' associations, resulting in a number of embarrassing problems for the BBC, which at the time was anxiously endeavouring to re-negotiate the licence fee on which it depended for revenue (110). As a consequence, *Law and Order* was only ever repeated once, 'very quietly' on a Sunday night in March 1980, just before the rights expired (114). The series was thence effectively 'disappeared' from the archives to be re-released on DVD at an all-day 'celebratory' event at the National Film Theatre (now BFI Southbank) in 2008 (2). As a result, although the series was kept alive in discussions about law and order in the criminal justice system, because no copies were in circulation it was largely forgotten in accounts of television drama in general and the television crime drama in particular (16–17). Fortunately, the re-release of the DVD and the inclusion of *Law and Order* in the British Film Institute (BFI) TV Classics series in an excellent monograph by Brunsdon has ensured that its significant role in the genealogy of the television crime drama is not forgotten here.

The four discrete but interrelated episodes of *Law and Order* were initially screened on Thursday nights during April 1978 at 9.00pm in a slot that bore the generic title of 'Play for Today'. As director Les Blair suggests in his contribution to the documentary feature *Criminal Minds* (a useful addition to the re-released *Law and Order* DVD), before the widespread use of video recorders, people would stay home for television events such as 'Play for Today', the title of which suggests something rather more culturally elevated than mere television 'entertainment'. Indeed previous television 'plays' had included such memorable TV 'events' as *Up the Junction* (1965) about working-class life in South London directed by Ken Loach with a script edited by Tony Garnett; *Cathy Come Home* (1966), which dealt with homelessness; and *Days of Hope* (1975), which unravelled the history of the General Strike in 1926, both also produced by Tony Garnett and directed by Ken Loach. Garnett's reputation as a producer of critically acclaimed social-realist television with an anti-establishment edge was therefore already well established by the late 1970s when he embarked on the *Law and Order* project.

Introduced to writer G. F. Newman by Troy Kennedy Martin, Garnett invited Newman, who had already written popular novels that portrayed the police in a less than flattering light, to write a script that would 'get behind the public relations' to reveal what the criminal justice system was 'really like' (*Criminal Minds*). In what could be taken as a pointed and rather unfair allusion to *The Sweeney*, Garnett suggests that what they did not want was yet another 'squealing tyres show' (*Criminal Minds*). Having produced the first script, 'The Detective', Newman was told by Garnett that it did not have a satisfactory ending – and a sequel was commissioned focusing on the activities of the character of Jack Lynn, 'The Villain'. The last two episodes, 'The Brief' and 'The Prisoner', were originally written as one, but subsequently sub-divided when they became too unwieldy.

Labelled as a series of plays, but touted as 'films' by *Radio Times* in its pre-publicity, a great deal of the debate about *Law and Order* related to its 'naturalistic' style and whether or not the series may be mistaken for a documentary. Apparently the label 'film' served to support this suggestion and became a contentious matter for debate. However, attaining this documentary look for what was in effect a television drama was not as easy to achieve as may be assumed. As director Les Blair suggests in his description of the process, the production of 'realism' was a highly wrought endeavour involving extensive use of location settings (including a recreation of the Metropolitan Police's own offices), natural lighting and sound, and a distant, observational camera, resulting in frequently obscured and partial views (Brunsdon 2010: 49). The results were impressive, providing a chilling and convincing portrayal of the 'ordinariness' of corruption and cruelty in the criminal justice system. What was even worse as far as the official representatives of that system were concerned was the fact that the series implied that the worlds of the police and the villains were so deeply imbricated as to make the two indistinguishable (10). The fact that the series went so far as to suggest that Sir Robert Mark's solution to the problem of police corruption – the internal investigation unit A10 – might also be 'on the take' simply added salt to already inflamed wounds.

In assessing *Law and Order*'s contribution to the drama of television crime, Brunsdon suggests that in its portrayal of the deep collusion between the institutions of criminal justice and the world of the criminals, *Law and Order* not only challenged any remaining faith the public may have in the criminal justice system, but also anticipates the critically acclaimed American series *The Wire* (HBO, 2002–8) in that both series point to endemic corruption in public life. As such, the original British *Law and Order* was very different from the subsequent British version of the American franchise, *Law and Order* (1990–2010) with which it shared a name and that also follows the career of an accused through the criminal justice system but from a very different moral perspective, as will be discussed in the next chapter.

G. F. Newman's *Law and Order* thus serves to illustrate a number of key points about the TV crime drama in general and the police procedural in particular at this time. First, by the end of the 1970s, the television crime drama might appear in a number of different formats including the episodic series as well as a filmic event in the style of what would later be called a mini-series or a tele-movie. Furthermore, the television crime drama was routinely at the forefront of experiments in style, whether this be in location settings or in the studio. Even more important is the fact that despite its reputation for conservatism and support for the establishment, the television crime drama frequently showed the police in a less than flattering light and could be very critical of the criminal justice system.

As a key figure in this critical push, Tony Garnett, producer of *Law and Order*, left the BBC and headed to the United States where he worked for a number of years, returning in the 1990s to spearhead other memorable and controversial TV crime dramas including

Between the Lines (BBC One, 1992–4) and the first season of *The Cops* (BBC Two, 1998–2001), each of which again presented a less than flattering portrait of the police. While the former once again dealt with corruption on the force, the latter used cinema vérité techniques in its dramatic portrayal of policing in a Northern town. However, although the programme won much critical acclaim, its portrayal of the police was so controversial that police support for the series was withdrawn. As Hilary Curtis reported in *The Guardian* ('It's a Cop Out', 8 October 1999), after seeing the trailers for the first series, the Greater Manchester and Lancashire Police decided that 'the journey through the mind and soul of the modern bobby ventured too close to the occasionally rotten heart of our boys and girls in blue' (Curtis 1999). This once again proved that Tony Garnett was determined to use the crime drama series as a vehicle for trenchant criticism of the established forces of law and order.

Garnett's key role in the history of the television crime drama in Britain points to the ongoing significance of the producer, a significance that was not lost on Horace Newcombe and Robert S. Alley when they declared television to be *The Producer's Medium* in 1983. And clearly this is a position with which Margaret Rogers (2009) would agree, given that in her comprehensive overview of the next major British police procedural to be addressed here, she divides the twenty-six year history of *The Bill* into four phases, each of which corresponding to the tenure of a different executive producer (Rogers 2009).

The life and times of *The Bill*

In Rogers' account, she singles out the contributions of Michael Chapman (1989–98), Richard Handford (1998–2002), Paul Marquess (2002–5), and Jonathon Young (2005–10) – but omits the work of earlier producers such as Lloyd Shirley (1984–7) and Peter Cregeen (1987–9). It is Michael Chapman, Rogers suggests, who was largely responsible for shaping *The Bill* as a police procedural with strong documentary overtones while Richard Handford's contribution included the introduction of the personal lives of the characters and the possibilities of romance in an endeavour to arrest falling ratings. For many of *The Bill*'s long-term followers, the tenure of Paul Marquess as executive director from 2002 to 2005 marked the nadir of the fortunes of this series. Hired with a brief to arrest sliding ratings, Marquess went even further than Handford in a bid to revamp the series to appeal to a younger audience. As Rogers reports, Marquess was well aware that *The Bill*'s primary audience was 'white men over fifty' and determined to change this by changing both the look and the focus of the series. This he succeeded in doing, by virtue of such sensational storylines as the firebombing of the Sun Hill police station – the central hub of the show's action – (this incidentally allowed for a change of decor) as well as an episode transmitted 'live' in order to mark the twentieth anniversary. By 2003 *The Bill* had successfully doubled its target audience in the sixteen to thirty-four year-old bracket and had also attracted more female viewers while having alienated many of its long-term devotees (Rogers 2009). In 2005, Jonathon Young returned the series to its social-realist roots, toning down the sensationalism while retaining the attention to interpersonal relationships. However, despite, or perhaps because of, Young's efforts, *The Bill* was cancelled in 2010, with the final episode, 'Respect', being shown in late August of that year.

In the documentary, *Farewell The Bill*, produced to accompany this final episode, Young makes some surprising claims. *The Bill*, he asserts, was the 'first' British television crime drama to embrace a documentary style and the use of a handheld camera. There was, he continues, simply nothing like it on TV at the time. Without wishing to diminish *The Bill*'s considerable achievements, Young's comments reveal either a lack of knowledge of the history of the television crime genre or the tendency to favour declamatory sound bites in this particular genre of promotional 'making of' programmes. For a start, the impulse towards documentary realism can be traced back to the very earliest days of television and the work of the documentary film unit at the BBC in bringing such series as *Fabian of the Yard* to the small screen. Attention to the working lives of police officers on the beat in working-class areas of London was also hardly innovative, having been apparent in the 1950s' series *Pilgrim Street* and *Dixon of Dock Green*. The focus on policemen working in pairs, first on foot and then in cars, and the extensive use of dialect to suggest authenticity, had been employed in *Z-Cars* in the 1960s and *The Sweeney* in the 1970s. The signature chases of *The Bill*, on both foot and in vehicles, to the accompaniment of squealing tyres, was one of the more well-remembered (and mocked) characteristics of *The Sweeney*. Even more interesting is the fact that in its references to police corruption, *The Bill* was following in the tradition of *Dixon*, *Z-Cars*, *The Sweeney*, and *Law and Order*, which had all addressed the problem at some point in their trajectory. As for the use of the handheld camera, this was a routine feature of the American police procedural *Hill Street Blues* (NBC, 1981–7), as will be discussed in Chapter 3.

With regard to police corruption, in the very first episode of the first series, the character of the immediately unlikeable detective sergeant

Burnside is introduced with the comment from station sergeant Cryer, 'How he got past Countryman, I don't know.' 'Countryman' is here a specific allusion to the unit set up by the Metropolitan Police to investigate corruption within the Flying Squad in 1978. It is hardly surprising then, as Margaret Rogers points out, that when *The Bill* first aired the police commissioner of the time objected to the 'unprofessional and unrealistic attitudes and actions' that were on show (Rogers 2009). However, by the end of Michael Chapman's tenure as executive producer in 1998, Metropolitan police surveys indicated that *The Bill* had become 'the main television police program[me] through which viewers [were] provided with an insight into the real world of policing' and that the Met were quite happy with the ways in which they were being portrayed (Rogers 2009).

Created by television writer Geoff McQueen, *The Bill* had started life in 1983 as a one-off drama entitled 'Woodentop' in the Thames Television Storyboard series on ITV. This self-contained television drama followed PC Jim Carver's first day on the job at Sun Hill police station. A series of twelve fifty-minute episodes was then commissioned for broadcast in what was identified as a post-watershed timeslot, thus enabling more violence to be shown and more 'adult' themes to be explored. This weekly fifty-minute episode format was changed to a twice-weekly thirty-minute format in 1988, increasing to three episodes a week in 1993 in an attempt during the Chapman era to emulate the pulling power of the early evening soap operas. In 1998, *The Bill* returned to an hour-long format that once again became bi-weekly in a return to serialisation during the tenure of Paul Marquess. In 2005, with the arrival of Jonathon Young as executive producer, the serial format was dropped and *The Bill* continued as series of stand-alone episodes at a 9.00pm post-watershed timeslot.

As is apparent from this outline, over the twenty-six years of its history, *The Bill* continually reinvented itself in terms of its format, overall tone and style in an effort to hold the interest of its audience as well as its ratings. Thus, as Rogers suggests, while at times *The Bill* appeared to have more in common with the working-class social-realist soap operas such as *Coronation Street* and *EastEnders*, at other moments it might be more like a situation comedy than a police drama (Rogers 2009). However, the documentary *Farewell to the Bill* reveals a desire on the part of producer Jonathon Young to make 'Respect' a statement of how *The Bill* should be remembered, that is, as a 'gritty' urban drama reflecting the contemporary problems of life and policing in multicultural London. As a result, this episode may have more in common with *The Wire* than anything else on British television at the time, suggesting once again the nature of the 'ongoing conversation' between the British and American police procedural.

The Bill, we are informed in what is the inevitably promotional and self-serving narrative of the *Farewell* documentary, always strove to be authentic in its iconography, using real police uniforms and equipment, and employing police advisors. This included a contribution from former senior policewoman Jackie Malton, who had also been an advisor to the Lynda La Plante series *Prime Suspect* that had debuted in 1991. In this authentic endeavour, the final episode emphasises the team effort involved in a case that begins with the death of a fourteen year-old on a dismal East London housing estate and ends with the arrest of the teenage gang leader at the centre of a network of terror, gang rape, and drug dealing on the estate. In terms of its subject matter and themes, 'Respect' is therefore highly reminiscent of the first season of *The Wire* in terms of its depiction of a depressed underclass in which crime is rampant, especially among the disaffected young, with the police portrayed as largely helpless in the face of endemic social malaise. Although the team at Sun Hill do get a 'result' in this particular case, it is clear that the societal problems they are addressing are much bigger than even they can handle.

The final scene of this last episode, filmed on the set of the Sun Hill police station, located as it was in a converted warehouse in South West London, begins with a press conference, during which superintendent Meadows (played by Simon Rouse) makes an emotional speech about the commitment of his officers to their job, and ends with an elaborate single take, reminiscent of the memorable opening shot of the American police drama *Hill Street Blues*. The camera follows DC Mickey Webb (played by Chris Simmons) from the pressroom, through the corridors, into the locker room, and out to the car park for a final crane shot of Sun Hill as Meadows leaves the police station and gets into his car. During the course of this single shot, all seventeen members of the main cast make an appearance in the company of numerous extras. The impression one is left with is that Sun Hill is still teeming with life, rather than about to meet its televisual demise. And the work of the police, it would appear, will never be done.

As this documentary demonstrates, the choreographing of this final shot required a concerted effort on the part of the technical crew and the cast, who rehearsed it repeatedly in order to get the timing right. The sequence was achieved using a steady-cam strapped to the body of a cameraman who was guided by an assistant along corridors and through doors, in a sequence oddly reminiscent of *The West Wing*'s ubiquitous walk and talk sequences, before backing onto a crane to be elevated for the final angled shot of the car park. In this technical endeavour, the skill needed to produce a look that is both aesthetically pleasing and yet also convincing in terms of its 'realism' is revealed. What is also evident is that like *Hill Street Blues*, *The West Wing*, and *The Wire*, this episode of *The Bill* was aspiring to the look and aesthetic of 'quality' television.

While it may be appropriate to conclude this section on the British police procedural with the demise of *The Bill*, I want to finish this chapter with a discussion of two series that serve to illustrate the ways in which the British crime drama uses and acknowledges the past of the genre in the inventions of the present. *Life on Mars* (BBC One, 2006–7) and its sequel *Ashes to Ashes* (BBC One, 2008–9), are crime drama series that not only illustrate the hybridity of the television crime drama, but also the ways in which these series constitute a reflection on the history of the genre and its relation to law and order issues in the United Kingdom.

Rising from the ashes

Life on Mars began the first of its two eight-episode seasons with a present-day cop transported back to the 1970s and a mode of policing intentionally reminiscent of *The Sweeney*. A spin-off sequel set in the 1980s, *Ashes to Ashes*, ended its three seasons with a farewell from George Dixon, formerly of Dock Green, in a gesture that acknowledged the history and legacy of the television crime drama in the United Kingdom. In making sense of the ending to these two linked series, in which it was finally revealed (not very convincingly it must be said) that all the central characters had been killed earlier in their careers on the force and that the action of both dramas had been played out in a kind of police procedural purgatory, one of the contributors to the blog 'Unreality Shout' noted:

> I loved the final touch of George Dixon, Dixon of Dock Green, doing the 'goodnight' after the credits. Presumably this links with resurrection, and the fact that the character of George Dixon was originally killed off in the Dirk Bogarde film *The Blue Lamp* (1950), only to be brought back to life in 1955 as the start of the BBC TV series, *Dixon of Dock Green*. (Anonymous n.d.f)

What is of interest here is that in making sense of the ending, this particular fan is very able to draw on the pre-history of the television crime drama. There is no doubt that this rear-view mirrorism was intentional since creators Mathew Graham and Ashley Pharoah acknowledge that their original inspiration for *Life on Mars* was the television crime dramas that they grew up watching and loving. As a result, *The Sweeney*, and to a lesser extent the American 1970s' series *Starsky and Hutch*, are clearly referenced in the iconography, setting, and cultural context of *Life on Mars* along with, inevitably, *Dixon of Dock Green*.[4]

The premise of *Life on Mars* is that after being hit by a car and falling into a coma, detective inspector Sam Tyler (played by John Simms) wakes up to find himself mysteriously transported back in time to the Manchester of 1973.[5] To make matters worse, he has been demoted and his new boss is DCI Gene Hunt (played by Philip Glenister) who Sam accuses of being an 'overweight, over-the-hill, nicotine-stained, borderline alcoholic homophobe with a superiority complex and an unhealthy obsession with male bonding' (01: 08). To which Hunt's typically arrogant response is 'You make that sound like a bad thing' (01: 08).

While the creators of the series were keen to deny the charge of nostalgia, Hunt began his on-screen career as an over-the-top parody of all the worst characteristics attributed to *The Sweeney* over the ensuing years. Actor Philip Glenister and writers Graham and Pharoah were clearly having fun sending up the political correctness of the present by means of a character who revels in outrageous rule breaking not only in terms of police procedure, but also with regard to sexuality, feminism, and race. As Stephen Lacey and Ruth McElroy suggest in the introduction of a collection of essays primarily devoted to *Life on Mars* (with some attention necessarily given to *Ashes to Ashes*), the series entered the public discourse of viewers and non-viewers alike in the form of debate about what the 1970s may mean for contemporary British society, especially in relation to policing (Lacey and McElroy 2012: 5).

In the opinion of Andy Willis, far from suggesting that the 1970s were the bad old days as seen from the perspective of a more enlightened present, the series appeared to valorise the 'instinctive rule-bending copper who gets results' as exemplified by DI Hunt (Willis 2012: 61). Contemporary policing, as represented by Sam Tyler, was thus implicitly criticised for being 'overly bureaucratic and obsessed with cumbersome procedures being followed to the letter by its officers' (Willis 2012: 61). In many ways, *Life on Mars* appeared to constitute a restaging of the ongoing battle in *The Sweeney* between the maverick cop Regan and his bureaucratic superiors, framed not in terms of class but as an implicit critique of the managerialism of the 2000s.

For Julie Gardner, a BBC Wales executive producer who had earlier worked on the spy drama *Spooks* (BBC One, 2002–11), *Life on Mars* represented what she intimated was a more American approach to making 'sexy' television with robust entertainment values, pace, wit, and a very 'clear definition of genre' (Gardner cited in Gardner and Parker 2012: 181). This last comment is of particular interest since it marks Gardner's refusal to label the series as 'science fiction' despite its time-travelling premise, an odd demur from a woman who had played a key role in the revitalisation of another BBC production, the iconic science-fiction series *Doctor Who*.

While *Spooks* and *Life on Mars* may indeed have represented an 'Americanisation' of British television in terms of their 'robust entertainment' values (Gardner and Parker 2012: 181), the effort to remake *Life on Mars* in the United States was in American TV scholar David Lavery's words a 'disaster', despite the fact that the ABC network endeavoured to shelter the series by pairing it with their ratings success *Lost* (ABC 2004–10). Comparing the original *Life on Mars* with *Lost*, which followed the fortunes of a group of travellers marooned on an island after an aeroplane crash, David Lavery described both series as 'richly inter-textual, open-ended, serialized, enigmatic mysteries that may or may not be science fiction' (Lavery 2012: 146). The American remake, however, was a bitter disappointment to Lavery, not least as a result of the casting of Harvey Keitel whose 'tired' performance Lavery considered to be but a 'pale imitation' of Glenister's ebullient Gene Hunt (147).

As far as the posters on the fan site *The Railway Arms* were concerned, while it may have been possible to translate the British series into an American setting in terms of the cultural reference points, the remake failed to do this adequately (Mills 2012: 137). For a start, setting the re-visioned series in New York indicated a complete lack of understanding of how the original setting of Manchester, as a regional city signifying 'The North', carried with it a range of very specific cultural connotations, although as one poster suggested, Chicago may have been a suitable substitute (136). For many posters, the prospect of a remake was offensive, signalling yet another instance of American cultural imperialism (137). In this case, the discourse around *Life On Mars* centred on its inherent 'Britishness' and an assumption on the part of the contributors to this discussion that this was in many ways untranslatable, depending as it does on a set of cultural assumptions that, as Brett Mills points out, were assumed to be so well understood by other British posters that they did not need to be delineated (ibid.). The moral of this tale is clear, that is, that for the fans of *Life on Mars*, television is still experienced and understood in terms of the national, a conclusion that is salutary at a moment when the transnational trade in television is presumed to be a marker of increased globalisation (Mills 2012: 142).

With their self-conscious allusions to the history of the British television crime drama, this discussion of *Life on Mars* and *Ashes to Ashes* serves to illustrate the cultural specificity of the police procedural as it has developed in the United Kingdom. However, these series also reveal that the British police procedural has not evolved without some cross-fertilisation, particularly in terms of its style and form, from other sources. Nor is this cross-fertilisation a recent phenomenon, as this chapter has indicated, with *Z-Cars* owing a debt to *Highway Patrol*, and the producers of *The Sweeney* wanting to emulate the *French Connection*, while the closing episode of *The Bill* recalls both *Hill Street Blues* and *The Wire*, both of which have been hailed as 'quality' television crime.

Conclusion

In an essay on the evaluation of quality in television that appeared in 1990, Charlotte Brunsdon suggested that within the British broadcasting context 'good' television had long been considered to be so on the basis of either its relationship with other art forms such as the theatre or literature, or its relationship to the 'real' (Brunsdon 1990a: 59). Thus television adaptations of literary works, or drama and television that reported on 'real' events, such as news and current affairs, were deemed to be of higher quality than other forms of television such as soap operas and game shows (60). 'Bad' television, according to Brunsdon's analysis of the prevailing discourse, is television that is perceived to be 'popular or commercial'. Thus the popular, commercially successful, imported American television drama series that appeared on British screens from the 1950s were inevitably assigned to the category of 'bad' television in Britain (ibid.).

What is of interest here are the ways in which such judgements of quality as identified by Brunsdon have played out within the history of the television crime drama and its reception. For example, those crime series that have adopted a documentary approach, especially when these have been based on 'real' crimes, have usually been well received by critics and viewers alike. So too have those crime dramas that adopt a social-realist aesthetic and a 'gritty' style, especially when this is coupled with a critique of law and order issues. Even more interesting are the accolades accorded to series that appear to be 'groundbreaking' in that they in some way divert from genre expectations, either in terms of form or representation, suggesting that the only 'good' crime dramas are the ones that break the rules. The series that do not appear to have been much valued by critics and commentators, are often those shows that are more light-hearted, cosy even, such as the period crime drama *Heartbeat* (ITV, 1992–2010) or *Midsomer Murders* (ITV, 1997–), which were and are (given the constant recycling of television crime on proliferating channels) popular with audiences. 'Good' crime drama as judged by the kinds of quality standards that Brunsdon identified in the 1990s are assumed to be confronting, unsettling and genre-busting while 'bad' crime drama is just the opposite, offering familiarity and reassurance in its formulaic repetition. However, as Brunsdon and many others have suggested, judgements of quality are actually judgements of taste, which begs the question: Whose taste counts? The debate about 'quality' in the television crime drama will be pursued in the next chapter with regard to the development of the American police procedural and its critical reception.

Notes

1. A Liverpudlian is a native of the city of Liverpool, located in the county of Lancashire in the North West of England.
2. According to the voice-over commentary to episode one, 'The Ringer', the red telephone box was loaded onto a lorry by the props department and followed the location shoot around, ready to be deployed whenever it was needed.
3. As noted in the voice-over commentary to 'Thin Ice'.
4. *Take a Look at the Lawman: Part One* (dir. Lancelot Narayan, 2006). Special feature of *Life on Mars* season one DVD.
5. The fact that *Life on Mars* was produced by BBC Wales for Kudos Films at the same time as BBC Wales was also producing *Doctor Who* was hardly incidental. As Stewart and Pharoah outline in their comments on the feature *Take a Look at the Lawman* (2006), having got one time-travelling drama on their plate BBC Wales was ready for another.

3 Quality Control: The American Police Procedural

While there are many points of comparison between the British and the American police procedural, given that both have reflected changing social attitudes to police and criminology within their different cultural contexts, this chapter will focus mainly on questions of form and style as they have evolved within the American television production environment. The series that will be dealt with here have, therefore, been selected on the basis that they mark significant moments in the evolution of the genre. Of course, any selection of 'significant moments' is to a certain extent subjective, especially for someone like myself who was watching these series in places where their resonance may have been very different from that experienced within the United States where they were originally developed and shown. Furthermore, as will become apparent in this analysis, some American television crime dramas have been taken more seriously and have been accorded a greater significance by academic and other critics over the years than others, with the inevitable result that there are many series that have been both overlooked and undervalued. This once again raises important questions about the criteria of value that have been used to assess the relative merits of television crime series over time.

When it comes to the American television context, Jane Feuer has argued that the distinction between good and bad television, or rather what she designates as 'quality' television and 'trash' television, can be traced to the early days of television when a sharp contrast was made between live anthology drama and the emerging forms of series television (Feuer 2007: 146). 'Quality' was, therefore, associated with television productions that carried the 'cachet' of legitimate theatre because of their liveness as well as their experimentation with story-telling and form. 'Trash' TV was television that adopted a series format, that is, a repetitive and predictable structure, a formula. While Feuer makes no mention of the status of the 'real' here, the point of this essay is to question why some forms of the 'real', such as reality TV, are less valued than others, such as documentary, with which they share many characteristics. As Charlotte Brunsdon noted in her earlier essay on the matter of quality and television, there are always issues of power in judgements of taste (Bunsdon 1990b: 73). In any determination of quality, it is, therefore, important to ask, 'Who gets to decide what is quality and what isn't?' Who are the arbiters of taste?

In 1996, American academic Robert Thompson would go so far as to argue that 'quality' series television had become a genre unto itself and could be identified as such because it shared a number of key characteristics. According to Thompson (1996: 14), quality television is television that:

- is not 'regular' TV in that it breaks the rules
- is produced by people of quality aesthetic pedigree outside of the field of television 'in other, classier media, like film'
- has undergone a 'noble struggle' before achieving success
- uses ensemble casts and multiple, overlapping plot lines
- has a 'memory' in that it refers back to its own history
- creates a new genre by combining old ones
- tends to be literary and writer-based
- is self-conscious
- tends towards the controversial with a liberal (left-wing) sensibility
- aspires towards realism
- includes social and literary criticism.

Thompson also suggested that quality television is television that attracts a blue-chip demographic, 'the upscale, well-educated, urban dwelling, young viewers [that] advertisers so desire to reach' (Thompson 1996: 14), raising the possibility that 'quality' television is the kind of television that a 'quality' audience (based on their consumer buying power) chooses to watch. In genre terms, quality TV, like Teen TV or Cult TV, is, therefore, a classification of television that depends on the perceived or intended audience rather than on its form, content, or themes. This is evident in the fact that the shows Thompson lists in his catalogue of quality include shows that belong to a number of different genres, including 'quirky' dramas such as the comedy drama *Northern Exposure* (CBS, 1990–5), the medical drama *St Elsewhere* (NBC, 1982–8), the legal drama *L.A. Law* (NBC, 1986–94) as well as such crime series as *Moonlighting* (ABC, 1985–9), *Twin Peaks* (ABC, 1990–1), and the police procedurals *Cagney and Lacey* (CBS, 1982–8) and *Hill Street Blues* (NBC, 1981–7). Revisiting the issue of quality in 2007, Thompson noted that while he could find a lot of shows on air that embraced the characteristics he had identified in 1996 as being those of 'quality' series television, many of these shows weren't any 'good', begging the question of what Thompson now thought was 'good' TV if 'quality' TV was no longer any guarantee of value (Thompson 2011: xx). This shift underlines Brunsdon's argument that it all depends on the criteria of value being applied, and by whom.

As this chapter will argue, critical evaluations of the American police procedural over the years have routinely invoked the criteria summarised by Thompson in 1996 in their assessment of the relative merits of a particular crime drama. In order to illustrate how such discourses have operated, particular attention will be paid to a number of series that are not discussed by Thompson, including Joseph Wambaugh's anthology series *Police Story* in the 1970s, Michael Mann's *Miami Vice* in the 1980s, and Dick Wolf's *Law & Order* in the 1990s. Finally, Jerry Bruckheimer's *CSI* (2000–) and David Simon's *The Wire* (HBO, 2002–7) will be compared in order to demonstrate the different critical reception that these two shows have received, given that they share many characteristics of the crime drama as a genre.

It may be noted that in the case of each of the series mentioned above, there is an immediate association with a particular producer or writer. This suggests that when it comes to notions of auteurism in television, the director is accorded less significance. What does matter, however, is the suggestion implicit in this naming that television can in fact be 'authored'. Just as the concept of the auteur/director was strategically deployed in film studies to recuperate cinema as an art form, so in television the attribution of a producer/writer serves to legitimate the (somewhat begrudging and slow to eventuate) appreciation of the television series as an art form. However, in line with Thompson's definition of quality TV above, it clearly also helps if the television 'auteur' has some form of 'aesthetic ancestry' outside of television, especially film. This was evident in *The New Yorker* television critic Emily Naussbaum's enthusiastic response to New Zealand film director Jane Campion's 2013 foray into the television crime drama with her seven-part series *Top of the Lake*, drawing comparisons with cult director David Lynch's 'visually daring' crime series *Twin Peaks* in 1990 (Nussbaum 2013: 106).

Attributions of authorship, however, obscure and devalue the fact that most television series may employ multiple directors and writers, and undergo a number of stylistic and even format makeovers within the period of their existence. While the executive producer, or more often these days the 'show-runner', may be a key figure in establishing the continuity of the show, as Caldwell points out, the production of a television series is still very much a collective enterprise (Caldwell 2008: 199). As a result, it is often tricky to talk about the stylistics of a television crime series as a whole, since it is quite possible to come across an episode that completely contradicts, or at the very least calls into question, any overarching authorial vision. This would include Troy Kennedy Martin's 'comic' episodes of *The Sweeney* discussed in the last chapter or, jumping ahead, the season five finale of *CSI* directed by Quentin Tarantino that attracted an audience of about 30 million viewers who were regaled with scenes of body trauma more typical of Tarantino's cult films than *CSI*'s more clinical scenes of forensic investigation (Bignell 2007: 161).

In considering matters of form, it should also be noted that in both the United States and the United Kingdom over the last sixty years, television crime dramas have adopted a number of different formats, sometimes even within the same series. These have included the anthology series, half-hour or one-hour episodic series with ongoing characters, as well as 'hybrid' series that have embraced both an episodic and a serial narrative, with story arcs that can last the length of a season or even continue across seasons in what has come to be called the 'long-form narrative'. Crime series have, therefore, varied in the degree of attention they have paid to the drama of the ongoing characters as opposed to the investigation of the crime. Such differences in form and focus reveal the ongoing tension between the competing pull of documentary and melodrama, entertainment and edification, as they have played out within the genre.

Another important aspect of both the British and the American police procedurals involves the portrayal of place. For example, in the British police procedural there has been the perceived distinction between police procedurals set in the North of the United Kingdom and those set in the South: a regional and metropolitan distinction that also has a class dimension. In the United States, location has also played a key role in the development and differentiation of the police procedural as a sub-genre. Here the distinction is more likely to be between East Coast crime and West Coast crime, or be between the urban and the rural, with the occasional excursion into more 'exotic' locales, such as Hawaii (*Hawaii Five-O*, CBS, 1968–80) or Florida (*Miami Vice*, NBC, 1984–9). Many American police procedurals, however, have taken as their setting 'the city', whether this be the Los Angeles of *Dragnet* (NBC, 1951–9), the New York of *Naked City* (ABC, 1958–63), the unnamed urban locale of *Hill Street Blues* (NBC, 1981–7), or a documentary approach to the city of Baltimore in *The Wire* (HBO, 2002–8).

From documentary to drama

The history of the police procedural both in Britain and in the United States reveals an early commitment to 'documentary realism' in the portrayal of crime on television, with implications for the judgements of taste involved. In the case of Britain, *Fabian of the Yard*, which was also shown on CBS television in the United States, offered an intriguing case study based as it was on the actual cases of a real-life detective who appeared at the end of every episode to endorse the verisimilitude of what the TV audience had just seen: an amalgam of actors reconstructing dramatic scenes shot on film in a studio and on location around London. In the United States, the commitment to realism in the police procedural resulted in the iconic series *Dragnet*, which also drew its stories from 'real-life' cases, recreated as half-hour dramas that were similarly shot on film at various locations in and around the city as well as on studio sets.

For David Marc, *Dragnet*'s serial format resulted in what he describes as a 'thoroughly familiar packaging formula' and he is particularly harsh in his criticism of the show and its creator, Jack Webb, arguably one of television's most significant auteurs (Marc 1984: 73). Jason Mittell, on the other hand, suggests that despite *Dragnet*'s historical and cultural importance, the show has long been undervalued and dismissed by media historians who have failed to take into account its unique textual style and complex vision of the American social order and ideology (Mittell 2004: 125). As a result, *Dragnet* has rarely been described as 'quality' television in America or 'good' television in other locations where popular American series TV is routinely dismissed as 'bad' television simply because it is American. This assumption, however, has more recently been challenged by the critical accolades accorded to such American 'quality' crime series as *The Wire* (HBO, 2002–8).

While the influence of *Dragnet* on the form and style of the police procedural was considerable, involving as it did a half-hour episode dealing with a single case investigated by a cast of ongoing characters, early crime drama series could, and did, take other forms. *Gang Busters*, originally created in 1936 by radio producer Phillips H. Lord, took a subtly different approach to the formula (Snauffer 2006: 9).[1] For a start, the series employed an 'anthology' approach, involving a different plot and a different set of characters in each episode. Second, while *Dragnet* focused on the investigation of a crime *after* it had been committed, thereby eschewing the need to show criminal activity on-screen, *Gang Busters* focused on the planning and execution of the crime. Like *Dragnet*, *Gang Busters* also involved assurances to the audience from creator Lord who would appear at the beginning and end of every episode informing the audience that the stories they were watching were 'true', based as they were on real-life police and FBI cases. Like *Dragnet*, *Gang Buster*s also ended with the punishment meted out to the offenders and the assurance that the law, if not justice, had prevailed.

According to the ratings, American audiences appeared to enjoy both series, which were broadcast during their first seasons on alternate Thursday nights, and both were renewed by NBC in the autumn of 1952 (Snauffer 2006: 10). However, for reasons that are not entirely clear, but that may have had much to do with Webb's ability to produce two episodes of *Dragnet* in as little as five days and to work cheaply, the network made the decision to cancel *Gang Busters* (Snauffer 2006: 10). This allowed *Dragnet* to become the dominant stylistic influence on the genre for the duration of the 1950s and, in the bargain, to have a lasting influence on the future of the genre. For example, even though the New York-based series *The Naked City* (ABC, 1958) had embraced a more liberal sensibility, including the possibility of flawed policemen, it stayed close to the *Dragnet* episodic half-hour formula and the documentary-style assertion that it too was presenting 'true' stories about a 'real' city.

Police Story – the weeping policeman

While the detective as hero became the standard for many TV crime series in the 1960s, the series that signalled a different direction for the police procedural as a sub-category of the crime genre in the United States was *Police Story* (NBC, 1973–8). Like the much earlier *Gang Busters*, *Police Story* also adopted an 'anthology' approach, each episode dealing with a different LAPD police officer working a case (although there were a few recurring faces). Like many earlier procedurals, *Police Story* also claimed to be an 'authentic' depiction of crime and policing, based as it was on the stories provided by a serving LAPD policeman, Joseph Wambaugh. Born in 1938, Wambaugh had already published two crime novels (*The New Centurions* and *The Blue Knight*), the first of which had already been made into a film and the second into what Wambaugh claims to be the first TV mini-series before producer David Gerbner contacted him about the creation of a new police drama series based on his own, and that of his fellow LAPD officers, experiences on the job ('Cop Talk' 2011).[2]

According to Wambaugh, Gerbner had a struggle convincing

the network to embrace the format of an anthology series given the popularity of the series format at the time, involving a cast of ongoing characters who investigated a different case every week ('Cop Talk' 2011). However, as far both Wambaugh and Gerbner were concerned, this was the only way to communicate the 'authentic' experience of policing with a focus on the 'story' rather than the stars. Relieved from the pressure of a recurring ensemble of actors, the writers were able to mirror a grimmer reality. As Wambaugh put it, 'if a cop had to die he died' ('Cop Talk' 2011). As a result, the series was allocated a later time slot, not because it was violent, but because the stories it told contained adult themes.

In terms of format, *Police Story* premiered with a two-hour movie-length episode, starring James Farentino as a 'hard-edged veteran recruited by a special task force set up to track down a killer' (Snauffer 2006: 83). Subsequently adopting a one-hour format, although the two-hour movie-length episodes did recur, the series focused on all aspects of police work, 'from the exhilarating to the mundane' (Snauffer 2006: 83). The featured cop(s) of the week may be old or young, male or female, on- or off-duty, both good and bad. However, the major innovation of the show, according to Wambaugh, was a shift in focus from the *work* of policing, to a concentration on the *experience* of policing. In an interview accompanying the re-release of the first season of *Police Story* on DVD, Wambaugh describes it thus:

> I wanted to get into the psychology of being a cop. I don't care about chases and shootouts and squealing tyres and sirens. That isn't what makes up police work . . . at least not the interesting part of the work to me. It's the psychology of the job; it's the psychology of the cop. It's what happens to him after being out there on the street and seeing not just the worst of people but ordinary people at their worst. What does that do to the cop? Does that make him prematurely cynical? If it does, how does he go home and deal with his family? I'm interested in all of that. ('Cop Talk' 2011)

As an illustration of the kind of story he wanted to tell, Wambaugh refers to an episode in the first season entitled 'The Wyatt Earp Syndrome' (after the Pima County deputy sheriff): the title of which refers to that moment in the career of a young cop when the weight of carrying a badge becomes immense and occupies his thoughts to the detriment of all other relationships. Apparently the 'actual' name for this well-known condition among serving police officers was 'The John Wayne Syndrome' (after the American film actor who starred in, among others, many Western films) but Gerbner and Wambaugh were obliged to change this in order to avoid being sued by Wayne ('Cop Talk' 2011).

'The Wyatt Earp Syndrome' opens with what were the opening and closing 'beats' of the series as a whole, a stylised radio call summoning police to the scene of the crime. We then follow the trajectory of young policeman, Curt Nations (Cliff Gorman), accompanied by a rookie sidekick, Hawkins (played by singer Smokey Robinson), whom Nations patronises unmercifully. After being called to rescue a child wandering onto the freeway, they are soon on the track of a serial rapist. As his obsession with catching the culprit mounts, Nations becomes increasingly estranged from his wife and daughter. Desperate to save their marriage, the wife makes an appointment for them both with the police psychologist, which her husband fails to attend, thus providing an opportunity for the expert to explain to her (and to the audience) the nature of the syndrome we are seeing acted out. It's a didactic but effective moment, providing a rationale for the obsessive behaviour we are witnessing. At this point, the episode could go either way with the more comforting option being an acknowledgement by Nations of his problems and reconciliation with his wife. Instead, Nations shoots his suspect in an unthinkingly enthusiastic act of violence after failing to wait for back-up. He then comes home to an empty apartment, his wife and child having left. As he breaks down in tears and weeps, the camera backs away down the corridor to take in his gun belt on the hall stand, attached to which is his police radio that crackles into life. It's yet another call to yet another crime scene, underlining the point of the episode that police work is relentless and all-consuming.

Shot in colour on location in Los Angeles and on studio sets, *Police Story* looks much like other television of the 1970s; it is nothing out of the ordinary, nor is the acting particularly memorable. Indeed, the performances are surprisingly muted, in what one assumes was a bid for social realism. What appears to have impressed viewers and critics alike, however, was the refusal to compromise on the portrayal of a grim job with even grimmer consequences for those who undertake it. There is no sensationalising, the camera drawing back at the moment of high emotion. The focus thus shifts from the individual characters and their story to the police radio emitting its formulaic call sign, evoking the ongoing and collective nature of police work.

As an anthology series, *Police Story* ran for five seasons, during the course of which at least three episodes generated their own spin-offs. Perhaps the most famous of these was *Police Woman* (NBC, 1974–8) starring Angie Dickinson who appeared in a first season episode of

Police Story entitled 'The Gamble' (to be discussed in Chapter 6). Less successful was the series *Joe Forrester* (NBC, 1975–6), which was based on a character played by Lloyd Bridges in a second season episode. And even less well known (it only lasted ten episodes) was the spin-off *Man Under Cover* (NBC, 1978–9) from the fifth season episode 'A Chance to Live' starring then teen idol David Cassidy as a fresh-faced cop going undercover in a high school, a premise that would be revisited in Stephen J. Cannell's more successful teen crime drama in the 1980s *21 Jump Street* (Fox, 1987–91). The latter starred a then unknown Johnny Depp as a member of a team of funkily dressed young officers going undercover in high schools and other youth hangouts, illustrating once again that for every bold new departure in the genre, there is almost always a precedent lurking somewhere in the past. It is, therefore, always advisable to be wary of the word 'first' in relation to any critical assessment of a television crime drama, although the temptation to greet every new show with the adjective 'ground-breaking' appears to be enormous, as this chapter will demonstrate.

In its attention to the emotional lives of the police, *Police Story* thus provides an important link between the documentary push of the police procedural drama in the formative years and the pull towards melodrama via an engagement with the personal lives of the serving policemen and women on and off the job. As will be suggested below, this melodramatic pull was to become much stronger during the 1980s in series such as *Hill Street Blues* and *Miami Vice*.

Hill Street Blues: mimesis and melodrama

According to John Thornton Caldwell, the history of American television in the 1970s and 1980s was marked by a shift away from what he describes as the entrenched 'homogenous, studio bound style of the 1970s dramatic telefilm' (Caldwell 1995: 58). This style Caldwell associates with such shows as Aaron Spelling's *Charlie's Angels*, Warner Bros.'s *Dukes of Hazzard* (CBS, 1979–85), and *CHiPs* (NBC, 1977–83), all of which he summarily dismisses on the basis of their tendency to place 'in front of the disinterested 35mm camera' what he describes as 'loaded objects and libidinous bodies' (Caldwell 1995: 58), including a 1969 Dodge Charger car, the chrome-laden motorcycles of leather-clad Californian highway patrolmen, and beautiful women.

This is not the kind of television crime that Caldwell takes seriously and that by default deserves some attention and recuperation. Although Thompson admits that he did indeed watch and enjoy *CHiPS* (Thompson 1996: 17), Caldwell is much more interested in the television style created and inspired by the more experimental work of independent television production houses such as MTM in the 1980s. According to Caldwell, when NBC 'bought' producers Steve Bochco and Michael Kozoll from MTM NBC was attempting to import both 'a look as well as an attitude' (Caldwell 1995: 61). The result was what is frequently, and to some extent justifiably, described as the 'ground-breaking' police procedural *Hill Street Blues* (NBC, 1981–7), which recombined existing genre elements in original ways.

In its attention to the routine of the cops on the job and its gesture towards documentary realism, albeit highly stylised, *Hill Street Blues* drew on its police procedural predecessors. However, as Caldwell points out, as a new hybrid form of crime drama, *Hill Street* also owed a stylistic debt to a number of other non-crime series from the 1970s, including the sitcom *M*A*S*H* (CBS, 1972–83) and the prime-time drama series, *Dallas* (CBS, 1978–91). While *M*A*S*H* demonstrated what could be achieved with an ensemble of skilled actors, *Dallas* took the family melodrama associated with daytime soap opera and trans-lated it into a glossy, large-budget enterprise involving big business, expensive decor, and explosive action. In the mining of both, Caldwell considers that *Hill Street Blues* constituted a 'premeditated stylistic breakthrough' in its endeavours to produce television that both looked and sounded different (Caldwell 1995: 63).

Getting that style on-screen and keeping it there was not an easy matter. One of Bochco's sources for the series was *Police Tapes* (1976), a low-resolution, black and white, small budget, documentary film about police on the streets by Susan and Alan Raymond (Caldwell 1995: 64). The major challenge for the director of photography on *Hill Street* was to achieve the same 'gritty' look in a studio using 35mm film. A review of the pilot episode reveals just how artfully this look was achieved using handheld cameras, minimal editing, and a strategic use of setting and performance.

In the first shot of the series, the camera unsteadily tracks the action through the station house into the meeting room for the 7.00am roll call – a scene that became the overture for every subsequent episode in a series that routinely followed the events of a single day at the station. This was a series that did not eschew such formulaic moves. The screen is crowded with movement; there is what Caldwell characterises as a kind of a 'visual chaos', repeated in the aural chaos of a soundtrack employing multiple and overlapping tracks (1995: 64). Apparently this was the gritty look and the messy sound that Bochco wanted to achieve and that Caldwell characterises as a wall-to-wall visual style that 'became a defining property both of each episode and of the ensemble of quality actors as well' (65). Note the telling use of the word 'quality' here. While the television critics were impressed, viewers at home, 'needed a little more time to make sense of it all' (Snauffer 2006: 116), thus revealing the potential gap between judgements of taste and the ratings, which has been an ongoing tendency in the reception of the television crime drama both in the United Kingdom and the United States.

As evidence of the enthusiastic critical reception that *Hill Street Blues* was accorded as quality television, Robert Thompson quotes 'one of America's most prominent and prolific novelists', Joyce Carol Oates, in her 1985 cover story for the widely read *TV Guide*:

> [It is] one of the few television programs watched by a fair percentage of my Princeton colleagues . . . [It is] one of the few current television programs that is intellectually and emotionally provocative as a good book. In fact from the very first, *Hill Street Blues* struck me as Dickensian in its superb character studies, its energy, its variety; above all its audacity. (Oates cited in Thompson 1996: 59)

This quotation is revealing in that it underlines the notion that 'quality' television is judged to be so on the basis that it is less like television and more like something else, in this case 'a good book', possibly one by Charles Dickens. At which point we may note the parallels with the evaluation and reception of the television series *The Wire* (2002–8), which was also described as Dickensian, as will be discussed in more detail below. Viewers of *Hill Street Blues* were thus reassured that what they were watching was quality television given that they were joining a quality audience (composed of Oates and her Princeton colleagues) in the process.

Members of the test audience for the pilot, however, found the show 'too confusing, too violent and too depressing' (Thompson 1996: 65). Not only were viewers presented with television that looked and sounded different from other drama series of the time, but it was television that dared to break genre expectations. The pilot, for instance, did not finish well with two of the central characters, Bobby Hill (Michael Warren) and Andy Renko (Charles Hill), having been shot by drug-dealers and left for dead in a deserted apartment building. This was not how a continuing crime series was supposed to end. And it didn't. After Bochco was given the green light for the series, Hill and Renko were revived for season one and the ratings began to slowly improve.[3] *Hill Street Blues* subsequently stayed on air for another seven seasons during the course of which it was nominated for seventy Emmy Awards, winning twenty-six, including Best Dramatic

Series four times. Meanwhile the popular ratings winner was *Magnum PI* (CBS, 1980–8), a crime series in a much chirpier mode, featuring a private eye played by Tom Selleck complete with floral shirts, shorts, and a frisky moustache romping through an exotic Hawaiian setting.

Tellingly, while much has been written about *Hill Street Blues* and its significant role in the 'canon' of acclaimed television crime series, rather less has been written about other 'popular' series of the time, except in relation to their gender politics. As Sandy Flitterman noted, following its premiere in December 1980, *Magnum P.I.* remained one of the top-rated shows in the United States for five years. This she attributed to the attraction of its central character, Magnum, played by Tom Selleck, who deliberately undercut the macho James Bond character envisaged in the original pilot, becoming in the process even more attractive to the show's 'preponderantly female audience' (Flitterman 1985: 46). In seeking to understand why *Magnum P.I.* has received such little critical attention when compared with the critical attention paid to *Hill Street Blues*, it may be salutary to note that television perceived to be targeted at a female audience, from soap operas to cooking shows, has tended to be critically undervalued and overlooked (van Zoonen 1994: 105; Bonner 2003: 1). This renders the inclusion of the ongoing melodramatic storylines typical of a daytime soap in a critically acclaimed crime series such as *Hill Street Blues* an even more interesting case study in the politics of taste. Clearly such melodramatic moves were acceptable in a 'gritty' police drama and may even contribute to the 'quality' of the series as a whole in its innovative hybrid form, just as long as that show was not obviously intended for a predominantly female audience.

While *Magnum P.I.* may have been the ratings success of the time, it was *Hill Street Blues* that would arguably be the most influential crime drama series of the period, not only in terms of its style but also in terms of its format. Although each episode of *Hill Street* might encompass one or two finite plot lines (Plot A and Plot B), the ongoing characters in the station would also be involved in a range of continuing plot lines about their various relationships (the proliferating plot Cs) that travelled across episodes, and even across seasons, thus establishing a format somewhere between the episodic series and the ongoing serial: a hybrid narrative form that would become the pattern for many television dramas to follow.

In terms of content, like many crime series before and after, *Hill Street Blues* confronted topical issues such as gang warfare, although the actual city in which the action was taking place was never identified. Like *Police Story*, the show focused on the 'real' experiences of serving police officers: the budget cuts, the possibility of burnout, and frequent public relations nightmares (Snauffer 2006: 117). Meanwhile one of the ongoing 'C' plots followed the love life of Captain Frank Furillo (played by the relatively unknown actor Daniel J. Travanti) as a recently divorced, recovering alcoholic, with a demanding ex-wife, a beautiful lover (public defender Joyce Davenport played by Veronica Hamel) whom he would subsequently marry, and a station to run. *Hill Street* thus combined matters of crime and policing (the realist dimension) with matters of heart (the melodramatic dimension) in a potent mix.

After the cancellation of *Hill Street Blues*, Bochco continued to develop crime series, including the ill-fated *Cop Rock* (ABC, 1990) – that endeavoured to capitalise on the 1980s' success of the music video network MTV by turning the crime show into a musical. This feat was more successfully achieved by the British TV series *Blackpool* (BBC One, 2004), a playful thriller set against the seedy, tawdry backdrop of a British northern seaside town. The American remake of *Viva Laughlin* (CBS, 2007) produced by and starring Australian actor Hugh Jackman was cancelled after only two episodes. Bochco's next successful foray into crime was *NYPD Blue* (ABC, 1993–5), which in its use of handheld cameras to vertiginous effect and its attention to the emotional lives of the serving policemen, can be seen as a continuation of the experiment with form and style of the police procedural that Bochco had begun in *Hill Street Blues*.

Miami Vice: the triumph of style

Another series to be developed in the 1980s that was to have an enduring influence on the aesthetics of television crime drama was *Miami Vice*, a crime drama frequently accused of taking an attention to style to excessive lengths, an interesting accusation since the same criticism may well have been made of *Hill Street Blues*. Although it has been suggested that the series began with a scribbled note from NBC TV president Brandon Tartikoff who wanted a show featuring 'MTV cops' (Snauffer 2006: 136), this was not the only inspiration for the show. *Miami Vice* creator Anthony Yerkovitch suggests in a commentary to the DVD re-release of the first season that his concept came not from the recently established video music television cable channel, MTV, but from a newspaper clipping about how Miami had become a centre for drug-smuggling in and out of America. This revelation, along with ongoing racial tension between white and Hispanic populations, rendered the city of Miami an attractive location for a crime drama with a very different kind of urban backdrop and look.[4] The comment also

signals the creator's intention to locate the show within the documentary (and culturally valued) conventions of television crime.

With its art deco mansions sparkling in the sunlight, aqua seascapes,
and pastel-clad undercover cops wearing designer shades, *Miami Vice*
not only looked very different from the more 'gritty' aesthetic of urban
crime shows such as *Hill Street Blues*, it also sounded different, too.
Following the MTV impulse, *Miami Vice* was one of the first television
shows to use recorded pop music and embed this into a soundtrack that
also included up to thirty minutes per episode of original electronic
music composed by Jan Hammer. For media academic John Fiske,
the use of this popular music, often accompanied by a montage of
voluptuous visual images, was merely an 'interruption in the narrative'
intended to seduce the eye (Fiske 1987: 255). Close attention to both
the music and the lyrics reveals that this was hardly the case and that
the musical tracks were often selected on the basis of how they might
provide a commentary on the action, however oblique.

One of the key examples in the pilot episode is the use of the track
'In the Air Tonight' by British artist, Phil Collins,[5] to accompany a
scene in which Crockett and Tubbs drive to a showdown with the
drug-dealers. The build-up of the tension is nicely evoked in the lyrics
('I can feel it coming'), leading to the inevitable Phil Collins' drum
roll, and the onset of the action. Eventually *Miami Vice* acquired the
distinction of being the first television crime drama to release its own
soundtrack album (as opposed to simply the theme tune). This went
to the top of the Billboard Charts in 1985 and stayed there for eleven
weeks ('The Music of Miami Vice' DVD extra 2005).

Fiske's dismissal of the pop music used in the series is typical of
a number of other commentators both at the time and since who
have suggested that *Miami Vice* suffered from an excess of style at
the expense of content. Caldwell (1995: 64–6) typically characterises
the series as 'designer video', a 'weekly ritual of style', in which the
dialogue hardly mattered at all, which is hardly true. Expressionist
in terms of direction, cinematography, lighting, cutting, and sound
design, *Miami Vice* was accused of being all about the conspicuous consumption of Armani suits and fast cars against a backdrop of high key
pastels with the occasional descent into neon-lit gloom. In the process,
the implicit critique of the conspicuous consumption on display, the
very careful use of bright light, deep shadows, and colour coding, were
overlooked. It was not unusual for plot lines to employ different visual
styles, a move that would be adopted many years later in the forensic
series *CSI*, which made extensive use of colour coding for its various
locations and intersecting plot lines (Turnbull 2007: 29).

The person responsible for the 'look' of Miami Vice was producer, Michael Mann. Born in Chicago, Mann undertook his film training at the London Film School after which he worked on television commercials alongside contemporaries such as Ridley Scott and Adrian Lyne, directors who would develop their own signature style in films such as *Bladerunner* (Scott, 1982) and *Flashdance* (Lyne, 1983). Significantly for this account of the crime drama series, Mann began his career in Hollywood writing scripts in the 1970s for such shows as *Starsky and Hutch* (ABC, 1975–9) and Wambaugh's *Police Story* before writing and directing his first feature film, *Thief*, in 1981. Mann, therefore, brought to *Miami Vice* (in Thompson's terms) a 'quality pedigree' acquired in the 'classier' medium of film. However, while Thompson mentions *Miami Vice* in passing, it is not one of the series that he discusses in relation his notion of 'quality TV' even though it satisfies many of the criteria he mentions, with the notable exception of 'realism'. *Miami Vice* was a crime show that largely eschewed a realist aesthetic.

With its atmospheric use of electronic music by Tangerine Dream to accompany the frequent travelling shots along wet roads illuminated by street lights and vivid neon, Michael Mann's earlier film *Thief* provided an acoustic and visual blueprint for *Miami Vice*. It is also worth noting that there's a bleakness and nihilism about *Thief*, a noir sensibility, which also found its way into the world of Crockett and Tubbs. In this way, *Miami Vice*, with its focus on a couple of cops in a fast car (recalling *Starsky and Hutch*) trying to come to terms with their emotional life and the demands of the job (recalling *Police Story*) set against a neon noir backdrop (like *Thief*), can be read as the logical outcome of Mann's earlier forays into the world of crime.

With an unprecedented budget of more than $1.3 million per episode, Mann aspired to the production values of a weekly feature film rather than a low-budget television series, although ironically this expense often appeared to be at the heart of critical devaluation of the show. Moreover, while it is easy to be seduced by the high style and the luscious visuals, a close reading of *Miami Vice* suggests that these should not be taken at face value. One of the few commentators at the time to notice the ironic gap between surface and reality was academic Jane Feuer who argued that far from being a frivolous exercise in style, *Miami Vice* was also dealing with overtly political issues, such as US involvement in Nicaragua in the episode 'Stone's War' (03: 02) (Feuer 1995: 103). Feuer's key point, however, was that *Miami Vice*'s use of visual excess constituted a form of 'complicitous critique': a 'knowingness' about what it was doing and why, in which the viewer was invited to participate (ibid.).

As evidence, Feuer cites a poolside scene where both male and female bodies are self-consciously flaunted for the pleasure of the camera's gaze while Crockett and Tubbs engage in the following conversation about the longeurs of a stakeout:

Crockett: I hate the waiting. I feel like a character in a Beckett play.
Tubbs: Since when do you know Beckett?
Crockett: Charlie Beckett, down on the corner, the shoeshine, writes plays on the side. (Feuer 1995: 103–4)

Miami Vice expected its viewers to know that it knew what it was doing, and to keep up with its tricky moves, even as these assumed a literary, even high-art, education.

For David Buxton, the style of the show was a visual manifestation of the vice in which everyone was implicated (Buxton 1990: 143). While Miami may look like a paradise, what lay beneath was much darker and more sinister. For Buxton, the *Miami* of *Vice* thus represents a fallen world, the end of the American Dream. Buxton considers it no coincidence that Sonny Crockett is a Vietnam veteran. In this world, the lines between good and bad have become so blurred that even the police, who are supposed to maintain the distinction, cannot locate them. In a telling two-part episode in season four entitled 'Mirror Image' (4: 22–3), Crockett suffers a bout of amnesia, forgets that he is a cop, and goes to work for a Columbian crime lord, at which point he is enlisted in a plot to kill his former partner, Tubbs.

While *Miami Vice* may have begun as a 'cynical attempt to juxtapose two police style heroes against a glamorous vice backdrop', anxiety about America's economic decline and moral breakdown during the Reagan years pushed the series into new and ambiguous territory (Buxton 1990: 158). Far from celebrating the conspicuous trappings of consumer wealth and style constantly on show, the series would illustrate in no uncertain terms the moral and economic decline that they indicated. As an illustration, Buxton works through the significance of Crockett's Ferrari that, while it allows the undercover cop to show off his driving skills, is also an object of critique, especially when he is driving through poor neighbourhoods where its status as a 'foreign' import is remarked upon (Buxton 1990: 159). *Miami Vice* was always alert to the politics of race and class, not to mention gender, as is revealed by a close analysis of its title sequence that foregrounded a tourist 'image' of Miami while the episodes themselves revealed the city's less glamorous underbelly. Writing in 1990, Buxton wondered where the crime series could possibly go post the nihilism of *Miami Vice* in an environment where television itself was fragmenting as the old broadcasting model gave way to new, more market-driven, forces.

One direction in which the crime drama series would proceed was towards increased cynicism about the job of policing in a society riddled by corruption from top to bottom. A more recent example of this trend (to be addressed later in this chapter) is David Simon's *The Wire* produced for HBO, a cable environment with a subscriber-based audience of comparatively 'affluent, middle class white Americans', a 'blue chip demographic' with implications for judgements of value and taste (Marshall and Potter 2009: 9). Another more conservative trend followed by the TV networks would see the police procedural continuing to present the police as heroes struggling to maintain law and order against the odds. With this in mind, it's interesting to note that when Dick Wolf, a former writer and producer on *Hill Street Blues*, was casting around for inspiration for a new television crime drama, he once again turned to the past.

Law & Order: back to the future?

Wolf's inspiration for his new series *Law & Order* was located in two earlier crime dramas: *Dragnet*, which Wolf would subsequently revive in a not altogether successful season in 2003, and *Arrest and Trial* (ABC, 1963–4) that Wolf would also go on to remake as a docudrama in 2000 (Snauffer 2006: 160). While *Dragnet* provided the format of a tight half-hour episodic drama focusing on the work of dedicated policemen whose private lives hardly mattered in their professional dedication to the job, *Arrest and Trial* (also produced by Webb), constituted a movie-length, ninety-minute, self-contained drama that encompassed both the police investigation and the subsequent trial. Starring Ben Gazzara as detective sergeant Nick Anderson and Chuck Connors as attorney John Egan, thirty episodes of this series were produced that had the distinction of being the first imported American show to be shown on the newly created BBC Two in the United Kingdom in 1963 (Briggs 1995: 413).

In opting for the one-hour, episodic format for *Law & Order*, Wolf was, therefore, swimming against the prevailing tide in the format of television drama. With the success of the prime-time series *Dallas* and *Dynasty* in the 1980s, and the appropriation of ongoing narratives into the crime genre, as in the case of *Hill Street Blues*, serial melodrama was the current trend in television crime drama. It is, therefore, hardly surprising that Wolf met with some difficulty in selling the concept of his new, determinedly episodic, series to the US networks. *Law & Order* was rejected by both Fox and CBS before being taken up by NBC, the original home of both *Dragnet* and *Arrest and Trial.*

Bucking current fashion and employing a tight episodic structure, *Law & Order* was ironically hailed by critics in the popular press as the most 'groundbreaking new series of the 1990s' (Snauffer 2006: 159), despite the fact that it actually marked a return to earlier manifestations of the television crime drama series. Within this tight structure, the first half of each episode would follow police investigation, and second half would follow the criminal trial, the shift in focus being heralded by a jarring sound that the musical director Mike Post described as 'The Clang'.[6] This sound, according to Post, was constructed from a number of other sounds, including that of a judge's gavel, a jail door slamming, and, bizarrely, the sound of five hundred Japanese monks walking across a hardwood floor (Schwarzbaum 1993). Despite, or perhaps because of, this ingenuity, the show was not an immediate hit and it took until the 1997–8 season for *Law & Order* to rate in the top twenty shows, eventually rising to number five in its eleventh season (Snauffer 2006: 163), once again illustrating the gap between the critical evaluation 'ground-breaking', and the popularity of a show in terms of its ratings.

In trying to explain this gap, Snauffer suggests that one of the reasons why *Law & Order* initially failed to appeal to viewers was because of its 'unique' documentary look (Snauffer 2006: 162). This claim can easily be challenged given the historical development of a genre in which a documentary look was hardly 'unique'. Furthermore, a close analysis of the first episode of the first season reveals that despite its claim to tell stories 'torn' from the headlines, *Law & Order* looks less like documentary and much more like most of the other American drama series that were on air at the time. As evidence of the show's intention to appeal to a wider audience, Snauffer notes that in an endeavour to give the show more 'sex appeal', the number of female characters in the third season (1992–3) was increased. Whether this move was about 'sex appeal', or an attempt to cash in on the success of other crime series featuring women in key roles, and/or the increasing prominence of women in the workplace, the ploy worked and the increase in the ratings was significant.

By the time that *Law & Order* was well established in its seventh season, Dick Wolf was invited to create a spin-off series. This resulted in *Law & Order: Special Victims Unit* (1999–), featuring a woman, detective Olivia Benson (Mariska Hegarty) in a central role. With its focus on sex crimes and the pursuit of the suspect who often proved to be seriously disturbed and/or dangerous, *Law & Order: SVU* was arguably more character-driven than its parent show, according to co-executive producer Neal Baer (Snauffer 2006: 164). By its third season, *Law & Order: SVU* was doing so well that a third spin-off series was proposed: *Law & Order: Criminal Intent* starring Vincent D'Onofrio as detective Goren. By season four of this latter series, it was apparent that D'Onofrio's health was suffering and Chris Noth, who had starred in the original first series, was brought in to share the load. In line with prevailing television trends at the time, a summer reality series was created by Wolf entitled *Crime and Punishment* in 2002, which failed to capture an audience. Hardly daunted, Wolf's next move was *Law & Order: Trial by Jury*, starring Jerry Orbach, in 2005, focusing on the work of the defence attorneys. However, following Orbach's death from prostate cancer during the filming of the third season, this series was not renewed.

After twenty years on air, in March 2010 it was announced that the original *Law & Order* would end while a new series, *Law & Order: Los Angeles* would begin. Only *Law & Order: Special Victims Unit* would continue. As an article in *The Huffington Post* noted, the original series of *Law & Order* was subsequently retired with the distinction of tying with the Western series *Gunsmoke* as the longest-running American drama series to appear thus far (Scott 2010). In 2013, interestingly, the only survivor from the franchise still on air was *Law & Order: SVU*.

Looking closely at the first episode of the original series, the format is clear, the action is intense, the scenes are succinct, and the editing is crisp. This is a series that moves fast, does not waste a moment of screen time, and puts the focus entirely on the case with little attention to the emotional lives of the police or legal teams. The episode begins in an emergency room where a young woman suffers a cardiac arrest. Her father, a former Vietnam medic, is immediately suspicious, as his daughter was presenting with little more than a case of bronchitis. The police, detective Mike Logan (Chris Noth) and sergeant Max Greevey (George Dzundza), take the father's concerns seriously, as Greevey reveals his own experience of a medical misdiagnosis. Their investigation leads them to a Jewish doctor who was in attendance at the scene. A controversial dimension to the crime is mooted as this doctor tells them that it is harder as a Jew to prove himself than it is for any other medical officer on the floor. Just when it would appear that he is the culprit, the investigation takes a different turn as it is revealed that the most senior doctor in the hospital was also present at the emergency and had obviously been drinking. In fact, it is revealed that it was the senior doctor who ordered the administration of the drug that caused the patient's death against the advice of his juniors.

Following the 'The Clang', the action relocates in the second half of the episode to the chambers of the prosecuting attorneys who find themselves up against a medical establishment keen to protect one of their own. The lawyers assemble their case and in a dramatic court-room finale, the accused doctor is asked to undertake a standard test for intoxication in front of the jury. He fails: the end. This is a drama series that expected its audience to understand the implications of the courtroom revelations. Justice, it is clear, will be done, although unlike the early *Dragnet* years, we no longer need a didactic voice-over to tell us this.

The history of the *Law & Order* franchise, which includes a telemovie, *Exiled* (dir. Jean de Segonzac; 1998) starring Chris Noth, and five video games developed for PC that adopt the episodic structure of the original series, demonstrates the ways in which the television crime drama as a genre continues to borrow from the past, diversify, reinvent itself, and proliferate across media platforms. Popularity and longevity, however, does not necessarily equate with critical acclaim, as the following comparison reveals.

CSI versus *The Wire*

As one of the most popular and highly rating television crime dramas ever produced, showing in many more countries than it is not, *CSI* offers an interesting contrast in terms of format, style, and critical reception with another new millennium crime series, *The Wire* (2002–8). Hailed by many critics, including *TIME* magazine, as 'the best television crime series of the 2000s' (Poniewozik 2009), *The Wire* only ever obtained modest ratings and has arguably been seen by more people on DVD than ever saw it on first airing. This chapter will, therefore, conclude with a comparison between *CSI* and *The Wire* in order to demonstrate how they illustrate, in their respective play with form, style, and aesthetics, very different approaches to telling stories about crime and policing.

For a start, it is important to note the very different contexts in which the two series were produced and viewed. *CSI* screened on the American network CBS where it was initially watched by more than twenty million viewers before going on to become 'the most watched TV series in the world' (Bibel 2012). *The Wire*, on the other hand, rated poorly for HBO, which marketed itself as a premium channel offering more sexually explicit and challenging material for mature audiences who would not normally watch network television, as signalled by their advertising slogan 'It's not television, it's HBO'

(Mittell 2010: 33). *The Wire's* audience may have been small, but it was 'quality'.

Partly as a result of this niche location, audiences for *The Wire* only ever peaked at approximately four million during its five-season run, dipping to below one million in its final season. Popularity, however, appeared to have little to do with *The Wire's* critical success. Indeed, the show's perceived lack of popular appeal and its small HBO audience may have been a significant aspect of its critical acclaim. Simon himself went so far as to suggest that 'ratings no longer mattered', since more people were watching the series than ever before through other mechanisms such as DVDs and downloads, both legal and illegal (Plunkett 2009). In one of his many literary analogies, Simon goes on to argue that television 'at this level' constitutes a 'lending library' from which you borrow on demand and 'read' at your leisure (ibid.). This suggests that quality television is something other than 'just' television.

Despite their different production contexts, and different audiences, *CSI* and *The Wire* have much in common. Like many police procedurals before them, both can trace their origins to a documentary impulse, however tenuous. In the case of *CSI*, creator Anthony Zuiker has told a production narrative about how the original idea came from his wife who was an ardent fan of a Discovery Channel show about real-life forensic detectives (Zuiker Interview, Paley Centre 2001). Zuiker subsequently spent five weeks following the work of the Las Vegas crime investigators before taking the idea for the series to Hollywood where it was picked up by producer Jerry Bruckheimer who had enjoyed major success with such films as *Flashdance* (dir. Adrian Lyne, 1983) and *Top Gun* (dir. Tony Scott; 1986). Bruckheimer had also been the producer of Michael Mann's first feature film, *Thief* (1981) and subsequent serial killer thriller *Manhunter* (1985). Bruckheimer had, therefore, worked with a number of directors whose visual style he wanted to bring to television, as reported by *CSI's* first director, Danny Cannon.[7]

Like *Miami Vice*, in its stylish 'neon-noir' colour coding, the first series of *CSI* produced by Bruckheimer in collaboration with Touchstone Pictures and CBS after the other networks (ABC, NBC, and Fox) had passed on it, did not look like documentary. Furthermore, while the producers and writers may have claimed a degree of 'authenticity' in the representation of forensic science, this has been challenged by real-life students and practitioners of forensic pathology, such as Daryl Vinall and Shelley Robinson (2007) who have questioned the 'accuracy' of the series on a number of levels. This includes not only the kinds of futuristic technology on display, but also the degree to which the crime scene investigators are involved in the case; although the investigators are supposedly 'specialists' in the lab, they operate like detectives in the field. Also doubtful is the pace at which the scientific evidence is processed, given that the timeline of each investigation is compressed to a scant forty-plus minutes of television time. In the opinion of the 'real' scientists, *CSI* is, therefore, far from realistic, although, as they somewhat grudgingly concede, this may make it much more entertaining than the real thing. However, for many commentators on the series, especially those within the discipline of criminology, the entertainment values of *CSI* are to be condemned since they resulted in an unrealistic expectation of the forensic evidence, its processing and certainty (Wise 2009).

The claims of *The Wire* to documentary authenticity were somewhat stronger given that the series evolved out of former Baltimore police reporter David Simon's own investigative research. This he initially turned into two true-crime books. The first of these, *Homicide: A Year on the Killing Streets* (1991), was the basis for the television series *Homicide: Life on the Street*, which Simon developed for NBC in 1992. This series ran for seven seasons before being cancelled in 1999. In collaboration with former homicide detective, Ed Burns, Simon wrote a second true crime book, *The Corner: A Year in the Life of an Inner-City Neighbourhood* (1997), which also became a television series, in this case a six-part mini-series (*The Corner*) created for HBO in 2000 that went on to win a Primetime Emmy Award for outstanding mini-series in that year. Not surprisingly, it was to HBO, with its niche audience, which Simon turned again when pitching yet another uncompromising portrait of the city of Baltimore, conceived once again in collaboration with Ed Burns.

The television format Simon elected to employ was that of a serial narrative consisting of thirteen episodes in the first of *The Wire*'s five seasons. This return to a serial format was an interesting move since, as Jeremy Butler suggests, serialisation had tended to be one of the least respected television forms, associated as it was with the long-running daytime soaps (Butler 2012: 40). However, 'critical favourites' like director David Lynch's 'off-kilter take' on the crime drama, *Twin Peaks* (ABC, 1990–1), and the long-running medical drama *ER* (NBC, 1994–2009), had arguably already paved the way for serial television that could also qualify as 'quality' (Butler 2012: 40), not forgetting, of course, *Hill Street Blues* and its soapratic storylines. Meanwhile, HBO had experienced success with such series as *The Sopranos*, which had earlier employed a serial structure over each of its seasons

(1999–2007), proving that HBO audiences were prepared to commit themselves to what David Lavery has described as the 'long-haul narrative' (Lavery 2010: 43).

Like *CSI*, each episode of *The Wire* would begin with what is described as a 'cold open', dropping the viewer into the middle of the action. This scene would be followed by a title sequence involving a montage of images that established the particular thematic and style of the show. In the case of *The Wire*, this was accompanied by the downbeat blues track 'Way Down in the Hole' (popularly known as 'Down in the Hole') written by Tom Waits and performed by a different singer in each of the five seasons of the show.[8] The images accompanying this track, like those of *CSI*, included an array of technological gadgetry. In the case of *The Wire*, this encompassed the electronic surveillance equipment used by the police in an endeavour to entrap the drug-dealers that gave the series as a whole its name. As this theme music reaches its conclusion, a quotation from one of the characters who will speak in the ensuing episode appears in black on the screen.

The action then plays out in scenes that appear to lack any particular significance within an overarching narrative that took some time to fathom. This was hardly helped by the frequent use of vivid street language that was not only hard to hear but hard to decipher. *The Wire* was a series that for some viewers would have benefited from subtitles or at least a glossary. To add to the sense of dislocation, individual episodes often ended inconclusively, rarely making use of the established formula of a cliffhanger to carry the viewer over until the next instalment. Simon's approach, he suggests in his voice-over commentary to the first episode, was intentionally more 'literary' than televisual.

What Simon appears to mean by a 'literary' approach is not entirely clear.[9] For a start, he suggests that *The Wire* marks a break with episodic series television in which narrative closure is achieved in one hour. Second, he implies that this has to do with both the length of the narrative arcs and the complexity of the characters. In each case, Simon's claims about *The Wire* should be carefully considered in relation to the development of the crime drama as a genre in which complex characters and a lack of narrative resolution have certainly featured before, as was the case in the British mini-series *Law & Order* and the American series *Hill Street Blues*. Viewers of *The Wire*, however, were required to 'read' the series as a cumulative narrative in which the significance of the parts would only be apparent in the end, and perhaps not even then. As Amanda Ann Klein suggests, the season finales to *The Wire* largely refused to offer the kinds of satisfactions that viewers had come to expect in television story-telling (Klein 2009: 179).

Klein's discussion of *The Wire* considers how melodrama as a dramatic mode usually works, and the ways in which *The Wire* does, and
doesn't, work within the usual conventions. As Klein points out, as a
form of story-telling, melodrama has long been employed 'as a means
of grappling with moral questions during times of moral uncertainty'
(177). As such, the pleasures of melodrama 'usually' involve stories
that are resolved through individualised solutions to social problems.
There is also usually a clear delineation between the moral positions
presented (there are good guys and bad guys) with an ending that
affords 'the catharsis of tears' and narrative closure (179). By way of
contrast, *The Wire*, Klein argues, offers little in the way of melodramatic pleasure in the end, leaving the viewer without a moral compass,
'lost in a thicket of values that they must parse on their own' (183).
As a result, she suggests, the audience is left feeling 'dissatisfied and
agitated', their anger, sadness, and outrage going unpurged (179–80).

While this may be construed as a 'bad thing', Klein offers the proposition that instead of offering a 'passive, satisfied viewing position', *The
Wire* constructs an 'active, socially engaged viewer', one who is grati-
fied to be challenged in this way, experiencing television, as she quotes
Simon himself as suggesting, not just as a form of 'relaxation' but
rather as a form of 'provocation' (188). This is a problematic argument
since it implies that viewers who watch 'ordinary' crime dramas are
neither active readers of the text nor socially engaged citizens. Despite
a defence of melodrama as a strategy to evoke empathy, in her assessment of *The Wire*'s refusal to offer melodramatic pleasure, Klein (and
indeed Simon himself) continue to reinforce the questionable hierarchies underpinning the concept of 'quality' television as television that
breaks the rules while espousing the more serious values of 'art'.

While Simon's narrative approach was often described by commentators as reminiscent of a nineteenth-century novel, it should be
noted that popular novels in the nineteenth century by authors such as
Charles Dickens were often first published in a serial format, a section
at a time. Dickens knew all about serial narrative not to mention the
strategic use of cliffhangers as well as the affective power of moments
of high melodrama. Simon, however, frequently refuted any suggestion that either his narrative approach or his critical world view could
be compared with that of Dickens, since, he claimed, his own vision
was much 'darker'.[10]

CSI, on the other hand, espoused the televisual episodic narrative
form with a vengeance. Each episode in the first season begins with
a pre-title teaser establishing the scene of the crime, usually involving a murder or suspicious death. The ensuing titles then present a

fast-paced montage that includes the faces of the central characters, as
well as data-filled computer screens, and computer generated image
(CGI) effects, such as an exploding apple or skull. The titles for the
original *CSI* set in Las Vegas are accompanied by the energetic pop
anthem 'Who Are You'[11] written by Pete Townsend and performed
by Roger Daltrey of the British band *The Who*, whose musical career
experienced something of a renaissance as a result.[12] Each episode
then unfolds in a series of short scenes as the *CSI* team conducts their
microscopic analysis of the crime scene, reconvening in their carefully
colour-matched laboratory to perform all manner of sophisticated
experiments involving the artful use of digital cameras, computer
imagery, and re-enactments to reconstruct what may, or may not, have
happened. The possibilities were usually played out in visually discrete
soft-focus flashbacks. Each episode concludes with the discovery of the
perpetrator who will be subjected to some form of moral, if not legal,
admonishment: a very different kind of episodic conclusion to that
offered by *The Wire*, which provided no such moral certainty.

In this artfully constructed episodic format, *CSI* thus offered the
narrative closure and satisfaction of earlier police procedurals such as
Dragnet and *Law & Order*. With its focus on the investigation of the
crime rather than on the emotional lives of the characters – although
these did come into occasional play – *CSI* was an episodic series,
one that one could drop into and out of without missing key plot
developments and very unlike *The Wire* in all its evolving narrative
complexity.

As a television crime series, what was initially most striking about *CSI*
was its look, which can be attributed to producer Jerry Bruckheimer
who in his first meeting with British director Danny Cannon apparently informed him that what he wanted for this series was a 'cinematic
look' in television. Shot on 35mm film and subjected to a high degree
of post-production colour manipulation, in each of its subsequent
franchise locations, including Miami and New York, *CSI* echoed
the style of Michael Mann on his first film *Thief* (that Bruckheimer
had co-produced) and the 1980s' television series *Miami Vice*. This
included the colour coding of scenes to distinguish different plot lines,
the use of neon-noir lighting effects, and the strategic deployment of
bright sources of light. The fact that Cannon was well aware of Mann's
work in this regard is evident in his voice-over commentary to the *CSI
Miami* pilot during which he notes that the look of a particular scene
was constructed as 'a tribute to Michael Mann'.[13]

As for the soundtrack, like *Miami Vice*, *CSI* also made skilful use
of popular music. For example in the episode from season two that

was called 'Slaves in Las Vegas' (02: 08), the eerie, ambient music of Icelandic band Sigur Rós accompanies Grissom's close examination of a naked female body in the autopsy room. This scene lasts two minutes and thirty-one seconds and is shot through filters casting Grissom's white coat and the body of the victim in a greyish blue light. I have argued elsewhere (Turnbull 2007: 30) that it is in scenes like this that we can identify one of the primary appeals of this series, and indeed the *CSI* franchise as a whole, as the camera invites us to share the gaze of the forensic examiner, to see what they see, albeit highly stylised, and to thus participate in the process of investigation, an invitation that was extended in the first of the many video games based on the series to be released in 2003. There were those, however, who suggested that the gaze the viewer is invited to share is more voyeuristic, and even pornographic, than forensic (Lury 2005: 56; West 2007: 141).

The look of *The Wire* is also highly wrought, although in this case it may best be described as 'gritty' – a term associated in Britain with the 'social-realist' style employed by British directors such as Ken Loach working on the earlier police procedural *Z-Cars*. As a police drama, *The Wire*, therefore, aspires to a style that works hard to achieve the appearance of 'no-style'. *CSI*, on the other hand, aspires to a visual style that may best be described as self-conscious artistry. While both styles involve a high degree of art in the accomplishment of their particular look, it is the former that most usually attracts the label of 'quality' because of its association with 'realism' and the kinds of 'liberal' social and cultural critique that are implicit within a 'documentary' approach to the problem of crime.

The first season of *The Wire* opens on the depressing streets of Baltimore as detective Jimmy McNulty sits with a drug-dealer on the step of a boarded-up, vacant property. They are discussing the murder of a young man with the unlovely street name of Snot Boogie lying in front of them. The ensuing action encompasses dismal street scapes and gloomy interiors, in particular the depressing basement in which McNulty's hastily assembled crime team make their temporary base as they try to unravel the complexity of Baltimore's drug-related crime culture. As Simon reveals in his voice-over commentary, the production design for the series was all about restraint in an attempt not to draw attention to a non-descript background. Stylistically, *The Wire* thus belongs to the legion of crime drama series that have combined location shooting with studio sets in order to tell stories about crime that endeavour to suggest a degree of authenticity by deliberately eschewing any hint of glamour in their depiction of people and place.

Although the appeal of the two series is very different, it is possible to appreciate the achievements of both. While *The Wire* presents complex characters trying to negotiate tricky moral landscapes on both sides of the law, *CSI* offers its viewers clear moral boundaries. While *The Wire* reveals the flaws in the systems and institutions supposed to support the workings of a democracy, *CSI* presents a criminal justice system that for the most part functions well. While *The Wire* suggests that our knowledge is only ever partial and limited, *CSI* celebrates the certainties of (usually) infallible science. While *The Wire* requires its viewers' attention for (approximately) thirteen consecutive hours per season, *CSI* offered its viewers forty-plus minutes of highly stylised television and the satisfaction of narrative closure in episodes that require little knowledge of what has gone before, although a familiarity with the history of the central characters certainly pays off for long-term viewers of the show, as is evident on the many fan websites. Perhaps most significantly, while *CSI* suggests that crime is usually the result of a moral failing on the part of the individual, *The Wire*, in the true spirit of noir, suggests that crime is systemic and society itself is the crime. The individual, good or bad, can do very little in light of the moral corruption that underpins the entire city, and that underpins American society in general.

Conclusion

While *CSI* and *The Wire* may share similar genre DNA, they are very different in terms of their ambitions and the kinds of pleasure that they offer to their respective audiences. In terms of ratings, *CSI* has been one of the most successful television crime series ever made. In 2009, the worldwide audience for *CSI* was estimated at 73.8 million (Gorman 2010). In 2012, for the fifth time, the show was nominated as the most watched drama series in the world (Bibel 2012). *The Wire*, on the other hand, was only ever a minor ratings success for HBO, although it has achieved global circulation, largely through the sale of DVDs. As *The Telegraph* reported in the United Kingdom, '*The Wire* has never won an Emmy and often appears to have been watched by more enthusiastic TV critics than viewers' (Anonymous 2009). *The Wire*, *The Telegraph* article went on to suggest, is the kind of show liked by people who 'would usually only watch a US crime drama with a peg on their nose', concluding that despite this select viewership (or perhaps because of it, as the discussion of quality television in this chapter may suggest) *The Wire* may well be responsible for changing the face of television (ibid.).

As this chapter has revealed, this is the kind of claim that has often been made for the television crime drama over the years. However, in assessing the validity of such claims, it is useful to know something about the history of television crime drama and the ways in which the genre has been critically evaluated. For a start, in relation to the history of the American police procedural as it has been sketched out in this chapter, *The Wire* belongs to a documentary impulse that can be traced back to *Dragnet*, through Wambaugh's *Police Story* and through Bochco's *Hill Street Blues*, extending the 'messiness' of the latter to a new level of mimetic confusion. But this is hardly an entirely new departure for television crime.

However, when it comes to a debate about the 'quality' and how this is attributed, the comparison between *CSI* and *The Wire* is salutary. In terms of the criteria associated with 'quality' TV as outlined by Robert J. Thompson in 1996 it may be noted that both *CSI* and *The Wire* are produced by people of 'quality aesthetic ancestry' outside the field of television. Both Bruckheimer and Cannon had a background in film production and David Simon a former life as a journalist and author of true crime. Both series make use of ensemble casts and multiple, overlapping storylines, although *CSI* does so to a lesser extent than *The Wire*. Both include social criticism and both recombine prior elements of the genre to produce something new and original.

So where do they differ? Clearly their difference lies in their respective ability to attract what Thompson describes as a 'blue chip audience' (1996: 14). Indeed, I may point out from personal experience that I have frequently found myself in debates about *CSI* and *The Wire* in which I have defended the former as 'quality' television only to have this defence ridiculed by colleagues who don't watch much television. Television that most people like, it would appear, can never be 'quality', a conclusion that suggests that the concept of quality, especially in relation to the television crime drama, is more than ready for some critical re-evaluation.

Notes

1. As noted in Chapter 1, *Gang Busters* was Lord's sequel to *G-Men* following a difference of opinion with FBI head, J. Edgar Hoover about the direction that the show should take.
2. The source here is Wambaugh's direct-to-camera interview with David Gerbner in the special feature 'Cop Talk' on the 2011 re-release of the first season of *Police Story*.
3. Wouldn't it have been interesting if this had been the premise for the American version of *Life on Mars*?

4. 'The Vibe of Vice' feature on DVD.
5. Phil Collins's (1981) song 'In the Air Tonight' is on the album *Face Value* that was released by Virgin in the United Kingdom.
6. 'The Clang' has a life of its own online and can be downloaded from: http://en.wikipedia.org/wiki/File:The_Clang.ogg [accessed 14 September 2012].
7. Danny Cannon Interview, *CSI* DVD, season one feature.
8. Tom Waits's song 'Way Down in the Hole' (1987) was released on the album *Franks Wild Years* by Island.
9. As described in his voice-over commentary to the twelfth episode in season one.
10. See, for example, Simon's Interview with *Vice* (Pearson and Philip 2009).
11. The original album release in 1978 by Polydor in the United Kingdom and MCA in the United States, *Who are You*, and the title of the song, 'Who are You' have no question mark.
12. I know this from experience. After one of those surreal conversations about 'Who are The Who?' with my then twelve year-old son, he went out and bought the 'Best of' CD.
13. Cannon in voice-over commentary to episode one, season one of *CSI Miami*.

4 The Detective as Hero

While the evolution of police procedural as discussed in the previous two chapters can be traced back to a 'documentary' approach to crime, the 'detective' as hero on television, including the gifted amateur, the private detective, and the maverick cop, has predecessors in crime fiction, as well as on radio and in film. Although different episodes of a series may be produced, written, and directed by different creative personnel, it is often the character of the detective that lends coherence to the series as a whole, inspiring viewer loyalty, which may even be enacted in forms of cultural tourism, such as 'The Inspector Morse Tour' of Oxford.

From the many screen incarnations of Sherlock Holmes to those of the more recent Inspector Wallander (who has already appeared in three different crime series, played by three different actors), the 'eponymous sleuth' has long been an established feature of the television crime landscape. As will be argued, the identification of a crime drama with its central character may, therefore, lead to a kind of 'branding' in terms of what viewers expect from a specific series, while also signalling the pre-eminent role of the primary investigator whose ongoing presence ensures a level of continuity, familiarity, and reassurance for the viewer, even when the detective may be faced with intractable social problems or seemingly unsolvable crimes.

With its origins in the world of finance and marketing, branding is defined as the process of creating a unique image in the consumer's mind for a specific product, and as such it can be associated with the celebrities who lend their name to particular advertising campaigns and promotions (Anonymous n.d.g). In her book, *Personality Presenters*, Frances Bonner demonstrates how television hosts have long constituted a form of 'brand', the British presenter Michael Parkinson being a case in point (Bonner 2011: 75). This concept of personality branding can be extended to include television crime shows that are named after a specific detective, although the resulting 'brand' may not always be entirely related to the central character. For example, the Scottish series *Taggart* (STV, 1983–), which after the demise of *The Bill* (ITV, 1984–2010) has the distinction of being the longest-running television crime drama in the United Kingdom, initially followed a team of detectives that were led by detective chief inspector Jim Taggart, played in his own brusque style by actor Mark McManus. Unfortunately, McManus died in 1994 during the filming of an episode (with his absence from subsequent scenes explained by the excuse that he was in constant meetings with the chief constable), and, in the event, the series continued as a police procedural with a focus on an ensemble of investigators and their Glasgow locale rather than the 'detective as hero' in the lead. With this cautionary tale in mind – in the sense that *Taggart* no longer features a character called Taggart – this chapter will pay attention to those crime dramas that have been associated with their central characters within a system of genre classification that began well before the emergence of television industry and that has continued to the present.

One of the key factors in the success of such series is clearly the 'attractiveness' of the hero, or indeed, the heroine. This does not necessarily equate with physical attractiveness, although that may well matter, but rather their 'appeal' as long-running characters with whom the viewer becomes familiar. In the early days of television research, American sociologists Horton and Wohl (2006 [1956]) elaborated on the concept of para-social interaction to describe the ways in which viewers assume a degree of sociability with the characters that they regularly see on-screen: a proposition that has been supported by the subsequent literature on fandom that reveals how fans of all kinds may develop an ongoing emotional relationship with characters on-screen even though '[t]he interaction, characteristically, is one-sided, non-dialectical, controlled by the performer, and not susceptible of mutual development' (Horton and Wohl 2006 [1956]).

An attraction to the central character as embodied by an actor who may or may not be familiar from other roles and contexts involves a range of potential pleasures. These include the recognition of a familiar face, the construction of a fantasy relationship with the character, and other forms of 'identification' with them and their fictional world, although the concept of identification is a complex one, as will be discussed later. Within this fictional world, the hero performs the role of guide, equipped with a usually reliable moral compass, who 'takes' the viewer on a weekly excursion into the world of crime, 'allowing' them to accompany him or her on the investigation, to see what they see, and to participate in what is often an epistemological quest for truth.

As such, the presence of the hero also offers the reassurance of the formulaic, the particular aesthetic frame through which the viewer may contemplate events that may be too disturbing in other contexts. However, while producers and writers obviously depend on audience investment in a central protagonist to the extent that viewers are prepared to follow their narrative trajectory across the course of an episode and even a season or a series as a whole, this is clearly not the whole story. The sleuth is just one of the various 'hooks' on which producers and writers endeavour to hang a successful TV series, but it is an important one.

In considering the role of the eponymous sleuth, attention will also be paid to the industry practices and manoeuvres that have impinged on the development of the TV crime drama as it seeks to attract and maintain an audience. For example, within the commercial landscape of American television in the early 1950s the three major American TV networks – ABC, NBC, and CBS – initially showcased drama within anthology series that were sponsored by large companies such as 'Philco, Revlon, Goodyear and Motorola' (Osgerby, Gough-Yates, and Wells 2001: 15). By the mid-1950s, the networks were gradually moving away from this strategy in order to become the licensees of their own shows so that they could profit both from the sale of available advertising space and the subsequent syndication rights (ibid.). The promise of syndication resulted in the demand for a reliable 'product': the continuous and repeatable prime-time series rather than the one-off drama that had been the staple of the anthology show. These new network shows were often produced by independent producers in conjunction with one of the major film studios.

Competition for early viewers was fierce, with the already familiar outcome even in the 1950s that those television series that did not catch on quickly being rapidly cancelled while those that did rate well being possibly mined for spin-offs or copied by rival networks.[1] In terms of copycat shows, a television series seen to be doing well on another network might well inspire a similar but different show on a rival network. This scenario demonstrates that the phenomenon of the spin-off and the copycat was a feature of the television landscape right from the start. One particular suite of crime drama series that illustrate the ways in which industry practices and audience tastes may play a role in the development of the genre are a cluster of shows that appeared in the 1950s and in the early 1960s featuring a private eye.

The private eye

Crime series such as *Richard Diamond Private Eye* (CBS, 1957–9; NBC, 1959–60), *Peter Gunn* (NBC, 1958–60; ABC, 1960–1), *Johnny Staccato* (NBC, 1959–60), and *Pete Kelly's Blues* (NBC, 1959) drew upon the long tradition of the private eye in other media and literary forms with which the audience for television in the 1950s would be presumed to be familiar. The private eye genre had been a staple of radio from the 1930s onwards as producers mined the emerging field of pulp and crime fiction for their narratives. Radio series based on the careers of such literary private eyes as Nero Wolfe (created by Rex Stout), Sam Spade (Dashiell Hammett), and Philip Marlowe (Raymond Chandler), not forgetting such British literary heroes as Hercule Poirot (created by Agatha Christie), The Saint (Leslie Charteris), Harry Lime (Graham Greene), and Sherlock Holmes (Sir Arthur Ignatius Conan Doyle), had proved to be very popular. The private eye had also made a successful transition to film, with Humphrey Bogart as the iconic hard-boiled private detective in films such as *The Maltese Falcon* (John Huston, 1941) and *The Big Sleep* (Howard Hawks, 1946) in which he played first Hammett's Sam Spade and then Chandler's Philip Marlowe.

Richard Diamond, Private Detective made its first appearance on NBC radio in 1949. Written and produced by a young Blake Edwards (who would go on to be the highly successful director of such comedy films as *The Pink Panther*), the show was sponsored by Camel cigarettes, although the sponsor would later change, as did the network. *Richard Diamond* subsequently moved from NBC radio to ABC in 1951 and thence to CBS in 1953, revealing the nomadic career of such independently produced shows. The radio version of the series starred popular actor and singer Dick Powell, who concluded every episode by serenading his girlfriend. Jazz and the use of diegetic music were a key feature of the show. When it came to translating Richard Diamond to the screen, it was Powell's own company, Four Star Television, which produced the television version of *Richard Diamond*, starring David Janssen for CBS (1957–9) and subsequently for NBC (1959–60). The televisual, noir-inflected, half-hour series eschewed any musical interludes.

The success of *Richard Diamond* as a 'modern, more updated hero', as compared to the rather dour sergeant Joe Friday of *Dragnet*, inspired NBC to develop yet another series in the same vein (Snauffer 2006: 22). In a canny move, the network turned to the original creator of *Richard Diamond*, Blake Edwards, in the hope of a similar but different show. Edwards obliged by inventing *Peter Gunn* (NBC, 1958–60, ABC, 1960–1), named for a well-dressed private investigator who spends most of his time at Mother's, a smoky wharfside jazz club. Peter Gunn, as performed by actor Craig Stevens, is impeccably groomed and suave, bearing more than a little resemblance to actor Cary Grant as he appeared in the Hitchcock thriller *North by Northwest* in 1959. As such, Gunn was 'cool' at a moment when 'cool' was indubitably 'hot' in the 1950s.

With its memorable modern jazz theme tune by Henry Mancini, which won both an Emmy and two Grammys, the soundtrack album for the show reached number one in the Billboard Pop LP charts and the show finished its first season on air at number sixteen in the ratings (Snauffer 2006: 24). This gave Blake the kudos to produce and sell yet another private eye series to CBS, *Mr Lucky*, for the autumn season in 1959 (Snauffer 2006: 24). Based on a film of the same name starring Cary Grant, *Mr Lucky* lasted only thirty-four episodes, largely because the network forced Edwards to make significant changes to the premise of the show because they were worried about the proposed setting of a floating casino. When the ratings inevitably fell, *Mr Lucky* was rapidly axed mid-season (Snauffer 2006: 25).

While Edwards may have been the creator of *Peter Gunn*, the show employed a number of different writers (including two women) over the course of its 114 episodes and was produced by the independent company Spartan Productions and filmed at Universal Studios. One of two cinematographers on the series was Philip H. Lathrop who, in keeping with the style of the time, once again imbued the series with a moody film-noir aesthetic.[2]. Like other nomadic, independently produced, and successful series, after two seasons on NBC *Peter Gunn* moved to the rival network ABC for its final season, leaving the slot open for yet another private eye on NBC, Johnny Staccato (Snauffer 2006: 25).

Johnny Staccato and *Peter Gunn* have much in common. Both feature a 'cool' private eye based in a jazz club and emulate a film-noir aesthetic. However, the two series are also significantly different, with *Staccato* being by far the 'darker' of the two. Played by actor and director John Cassavetes who was much feted as a member of a new wave of independent filmmakers, Staccato is much edgier than the suave Gunn. Jazz is also accorded a more pre-eminent status in the show as signalled in the opening titles by a striking piano keyboard accompanied by a moody jazz theme. The DVD re-release in 2010 goes so far as to blurb Johnny Staccato on the cover as 'Television's Jazz Detective'. Within the diegetic of the show, Staccato is a would-be jazz musician, although close observation of Cassavetes' hands on the keyboard suggests that it is not his piano playing that we hear on the soundtrack. Unlike Gunn who lived in a glamorous, Hollywood-style apartment (although the location of his operations was never clearly identified), Staccato spends his time in the smoky and hip Greenwich Village (on the west side of Lower Manhattan in New York City) jazz club known as Waldo's, although the musicians featured on the show would have been easily identified by jazz aficionados as West Coast musicians local to the area of Los Angeles where the series was actually filmed.[3]

The prevalence of jazz within these early crime series indicates the significance of music to establishing the tone of these shows in order to appeal to their intended audiences. At which point it is also worth noting that while considerable attention has been devoted to the role of jazz in film, relatively little has been accorded to the role of jazz in television, or indeed to any of the music used in television drama, with the exception of John Fiske's rather dismissive comments about the use of popular music in *Miami Vice* during the 1980s (Fiske 1987: 255). As is evident in an interview with musician W. G. 'Snuffy' Walden, the creator of musical scores for television series such as *thirtysomething* (ABC, 1987–91) with its pop/rock soundtrack created to appeal to a 'blue-chip demographic', long before *Miami Vice*, producers often devoted a considerable degree of attention to the sound design of a television series (Kaye 2011: 222). Television music, whether diegetic or non-diegetic, has rarely been considered in any concerted way, even though, as Karen Lury points out, television has always been an 'audio-visual' medium in the home (Lury 2005: 58). Even more interesting is the fact that jazz in the TV crime series discussed here was not simply part of the backdrop, but it was also part of the story. For example, in an episode of *Johnny Staccato* directed by Cassavetes, a young Martin Landau guest stars as a composer who has taken revenge on a jazz musician who has stolen his song.

In common with many television series of the time, *Johnny Staccato* regularly featured up-and-coming film stars in guest roles. In the episode 'Nature of the Night' (1: 05), a fresh-faced Dean Stockwell (now better known for his roles in *Quantum Leap* and *Battleship Galactica*) plays a disturbed young barman, Dennis, who suffers a nervous breakdown following the departure of his ambitious wife who wants to be a movie star. Dennis works out his demented rage by slash-ing the faces of pretty blonde women. In a vertiginous finale, Staccato confronts Dennis on a ledge perched high above the street, giving the police time to forestall the latter's suicide attempt. The scene is shot at night, the black-and-white cinematography is expressionistic, and the images are carefully framed, employing off-beat angles. It is very 'noir', proving that 'excessive style' was achievable on television in black and white long before *Miami Vice* was accused of taking this too far.

What is also interesting to note about the shows described above is the attention paid to the psychology of the characters and their motivations. If one adds into the mix the attractiveness of the male stars, and the frequent appearance of stylish women as both ongoing characters and guest actors, it is not hard to understand how these shows might appeal to both male and female television viewers. The fact that *Johnny Staccato* lasted for only twenty-seven episodes of a season planned to be thirty-nine episodes in length had less to do with the ratings than with the desire of John Cassavetes to be released from the show. Cassavetes had only agreed to undertake the part because of the debts he had incurred while making his own independent film *Shadows* (Snauffer 2006: 25). After Cassavetes' idea for an episode about a fellow musician's drug addiction was rejected by both the network and the sponsors (presumably because the conservative networks perceived this drug-taking as too hot a topic to handle on television), Cassavetes was freed from his contract in time for the release of *Shadows* that his work on *Johnny Staccato* had helped to finance (Snauffer 2006: 27).[4]

What the *Johnny Staccato* example reveals is that while ratings clearly mattered, other factors, often both political and personal, may impinge on the creation of a television show and inevitably on the development of a genre. The defection of Cassavetes also serves to illustrate that film at this time was perceived as the more legitimate medium for a would-be young director with artistic aspirations. As the debate about 'quality' TV reveals, largely because of its commercial success and popularity, television crime drama has taken some time to be accepted as anything other than 'trash', despite the fact that there were television auteurs such as Jack Webb, the creator of *Dragnet*, with credentials in both film and radio, who may well have had grand ambitions for the medium.

While there is conflicting evidence about whether *Dragnet* was cancelled in 1959 because of falling ratings or because creator Webb was bored with the series and had decided to pursue other projects, Webb's next project for NBC, *Pete Kelly's Blues* (1959), featured yet another private-eye series and jazz. Even before and during the time that he was working on *Dragnet*, Webb had starred in two private-eye series for radio, *Pat Novak for Hire* (1947), and one that he himself had created in association with Richard L. Breen, the original *Pete Kelly's Blues* (1951) (*Pete Kelly's Blues* n.d.). While the latter only amounted to thirteen episodes as a summer replacement series for NBC radio, it was another a radio series that Webb wanted to move to the screen, producing, directing, and starring in a successful film version in 1955 that featured legendary jazz singers Ella Fitzgerald and Peggy Lee in small but significant dramatic roles – as well as singing (*Pete Kelly's Blues* n.d.). (Peggy Lee was even nominated for an Oscar for her cameo.)

As a lifelong fan of jazz music (Webb's first wife was jazz singer Julie London, and he began his radio career playing late night jazz on the San Francisco radio), Webb was able to secure the services of a number of respected jazz musicians for his original radio series with whom he hoped to bring jazz music to a mainstream audience (*Pete Kelly's Blues* n.d.). Set in a Kansas City speakeasy (an establishment selling illegal alcohol during the Prohibition era in the United States in the 1920s), each episode would involve Kelly in a case that he would have preferred not to have taken, favouring to play in his band rather than deal with gangsters and G-men, a.k.a government agents. Each episode would feature two musical interludes in the ensuing action. The subsequent television series starred William Reynolds as Kelly, a trumpet player and leader of Pete Kelly's Big Seven. Only thirteen episodes were made, which following Webb's penchant for formulaic titles, were entitled 'The Steve Porter Story', 'The June Gold Story' and so on. Like Johnny Staccato, most of Pete Kelly's cases were directly related to the jazz club locale (*Pete Kelly's Blues* n.d.).

The early development of the private eye series featuring jazz thus illustrates a number of key themes in the development of the television crime genre. First, one can note the copycat nature of these early network television crime dramas, keen as they were to capitalise on the success of rival shows. Second, one can note the repetition of specific tropes, not only that of the private eye, but also the use of music for setting the tone and ambience of the show, a move that anticipates the attention paid to music in subsequent highly stylised series such as *Miami Vice* and *CSI*. Last, but by no means least, these early crime series demonstrate the imbrication of the American film and TV production industries, not only in terms of commonalities of style, but also the cross-over of personnel. While Jack Webb was a TV auteur who managed to straddle both media, he has hardly been accorded the esteem granted to a film director such as Cassavetes, possibly because Webb's major output was series television rather than what Thompson has described as the 'classier' medium of film (Thompson 1996: 14).

While the television private detective series continued to evolve on American screens through the 1960s with a watchful eye on the success of such British heroes as James Bond and the feisty female characters that were appearing in *The Avengers* with the latter inspiring one of the 'first' female private eyes on-screen, the title character of *Honey West* (ABC, 1965–6), who will be discussed in more detail in Chapter 6, the most significant private eye series to follow was *The Rockford Files* (a.k.a *Rockford*) (NBC, 1974–80) – significant because in this instance the writer, Stephen J. Cannell, deliberately set out to subvert a genre (Snauffer 2006: 91).[5]

The Rockford Files: subverting genre

While there are many different and competing stories of origin for *The Rockford Files* (Snauffer 2006: 56; Robertson 1995), it is unarguable that the series emerged during a Writers' Guild strike in 1973. During this time, Cannell had been working on the detective series *Toma* (ABC, 1973–4) for Universal Studios. Produced by Roy Huggins, who had earlier created such successful series crime series as *77 Sunset Strip* and *The Fugitive* (ABC, 1963–7), *Toma* had been dogged by a number of problems, including the reluctance of its star, Tony Musante, to continue (Robertson 1995). As a result of various interruptions to the production schedule, a mid-season replacement was needed fast (Snauffer 2006: 90). After Huggins reportedly chose the name Tom Rockford (later changed to Jim) from the Universal Studios' phone directory, the decision was made to introduce the character in an episode of *Toma* before launching him into his own show. According to Cannell's story of origin, because he thought *Rockford* was simply going to be a 'filler', and because he didn't think people really cared what he did as long as he produced a workable script, when given the task of writing the pilot, Cannell decided 'to break every cliché he could think of in private eye fiction' (Snauffer 2006: 91). And so he did. Because private eyes are usually loners and rarely have a family, Cannell gave Rockford a father, who is a blue-collar truck driver who shares Jim's mobile home and domestic woes. Because private eyes are normally brave and morally impeccable, Cannell portrayed Jim as something of a coward who would rather run than fight – with his gun usually located in the cookie jar. Instead of being serious and dark, Rockford was wry and funny. Furthermore, rather than being about a 'serious' crime and the operations of the law, *Rockford* was all about justice. A typical *Rockford* plot would involve an acquaintance or friend coming to Rockford for help in sorting out a situation in which they had become the victim of a scam. Rockford would then set up his own elaborate con to out-con the conners in ways that anticipate more recent series such as *Hustle* (BBC One, 2004–12).

Although the NBC network apparently loathed both the character and the script, they changed their mind when Huggins secured the commitment of actor James Garner to play Jim Rockford. Huggins had earlier created the successful comedy Western series *Maverick* (ABC, 1957–62), starring Garner, and there is no doubt that the genial characters of Brett Maverick and Jim Rockford share similar cultural DNA. However, while Maverick is a sly trickster, Rockford is irritable, put-upon, and un-heroic, and he has a nosy parent who is always telling him what to do. The first episode of *The Rockford Files* aired in March 1974, rating well and receiving a good critical reaction (Snauffer 2006: 92). NBC ordered a full season for the autumn, and *Rockford* continued for a further five years, winning an Emmy in 1978 for Best Dramatic Series.

In terms of its play with genre, long before Bart Simpson wrote a different set of lines on the blackboard every week, every episode would begin with an opening credit sequence in which we heard a different telephone message on Rockford's answering machine, merely confirming what we knew about the character, his shady associates, and money problems. At the prompt, 'This is Jim Rockford. At the tone leave your name and message. I'll get back to you', we hear such messages as: 'Jim, it's Norma at the market. It [your cheque] bounced – you want us to tear it up, send it back, or put it with the others?' (Rockford 01: 01). The humorous tone was thus established at the outset with the title sequence providing a neat hook for the series as a whole, while enacting one of the key attributes of the long-running episodic series – that it would be exactly the same as last time, but also completely different.

It would be wrong, however, to simply dismiss *Rockford* as a comedy-crime drama. Once again, the morphology of a long-running series with multiple writers and directors inevitably led to a variation in both tone and style with some episodes being quite dark – as was the case with 'The Hammer of C Block' (02: 14; a covert version of Raymond Chandler's *Farewell, My Lovely*). This episode, which guest-starred singer/actor Isaac Hayes (who would later go on to be the voice of Chef in *South Park*), opens with Hayes singing the melancholy 'Gandy's Theme', a song that Hayes had composed especially for the series in yet another instance of a strategic use of the musical score to tell the story. As a musician, Hayes had already won both a Grammy and an Academy Award for the soundtrack music he had composed for the successful blaxploitation movie *Shaft* (1971) in which he also had a cameo role. Hayes' guest performance in *Rockford* would, therefore, have been a major drawcard for this episode given his high media profile at the time.

In this episode, Hayes plays Gandolf Fitch who has (wrongly it turns out) served twenty years in prison for the murder of his wife. Gandolf met Rockford in jail (another interesting wrinkle to Rockford's shady past) and wants Jim (whom he always addresses as 'Rockfish', one of the lighter beats of an otherwise dark episode) to track down his wife's killer so that he can enact his own revenge. When Rockford leads Fitch to the truth – the knowledge that his wife concealed the birth of his two children and committed suicide because of the beatings he regularly inflicted upon her – Fitch is broken, and the episode concludes with the desolate Fitch rejected by his offspring and facing an uncertain future. All Fitch has, Rockford consoles him, is his freedom, which is hardly much comfort to a man who has lost everything, even hope. *The Rockford Files* was thus not only genre-bending and funny, but it could also be serious in terms of its social commentary.

As a private eye series, the *Rockford* format involved self-contained episodes and an absence of narrative arcs across the seasons (except in the case of the occasional double episode). There was, however, an ongoing cast of characters, not all of whom appeared in every episode but each of whom had an ongoing relationship with Rockford. Filmed partly on studio sets, the series made considerable use of the 'real' Los Angeles' locations visited by Rockford in his iconic gold Pontiac Firebird, which in a commitment to authenticity, Garner himself drove even when this involved chases and stunts. With such memorable episode titles as 'The Oracle Wore a Cashmere Suit' (03: 02) written by future television auteur and creator of *The West Wing*, David Chase, and 'Dwarf in a Helium Hat' (04: 17) written by Cannell and Chase, *Rockford* broke the mould of the noir-inflected private eye series. *The Rockford Files* can thus be read both as a response to the history of the PI genre and as a result of industry practices within a specific historical moment when the opportunity to come up with something new presented itself. A similar trajectory for re-invention can be observed in the career of the 'amateur sleuth', or 'consulting detective' as Sherlock Homes prefers to describe himself to Dr John Watson, who will be his associate and the fictional narrator of their cases, in the first days of their collaboration (Conan Doyle 1967b [1883]: 160).

The consulting amateur: the case of Sherlock Holmes

Although there have been a number of British television series that have featured an eponymous private eye, these have been few and far between, with one series in particular, *Shoestring* (BBC, 1979–80), demonstrating an ironic, post-*Rockford*, take on the genre. In this two-season show, which ended when actor Trevor Eve left to pursue other projects, Eve starred as former computer technician, Eddie Shoestring, a 'private ear' hired by the (then) fictional Radio West in Bristol. Much of the humour of the series derived from the setting: the incongruity of a private eye mooching through the nether regions of regional Britain. Nevertheless, while there have been other British private eyes, including P. D. James' Cordelia Gray in *An Unsuitable Job for a Woman*, the British corollary to the independent investigator on television has been that of the amateur sleuth in fiction, on radio, and on television.

While Agatha Christie's literary creations, Miss Marple and Hercule Poirot, have been staples of the television landscape since the early days of television, reinvented with different inflections in different eras, the character whose trajectory best illustrates the interplay between industry imperatives and the genealogy of the television crime drama genre is that of Sherlock Holmes. Although Holmes may occasionally have taken a fee for his services as consultant detective, he is nevertheless an exemplar of the 'amateur' who does what he does because of his love of investigation and the ratiocinative process rather than because of pecuniary reward. Indeed, at the start of the short story, 'The Speckled Band', Dr Watson writes, 'working as [Holmes] did rather for the love of his art than the acquirement of wealth, he refused to associate himself with any investigation which did not tend towards the unusual, and even the fantastic' (Conan Doyle 1967 [1883]: 243).

In this instance, rather than begin at the beginning, it is interesting to look at where the television career of Sherlock Homes had arrived by 2012. An article in the British newspaper *The Independent* in February of that year notes that the BBC had recently threatened legal action against the American TV network CBS over a planned new series entitled *Elementary*, starring actor Johnny Lee Miller as an updated Sherlock Holmes and actress Lucy Liu as Dr Jane Watson re-imagined in contemporary New York (Sherwin 2012). Producer Sue Vertue is quoted as saying, 'We have been in touch with CBS and informed them that we will be looking very closely at their finished pilot for any infringement of our rights' (Sherwin 2012). The rights in question were to the successful series *Sherlock* (BBC One, 2010–)

Figure 4.1 Sherlock Holmes (Benedict Cumberbatch) and Dr John Watson (Martin Freeman). Credit: Photofest

created by Vertue's husband, Stephen Moffat, and co-writer Mark Gattis and featuring Benedict Cumberbatch as an updated Holmes in contemporary London (see Figure 4.1).

The idea of re-imagining Holmes in a twenty-first-century setting apparently came to Moffat and Gattis during one of their frequent train journeys from London to Cardiff while they were both employed as writers on the long-running (and also re-imagined) cult TV series *Doctor Who* (Leader 2010). A diehard fan of Conan Doyle's hero, Moffat re-creates their train conversation in his foreword to the invaluable reference book, *Sherlock Holmes on Screen*, compiled by Allan Barnes. In this book, Barnes amasses a wealth of evidence to suggest that Sherlock Holmes may well be the fictional character with the most screen incarnations in the history of the moving image. Holmes is cast as the foremost hero of a post-Darwinian era, championing the triumph of science over superstition, and as 'the first pop icon' of the modern age (Barnes 2011: 8). Even more suggestive for a discussion of the television crime drama as a genre is the argument that the coincidence between Conan Doyle's creation of Holmes in the late nineteenth century and the emergence of film as a medium meant that one can observe 'almost every historical, cultural and technological development in the moving image purely through the changing representation of Holmes on screen' (Barnes 2011: 8).

To this end, Barnes provides a chronology, beginning with the publication of the first Holmes story in 1887, and the 'first' screen representation of Holmes in the Mutoscope peepshow *Sherlock Holmes Baffled* (1900). Setting aside the cinematic portrayal of Holmes, the character's 'first' television appearance is given as a 1937 teleplay of the story *The Three Garridebs* produced at the NBC Radio City Studios in 1937, which would have been seen only by a very early television audience numbered only in its hundreds (290).

According to Barnes, this production involved three very small sets and two pre-filmed inserts: one of the London skyline and the other being a sequence filmed partly in Central Park as Watson and Holmes take a hansom cab. *The New York Times* approved of this excursion into the new medium, noting that 'the ingenious welding of film and television production offered an interesting glimpse into the future of a new form of dramatic art' (291). And so it did, this production suggesting not only that Sherlock Holmes may well transfer to television, but that American producers and audiences were as keen on relocating the British sleuth to the United States then as they appeared to be in 2012 with the new series, *Elementary*. As further evidence of the American penchant for Holmes, the character made yet another early appearance on American television in an adaptation of 'The Speckled Band' for the Anthology series *Your Show Time*, which was sponsored by Lucky Strike cigarettes and aired on CBS in 1949.

The 'first' Sherlock Holmes series was also made for American television. Produced by Sheldon Reynolds, the series aired on NBC-affiliated stations on Monday nights from 7.00pm to 7.30pm from 18 October 1954 (181). In an endeavour to keep production costs down, Reynolds based his production company in Paris, although he made frequent use of film inserts featuring London landmarks (ibid.). With an eye to the successful series of fifteen Holmes films starring Basil Rathbone made from 1939 to 1953, Reynolds determined that his television Holmes would be closer in age to the Holmes of Conan Doyle's original creation. To this end, he chose actor Ronald Howard, who was 36 years old at the time. Most of the episodes were not based on Conan Doyle stories (probably for copyright reasons), but were complete inventions. This included an episode with the intriguing title 'The Case of the Careless Suffragette'. Thirty-nine episodes were produced at the rate of one twenty-five minute film every four days, a breakneck speed that actor Howard found particularly exhausting (185). While this series has all but been forgotten, Barnes notes that Howard's Holmes ranks only behind Jeremy Brett in terms of total television screen time. This early series is, therefore, long overdue for re-evaluation, given that it has largely been forgotten, especially since, as Barnes suggests, it was a loving form of Holmes 'pastiche' (180).

While there have been many other television Sherlocks since 1955, it is Jeremy Brett's Holmes who many regard as the 'definitive' television Holmes and whose continuing popularity is indisputable. In Australia in June 2012, the version starring Brett was again showing on the public service broadcaster (ABC1), albeit in an early afternoon slot with a 'catch-up' service available from the ABC's online service, *iview*. Developed for television in 1984 by writer John Hawkesworth, the first of the Brett/Holmes series, *The Adventures of Sherlock Holmes*, was produced for Granada on the commercial network ITV.

In his account of the series, Barnes makes two important points. The first is that the series owed its genesis to the success of an earlier lavish period drama adapted from a literary work made for Granada and screening on ITV from October to December in 1981, *Brideshead Revisited*. This series (subsequently remade as a film in 2008), has been identified as belonging to a cycle of production commonly identified as 'heritage television' (24). As Lez Cooke suggests, such series:

> were usually literary adaptations, evoking a period of history when Britain was still 'Great', possessing an Empire, and where everyone not only knew their place in the social hierarchy but where everyone was (apparently) content with their lot. (Cooke 2003: 157)

These series were imbued with nostalgia for a lost and safer world, even if this only ever existed in the imagination. The second key factor in the development of a new and lavish Holmes' production was the fact that the British copyright to the Holmes' stories had expired in 1980 (fifty years after Doyle's death). This encouraged producer Michael Cox to envisage the making of a 'definitive' series of adaptations, 'in colour, for a new generation of viewers' (24).

Thirteen fifty-minute episodes were produced for the first season, entitled *The Adventures of Sherlock Holmes*, beginning with 'A Scandal in Bohemia' and ending with 'The Final Problem' in which Holmes and Moriarty plummet to their 'death' over the Reichenbach Falls in Switzerland. In keeping with the fidelity of the series as a whole to the Conan Doyle canon, this latter scene was filmed 'in situ' at the waterfalls on the Reichenbach stream, a decision that demonstrated a desire on the part of the producers to be as 'authentic' as possible. However, such authenticity came at a considerable price, leading to an attenuation of the subsequent season two because of a blow-out in production costs.

While the popularity of the Jeremy Brett series has now been assured (a box set of the re-mastered complete collection was re-released in 2009), the initial response to the first season was only moderately enthusiastic; the highest rating episode attracted 11.23 million viewers in the United Kingdom (27). Nevertheless, the show was sufficiently successful to ensure a second season – *The Return of Sherlock Holmes*, which comprised of eleven fifty-minute adaptations of Doyle's original stories. Although a further two episodes were planned, Brett's illness during the latter part of the shooting coupled with the massive overspends resulted in a reduced number of episodes (eleven instead of the planned thirteen).

Looking closely at the composition of the Brett version of the Holmes' adventures as they progressed over the following decade, it is not easy to understand the logic of what went to air and when without considering some of the stories behind the scenes, including Brett's failing health, Granada's production practices, and ITV's programming strategies. The format of the series is thus revealed to be less a case of strategic planning and more a set of tactical moves in order to manage a difficult production schedule. As it is, programming varied between splitting the first thirteen episode series over 1984 and 1985, to screening only one telemovie in 1992, two in 1993, as well as a final series of six episodes in 1994.[6] Not surprisingly, given the American predilection for Holmes, the series also screened on PBS (the Public Broadcasting Service) in the US Service and, in 1991, the third series of six episodes comprising 'The Case-Book of Sherlock Holmes' was co-produced with the Boston Public Service Broadcaster WGBH (Anonymous n.d.h).

The performance of Brett as Holmes was clearly the major attraction of the show, both then and now, with the lavish period setting enhancing the series' ongoing appeal. However, with the benefit of hindsight, it is clear that the series closely resembles other British television productions of the 1980s in terms of its aesthetics and form. As Barnes and others have illustrated, the desire to be true to Conan Doyle's original creation meant that the designers of the show went to great lengths to ensure a degree of 'authenticity' in the production, even styling and positioning Brett to echo the original illustrations of Holmes by Sydney Paget that accompanied the 1891 publication of Doyle's story 'A Study in Scarlet' in *Strand* magazine (Anonymous n.d.i). Brett himself conducted extensive research on the character that he continued to play until 1995 when he died after what had been a protracted series of illnesses at the age of fifty-nine (Gussow 1995). Such attention to detail and fidelity to the literary origins of Holmes was clearly part of the series' 'quality' aesthetic despite the fact that the show originally appeared on a commercial channel. It was also possibly part of the pleasure for an audience already familiar with the stories and keen to see how these may be realised on-screen.

At his most ebullient, Brett's Holmes is a mercurial trickster, swirling through the streets of London or skipping across the British countryside with his stalwart amanuensis, Dr John Watson, trudging dutifully in his wake. Played in the first series by David Burke and in subsequent episodes by Edward Hardwicke, this rather humourless Watson manifests as the straight man to Sherlock's antic sleuth. While the psychology of Holmes and the nature of his relationship with Watson have exercised the critics ever since their first appearance in print, the primary appeal of this series and indeed of all the other representations, is the character of Holmes as a sleuth.

Of particular interest to students of media and communication is the suggestion that Holmes is an adept semiotician, able to read the 'signs' that others simply don't see. And indeed, long before forensic science became a staple of the modern police procedural, Holmes was using a test tube, a microscope, and crime scene analysis to aid him in the process of investigation. When Watson first meets Holmes in Conan Doyle's story 'A Study in Scarlet', Holmes is discovered in a chemical laboratory at a nearby hospital where, to his great delight, he has just discovered a means of isolating haemoglobin, thereby making the identification of a blood stain possible. While Holmes' prescient use of science has ensured his ongoing location at the cutting edge of crime, there are clearly other aspects of his character, along with the 'format' of his criminal investigations, which have continued to appeal to audiences across the years.

Sherlock in the twenty-first century

For Moffatt and Gattis, the desire to update Holmes to a contemporary setting was based on what they perceive as the central 'core' of the Holmes stories, which Gattis describes as 'thrilling, funny, silly, strange, wonder pieces of exciting adventure' (Gattis cited in Leader 2010). For them, the previous 'respectful' period adaptations were a distraction from what they regarded as the essential qualities of the Holmes' stories. In devising their version of Holmes, they, therefore, took inspiration not from previous television adaptations, but from a film directed by Billy Wilder entitled *The Private Life of Sherlock Holmes* (1970), which encapsulated the 'perfect combination of reverence and irreverence' they wished to emulate (Leader 2010). For example, in the film there is a great deal of rather pointed speculation about Holmes' sexual predilections, with Watson acutely embarrassed by the suggestion that they are a 'couple' – a trope that Moffat and Gattis also relentlessly exploit for humorous effect.

Like Sheldon Reynolds before them, Moffat and Gattis also decided to make Holmes as young as he is in the earliest Doyle stories and cast Benedict Cumberbatch who was then aged thirty-four: an actor whom Barnes describes as having already achieved a reputation for playing 'tortured, highly intelligent outsiders' (Barnes 2011: 169). While the first Brett series opened with the story *A Scandal in Belgravia*, Moffatt and Gattis decided to begin at the beginning of the Conan Doyle canon with 'A Study in Scarlet', which they playfully retitled 'A Study in Pink'. This opening gambit allowed them to make a significant link between the nineteenth-century return of Dr John Watson of the Fifth Northumberland Fusiliers from the war in Afghanistan with the return of the twenty-first century major John Watson from the contemporary 'unwinnable' war in Afghanistan. It also allowed them to place actor Martin Freeman as Watson centre stage at the opening of the series, as he is in the original Conan Doyle story: a canny move since for younger viewers Freeman would already be associated with the edgy comedy series *The Office* (BBC Two, 2001–3) and about to achieve an even bigger fan-following, deriving from his role as Bilbo Baggins in *The Hobbit* (dir. Peter Jackson; 2012).

In the Moffat and Gattis version of Holmes and Watson's first encounter, we meet Holmes not in a laboratory isolating haemoglobin, but beating a corpse with a riding stick (an incident briefly alluded to in the short story 'A Study in Scarlet'). This scene immediately signals Holmes as strange, and even manic. This perception, which is sustained in Cumberbatch's performance of Holmes as an erratic, brilliant, fast-talking, individual who may or may not suffer from Asperger syndrome but who clearly has difficulty relating to people on an emotional level, even if he is good at reading their motives. Instead of smoking an iconic pipe, Cumberbatch's Sherlock wears nicotine patches; instead of writing a diary, Freeman's Watson is writing a blog and, in the process, Holmes becomes something of an Internet sensation. Instead of writing letters back to Holmes, Watson shows him around a crime scene using Skype on his laptop computer. Indeed, the use of new technology, including mobile phones, global positioning system (GPS) technology, and the clever use of text on-screen, placed this particular version of Holmes firmly in the twenty-first century. *Sherlock* also updated Conan Doyle's Victorian attitudes to both sex and the monarchy as the playful adaptation of the Conan Doyle story, *A Scandal in Bohemia*, re-imagined as 'A Scandal in Belgravia', revealed in a screenplay involving nudity, a lesbian dominatrix, and a female 'royal' client.

While the original Doyle stories may have been the inspiration for *Sherlock*, what appears to have won over audiences and critics alike was the combination of 'reverence and irreverence' that Gattis and Moffatt exhibited in their updated version of Holmes. For those aware of the Conan Doyle stories and any of Holmes' on-screen appearances, there was the pleasure of recognition. For those who had never encountered Holmes before there was the delight of discovery, and the possibility of making a comparison with yet anther recent British-American rein-vention of Holmes at the time as embodied by American actor Robert Downey in Guy Ritchie's film (*Sherlock Holmes*, 2009).

In terms of format, the original plan for *Sherlock* was to create a series of one-hour telemovies for the BBC. However, after viewing the one-hour pilot, the BBC executives ordered a series of three ninety-minute films: a move apparently inspired by BBC One's previ-ous success with *Wallander* (2008–): the crime drama series based on Swedish crime writer Henning Mankell's Inspector Wallander series (Barnes 2011: 169). Clearly there was a perception that the audience 'liked' this film format. While it may appear to be rather a jump from *Sherlock* to *Wallander*, what both had in common was their status as 'literary detectives' as well as their high production values, which helped to establish their status as 'quality' television.

Literary detectives and maverick cops

Like Sherlock Holmes, both *Maigret* (BBC, 1960–3) and *Wallander* (BBC One, 2008–) are literary detectives who began life on the printed page: the former in the novels of Belgian crime writer, Georges Simenon, and the latter in the books of Swedish crime writer Henning Mankell. These two series bookend a range of British television crime dramas over the intervening years that began life in print. While the 'literary' detective is clearly popular on both sides of the Atlantic, I want to focus here on a cycle of British productions that begin in the 1970s and that continue to the present day based on adaptations of British crime novels that feature heroic police detectives in the lead in order to illustrate some of the issues that may arise for both the pro-ducers and the audience in the translation from page to screen.

Detective, later commander, Dalgliesh first appeared in P. D. James's debut crime novel, *Cover Her Face*, in 1962. In 1983 he arrived on television as portrayed by actor Roy Marsden in a six-part adapta-tion of James's *Death of An Expert Witness* (ITV, 1977). Twenty-one years later, Dalgliesh was played by Martin Shaw in a two-part adaptation of *The Murder Room* (Anonymous n.d.j), suggesting that, like Sherlock Holmes, the (literary) character of the detective and their milieu may be the primary attraction of a television series that producers hope will outweigh allegiance to particular actors in the role, in much the same way that allegiance to the cult TV series *Doctor Who* has allowed for at least twelve (and counting) incarnations of the eponymous Doctor. Other significant literary detectives would include Ruth Rendell's Inspector Wexford in a series clearly intended to capitalise on the fame and popularity of the literary author as a brand, *The Ruth Rendell Mysteries* (1987–2000), R. D. Wingfield's Inspector Frost in a series entitled *A Touch of Frost* (1992–2010), the Yorkshire-based duo *Dalziel and Pascoe* created by Reginald Hill (BBC One, 1997–2007), Ian Rankin's Edinburgh-based detective *Rebus* as played by two actors, John Hannah and Ken Stott, to very different effect (ITV, 2000–7), and Val McDermid's clinical psychologist, Dr Tony Hill, in the series *Wire in the Blood* who is a 'specialist' and profiler, assisting the police (ITV, 2002–8).

While the producers of such series have the possible advantage of the audience's pre-existing familiarity with the characters, they also face the challenge of meeting audience expectations in terms of the series' fidelity to the original text for those who have read them. As has been illustrated in studies of the *Lord of the Rings*' audience, such prior knowledge enables the audience to enact their scholarship so that even if the on-screen narrative diverges from the original, there is pleasure to be had in recognising this (Turnbull 2008). At the same time, the success of the television detective may boost sales of an author's works, as was certainly the case following the recent *Wallander* adaptations for BBC One. New editions of Mankell's books appeared in prominent bookshop displays with Kenneth Branagh's pale, pink-eyed version of Wallander on the cover. In the case of *Inspector Morse*, the Morse of the TV series is a considerably more likeable and less misogynist character than that of Colin Dexter's original, at the same time as the casting of John Thaw brought an interesting new edge to the series given his previous major role as the hard-bitten Regan in *The Sweeney*. Despite being played by the same actor, Regan and Morse could not be less alike with Morse portrayed as middle-class, unfit and having a penchant for opera and classical music. The only characteristic the two characters appear to have had in common is their (doomed) attraction to intelligent women.

Morse's other attractions included his Oxford setting, which cast a 'heritage' gloss over the series, and his vintage Jaguar car, which from personal memory was of key interest to the male viewers of my acquaintance at the time. Thus, during an era of increasing manage-rialism in the 1980s when the police were rewarded with successive pay rises by the conservative Thatcher government for their efforts in dealing with various forms of civil unrest and protest, according to Helen Davis, *Inspector Morse* represents something of a throwback, 'an elegant return to the crime detective story in a fictional world unaf-fected by rioting miners or belligerent politicians' (Davis 2001: 137). As such, the series portrays the work of the police as an ethical public service with the 'cerebral, melancholy' Morse owing more to Britain's literary heritage than he does to the world of television crime drama of the grittier kind (ibid.). The series is therefore imbued with what Davis identifies as an overwhelming sense of nostalgia in its portrayal of a man who finds himself out of step with the world in which he lives. Like many other television series based on a literary figure, *Inspector Morse* is more successful as a character study of its eponymous hero than as a study of crime in the contemporary world.

Morse is inherently a loner, even though he is usually accompa-nied on his investigations by sergeant Lewis who is marked by his Geordie accent as belonging to a different class and social world to the Oxford-educated Morse. 'I could have had a first,' Morse confides to a colleague, except for the fact that he dropped out without com-pleting his degree after suffering a broken heart, thus reinforcing the supposition that Morse is an emotionally vulnerable man ('The Last Enemy' 03:02). Far from being a hindrance, Morse's lack of success in establishing a relationship with the many attractive and intelligent women with whom he comes into contact evidently constituted part of his appeal. In her study of the female audience for Morse, reveal-ingly entitled 'In Love with Inspector Morse', Lyn Thomas (1997) suggests that as a result of his failure to sustain a relationship, Morse is always available for an imaginary romance with the (female) viewer. Interestingly, Inspector Kurt Wallander is similarly unsuccessful in his dealings with the opposite sex, only one of the many parallels that can be drawn between these two detective heroes, and with the many other literary detectives where this trope of the middle-aged lonely sleuth 'unlucky in love' has long been standard.

Morse and Wallander

Wallander is another world-weary detective appalled by the violent crimes he is called upon to investigate that he also perceives to be symptomatic of contemporary social decline. Like Morse, Wallander is melancholy and alone, although unlike Morse he does have a daughter, Linda, with whom he has a loving but often tetchy relationship. Wallander also has a difficult relationship with his ageing father, Povel, a landscape painter who rages against the fog of Alzheimer's, which gradually overtakes him. However, while Wallander and Morse both signal their middle-class aspiration through their love of opera in the books, the producer of the British television version of *Wallander* decided to drop this particular affectation precisely because it would make Wallander too similar to his on-screen predecessor Morse (Jarossi 2008) – a potential overlap that publications like the British *Radio Times* were more than happy to invoke in punning feature articles announcing the arrival of the new Swedish 'Inspector Norse' (Anonymous n.d.k). Both Wallander and Morse suffer from diabetes and have to deal with their recalcitrant bodies, viewers being party to their physical discomfiture in ways that are clearly intended to evoke sympathy for their human failings. While Morse dies of a heart attack in the final episode of the series, it is foreshadowed that Wallander will also come to an untimely end in series four as the character, following Mankell's literary lead, succumbs to Alzheimer's disease.

By the time that *Inspector Morse* ended in 2000 with the 'death' of Morse, the series had amounted to thirty-three 100-minute episodes.[7] With at most five episodes shown per year in 1991 and 1992 and as few as one per year in 1995, 1996, 1997, 1998, and 2000, the appearance of *Morse* during this time frame therefore constituted something of a television event, even in those territories such as Australia where it was shown not on the commercial network, as in the United Kingdom, but on the public service network, the ABC, where an older and predominantly Anglo audience for *Morse* (and 'quality' TV) may be imagined to congregate. During its time on air *Morse* also received a number of awards, confirming its 'quality' status, including a Best Actor BAFTA for John Thaw in 1989 and a BAFTA Best Drama Series in 1993 (Anonymous n.d.l).

The adjective 'quality' again deserves some explication here since as Liz Thomas points out, *Morse* had the unusual distinction of being a TV show that was perceived to be a 'quality' drama at the same time as it was extremely popular (Thomas 1997: 185). As was noted in previous chapters, the concept of 'quality' in relation to television is by no means clear-cut. In the British context, the concept of 'quality' may include a conventional 'high art' discourse that would usually discount the medium of television altogether. However, within the television industry itself, there are also professional codes and practices that would value genres that embrace a 'realist paradigm' above those that are perceived to be more fanciful, and/or melodramatic (Brunsdon 1990a: 61). As has been demonstrated, the particular relevance of the 'realist paradigm' to the evaluation of the television crime drama is evident in the fact that those series that espouse realism (especially social realism) are routinely more highly regarded than crime dramas that are perceived to be more stylised, formulaic, and entertaining. The only exception here would appear to be the 'period' crime series that is perceived as quality by virtue of its heritage status and production values. To this list, I would like to add an additional criterion of value, and that is the pre-existence of the television detective in crime fiction, with the literary origins of the detective conferring on 'him' (and it is most often a 'him') a status to which the made-for-television detective may not aspire.

From 1994 to 2007 all nine of the Wallander crime novels were made into a series of Swedish language films starring Rolf Lassgard as Wallander. From 2005 to 2006, thirteen new stories starring Krister Henriksson as Wallander and Johanna Sällström as his daughter Linda were produced by Yellow Bird productions, Mankell's own production house later sold to Danish media house Zodiak Entertainment in 2007 (Anonymous n.d.m). In 2008, Yellow Bird announced that thirteen new Swedish-language Wallander films would be made starring Henriksson. The first in the series, *The Revenge*, was given a cinematic launch in Sweden before its release on DVD. Yellow Bird is also one of the producers of the English-language version of *Wallander* starring Kenneth Branagh and made for BBC Scotland, which premiered on BBC One in November 2008. Season two (2010), season three (2012), and a planned final season four have been constructed as a trilogy of made-for-television movies. This last point brings us to the relationship between televisual form and perceptions of quality.

Inspector Morse and *Wallander*, particularly in its British incarnation, represent a move away from the weekly half-hour or one-hour episodic crime series that may unfold over a season of thirteen or twenty-six weeks to the construction of a TV crime series as a sequence of telemovie events. The production values of these made-for-television films is consequently very high. The first series of *Wallander* starring Branagh had an initial budget of six million pounds, with half coming from the BBC and the other from a pre-sale co-production funding agreement with the American public broadcaster network WGBH Boston and the German ARD Degeto (Thomas 2008). The series also received a tax deduction for location filming undertaken in Sweden (Armstrong 2008). *Wallander* premiered on 30 November 2008 on BBC One and attracted an audience of just over 6.5 million, coming eighth in the ratings for the network on the weekend, some four million behind *Strictly Come Dancing* (Anonymous n.d.n), an outcome that underlines the point made in the previous chapter that 'quality' television is not necessarily television that is popular with a large audience.

Like *Morse*, the English-speaking version of *Wallander* was greeted with critical acclaim, with a British Academy Film and Television Arts (BAFTA) Best Actor Award for Branagh in 2009 as well as a number of craft awards for production design, sound, and lighting (Anonymous n.d.o). Branagh's presence as a producer and an actor, given his credentials in direction and acting in theatre and film, clearly added to what was the promotion and reception of the series as 'quality' television. Nonetheless, a review of the third series on *The Guardian*'s online TV and Radio Blog prompted a heated online debate on the merits of the Branagh adaptation with a number of posters preferring the Swedish-language television version starring Krister Henriksson instead. As the anonymous author of the original blog post notes, another Swedish version of *Wallander* staring Lassgard was about to start screening on BBC Four at the end of July 2012 that would further fan the flames of the debate (Anonymous n.d.p). For one commentator, the proliferation of Wallander adaptations only served to prove that 'detective fans have a limitless capacity to re-watch the same plots', arguing that this is either because they have forgotten who the perpetrator may be, or that they don't mind knowing. While this comment appears to assume that that crime fiction readers and crime drama viewers are only interested in plot, as has been suggested there are many other aspects of the narrative that may appeal, including the setting. Furthermore, far from being a disincentive, familiarity with the literary original or a previous screen incarnation may well be an incentive since there is much pleasure to be derived from considering how the latest adaptation shapes up.

There may be other reasons for watching, too. While Lyn Thomas describes the ways in which women may fantasise about a romantic engagement with Morse, a male participant in Stijn Reijnders's study of crime show tourism identified with Wallander on the basis of his unhappiness:

We are just similar. I had also had a divorce. The guilt you feel to your children. And I had to raise them ... When it's too much for me, I grab a bottle of wine or glass of whisky and listen to opera ... Kurt [Wallander] has a lot of feelings that I like about him. He thinks about things. (Reijnders 2010: 47)

Important to this person is their emotional connection with an on-screen detective facing the same kinds of problems in the conduct of their lives. In this case, the motivating crime narrative becomes an opportunity for an encounter with a familiar, like-minded character with whom the writer may indeed have a form of 'para-social' interaction.

Such an interest in, and identification with, the character of the detective may carry over into a desire to enter into their 'fictional space' by visiting the 'real' world in which their 'fictional' activities are carried out. Such forms of cultural tourism are hardly unusual. As Nicola Watson has demonstrated, cultural tourism has long encompassed a visit to the home of William Shakespeare in Stratford-upon-Avon or a visit to the Haworth parsonage – the home of the Brontë sisters (Watson 2006), and I recall once conducting my own improvised tour of 'Wessex' on the back of a motorcycle in the early 1970s in pursuit of Thomas Hardy's fictional world. From the start of the twentieth century, such cultural tourism may also encompass a love of crime fiction, with regular pilgrimages to 221b Baker Street, the fictional home of Sherlock Holmes. According to Reijnders, while these pilgrimages usually originate with 'fans', it is not long before local authorities may need to step in to help manage the wave of interest while also capitalising on the possibilities that such cultural tourism may bring to their region (Reijnders 2010: 42).

Since 1996, the Oxford Information Centre has offered visitors to the city an Inspector Morse Tour that, reflecting the now worldwide popularity of the series, apparently attracts an international audience (Reijnders 2010: 38). The tour encompasses Morse's police station, the courtyard where he had his heart attack, and the pub of The Randolph Hotel (now renamed The Macdonald Randolph Hotel), which has been officially renamed 'The Inspector Morse Bar'. Meanwhile, over in Sweden, readers of the Mankell books started approaching the tourist office in Ystad, Wallander's 'home' town as early as 1992. As the number of visitors have increased, augmented by the popularity of the various films and TV series both in Sweden and overseas, the tour now encompasses a visit to Wallander-related sites on an old fire engine (Reijnders 2010: 43). Not to be outdone, fans of Ian Rankin's character Inspector Rebus can download a virtual tour of Edinburgh conducted by Rankin on their iPhone from Rankin's own website that arguably provides an even more intimate connection to the reality of a fictional character (Anonymous n.d.q). In attempting to explain the phenomenon of the 'TV detective tour', Reijnders draws upon the notion of the pilgrimage, the history of cultural tourism, and the concept of *lieux d'imagination*, or places of the imagination. He argues that 'by visiting these locations and focusing on them, tourists are able to construct and subsequently cross a symbolic boundary between an "imagined" and a "real" world' (Reijnders 2010: 48).

In terms of the television detective as hero, this kind of audience activity therefore suggests an engagement with a character that transcends the specifics of any one investigation or case – or, in the case of Sherlock Holmes and Wallander, even the performance of one particular actor as the eponymous detective, although viewers may have their favourites, a fact of which the producers of such shows are well aware. Nor does the detective have to be particularly good at their job. As Morse suggests in the first episode of the TV series: 'I stumble along . . . around . . . and sometimes I stumble in the right direction.' What sustains Morse is his doggedness and reliable moral compass, not his brilliant mind and powers of deduction. On the other hand, there are detectives who do indeed exhibit extraordinary powers of deduction or have particular forms of specialist knowledge or skill and it is to this particular group that we shall turn in the next chapter, particularly as it once again demonstrates the ways in which the television industry may respond to current trends and public interest.

Conclusion

In terms of the television industry, the popularity of the detective in literature or on radio has clearly been an important factor in the development of subsequent television series since the early days of the medium. The currency of the private eye in American and the 'amateur' detective in British fiction offered television producers and creators the opportunity to reacquaint audiences with a literary character with whom they were already familiar and in whom they may already had an emotional investment. In the case of more recent series such as *Wallander*, an already existing and proven attachment to the eponymous detective clearly provided some element of security in launching the project. By the time that the BBC One series was pitched, twenty-five million copies of the Wallander series had been sold worldwide (Churchill 2008). While book sales may ensure potential audience interest in the project, as the online debate about Branagh's performance as Wallander indicates, the success of any adaptation is not a given, especially since in this case Wallander had already been adapted in Swedish. However, given that only a 'minority' audience may be prepared to watch television with subtitles, this would be a risk well worth taking in the endeavour to achieve global

sales of an English-language adaptation to those regions more resist-
ant to the Swedish originals. In the transnational trade in television,
some series clearly travel better than others with the British and the
American product having a much higher circulation in the global
traffic in crime drama.

From the early adaptations of the private eye genre through to the
most recent adaptations of Sherlock Holmes, fictional representations
of crime on-screen have been an enduring feature of the television
landscape. In the process, the detective as hero has taken many different forms, although as will be discussed later (Chapter 6) the question
of gender has been an ongoing issue in the debate about television
crime. Given how many women are successful crime writers, the
relative absence of female sleuths on television has been an interesting
anomaly that perhaps says more about the practices of the television
industry and culture than it does the popularity of the female detective as hero. With the 'breakthrough' of feminist crime writers such
as Marcia Muller, Sara Paretsky, and Sue Grafton in the 1970s and
1980s, it is surprising that an eponymous feminist detective or private
eye was so slow to appear on television, although, as will be revealed,
the role of women in television crime did indeed begin to change as an
effect of the second wave of feminism during the 1980s.

Notes

1. An early example of the spin-off phenomenon is the successful
   private eye series 77 *Sunset Strip* (ABC, 1958–64) created by writer
   Roy Huggins and produced by Aaron Spelling for Warner Bros.
   Studios, which spawned three more-or-less successful spin-offs:
   Bourbon Street Beat (ABC, 1959–60) set in New Orleans, *Hawaiian
   Eye* (ABC, 1959–63), and *Surfside 6* (ABC, 1960–2) set in Miami.
2. Lathrop would go on to a distinguished career in television and
   film, including Blake Edwards's *The Pink Panther*.
3. These observations are courtesy of jazz fan and former resident of
   Los Angeles Richard Thompson who was also an aficionado of
   these series in the 1950s and 1960s.
4. After viewing *Shadows* in the context of Cassavetes' work on *Johnny
   Staccato*, my personal opinion is that *Johnny Staccato* is by far the
   more interesting and successful project. But then I am biased.
5. It may be noted that Cannell had been a writer on Jack Webb's
   police procedural *Adam-12* (NBC, 1968–75) before embarking on
   Rockford.
6. In 1984, the first seven episodes of the *Adventures of Sherlock Holmes*

went to air in consecutive weeks from 24 April to 5 June. In 1985, the remaining six episodes aired from 25 August to 29 September. In 1986, seven episodes of *The Return of Sherlock Holmes* went to air from 9 July to 20 August. In 1987 a feature-length, stand-alone episode, 'The Sign of Four', was shown on 29 December. In 1988, the final five episodes of *The Return* were showing, culminating in yet another feature-length episode, 'The Hound of the Baskervilles', on 31 August. The third series, *The Case-Book of Sherlock Holmes*, comprising only six episodes, was broadcast from 21 February to 28 March in 1991. In 1992 only one telemovie, *The Master Blackmailer* (2 January), appeared, and in 1993 there were two, *The Last Vampyre* (27 January) *and The Eligible Bachelor* (3 February). The final series of six episodes, *The Memoirs of Sherlock Holmes*, were screened from 7 March to 11 April, culminating in 'The Cardboard Box'.

7. The series was produced by Zenith Productions and Central Independent Productions for ITV.

5 The Specialists

While the police procedural and crime drama featuring a police detective, gifted amateur, or private eye have long been staples of the television crime drama, there is another sub-genre of crime shows that cluster around a different set of investigators. These are the shows that focus on the work of the 'specialist' who may bring to the case in question a particular gift or knowledge set that equips him or her with the necessary powers to solve the crime. Once again, this is a sub-genre that can be traced to other popular representations of crime, including pulp magazines, radio series, film, and crime fiction, as these too have mirrored, and sometimes anticipated, social and scientific developments in the field of crime and its detection.

While it is interesting to identify these points of origin within the complicated root system of the television crime drama, it is also important to consider how these specialist series have emerged not only in relation to changing practices of criminal investigation, but also in relation to specific production contexts and audience tastes – especially in the last decade of the twentieth century when the 'turn' to the specialist in forensics and profiling became a significant trend in the development of the genre. For example, the figure of the rational scientific forensic investigator arguably begins with Sherlock Holmes isolating haemoglobin in a laboratory in *A Study in Scarlet* to resurface on American television in *Quincy, M.E.* (NBC, 1976–83) during the 1970s, to appear again in the 1990s in the British series *Silent Witness* (BBC One, 1996–), and to pop up at the start of the new millennium in the form of Gil Grissom in *CSI* (CBS, 2000–), a character and a series that rapidly became one of the most popular television crime dramas in the world and that had a profound influence on both the look and the form of the television crime drama.

In his reading of character and motive, it is also possible to argue that Sherlock Holmes anticipates the work of the criminal profiler whose job depends not just on an interpretation of the physical evidence, but also understanding the psychological and subconscious desires that motivate criminal behaviour. With his intuitive leaps of logic, Holmes prefigures the work of those investigators who arrive at the 'truth' by some form of psychic power that may or may not be paranormal, as in such recent series as *Medium* (NBC, 2005–9; CBS, 2009–11). Finally, Holmes can be identified as the prototypical 'detective on the edge', the unstable but brilliant loner, who has to deal with his own demons (Conan Doyle implied that Holmes' occasional cocaine use was the result of incipient depression and boredom) in the course of his investigation.

In tracing the genealogy of these series, this chapter, therefore, considers the British and the American shows that have featured such specialists, noting in passing that there appear to be some interesting disparities between the two. For example, while the American shows *Bones* and *Quincy, M.E.* have adopted what may be described as a 'playful' engagement with the science of forensics, which is perhaps best exemplified by the extremely stylish *CSI* as a form of diverting screen entertainment, British series such as the long-running *Silent Witness* in its pre-*CSI* period adopted a much more sombre tone, underlined in some cases by the adoption of a quasi-documentary, realist style. These are crime shows that take serious crime very seriously, especially when it involves the abuse and/or murder of women and children, although the entertainment factor is still, of course, paramount, since if viewers 'turn off' then the show will simply be cancelled. As the case of *CSI: NY* discussed later in this chapter suggests, there is a delicate balancing act involved.

Another interesting aspect of these 'specialist' shows is the precise relationship that their central protagonist may have with the forces of law and order. Are they, for example, simply a 'consultant' who offers insight and advice? Or do they 'cross the line' and become more central to the investigation in ways that would be unlikely in 'real' life, but that within the realm of the television crime drama affords them a more heroic role within the narrative? As a result, the specialist may, therefore, be something of a loose cannon, an investigator who operates outside of the confines of the law when they consider this necessary to protect the interests of the victim. The most compelling example of this kind of vigilantism in recent times is the 'blood-spatter expert', Dexter, who not only carries out his own investigations but who also metes out his own form of terrible justice. *Dexter* the series, however, was not simply a grim portrait of a serial killer at work, but it was rather a playful hybrid of black comedy, horror, and crime in which the entertainment values were clearly to the fore. As such,

Dexter makes for an interesting comparison with the British series *Luther* in terms of style and tone, begging the question, 'Do the British take their specialists more seriously?' This chapter establishes the groundwork for such a comparison.

Forensic traces

In her study of the science employed by Sherlock Holmes, E. J. Wagner notes that at the time of Holmes' appearance in 1887 forensic science was 'largely a function of the medical profession', variously described at the time as Medical Jurisprudence or Legal Medicine, and suggests that an accurate understanding of fingerprint and other trace evidence (such as hairs and lipstick stains) lay somewhere in the future (Wagner 2007: 4).[1] But not very far in the future, since, in 1896, Sir Edward Richard Henry, 1st Baronet of the Bengal Police created the Henry Classification System enabling police to identify criminal suspects using their fingerprints – a system that remained in place for some hundred years, although the technologies employed over this time underwent some modifications (Watson n.d.). While histories of forensic science may cite much earlier incidents of the use of scientific methods in the investigation of crime, it was not until the twentieth century that these became routine for the majority of the police force. Nevertheless, the potential use of forensic science was already on the radar in the 1880s, and Conan Doyle was prescient when he equipped his fictional detective Holmes with a microscope and an enquiring, scientific mind. Nor in his dedication to the science of observation was Holmes alone for long.

In 1905 the British crime writer Richard Austin Freeman, who had himself trained as an apothecary and as a medical doctor, introduced the character of Dr John Thorndyke, who would go on to become the hero of some fifteen books, one of which was entitled *A Silent Witness* (1914), prefiguring the title of the long-running British forensic series *Silent Witness* (BBC One, 1996–) by more than eighty years (McAleer 1999: 169). A 'typical' Thorndyke mystery would unfold according to a reliable formula: A young doctor, lawyer, or other acquaintance would find himself in 'mysterious circumstances' and call on his former tutor Thorndyke for assistance. Dr Thorndyke would then devise a scientific solution or experiment that would lead to the solution of the mystery, one that often involved research into some obscure topic, such as pond fauna, archaeological anthropology, or Egyptology. Apparent from this brief description is that while Freeman offered his readers a predictable narrative structure, this would be enlivened

by the introduction of 'new' specialist and scientific knowledge calcu-
lated to engage, entertain, and possibly even educate the reader in the
process of reading the story. In other words, the origins of the episodic
forensic crime series can be traced back to this early instance of detective fiction.

Inevitably, as the use of forensic methods by the police became
more routine, forensic science began to play a more prominent role
in screen depictions of crime. It may be recalled that TV auteur Jack
Webb had himself played a forensic examiner in the film *He Walked
by Night* (dir. Alfred L. Werker; 1948), which inspired the creation of
Dragnet. In this film we see him dusting a car for fingerprints and also
engaged in the process of constructing a photofit image of a criminal
using transparencies overlaid on an overhead projector – a state-of-
the-art technology at the time. However, the first American television
series to put a forensic investigator front and centre rather than in the
background or on the wing was *Quincy, M.E.* (NBC, 1976–83).

Quincy, M.E.

Like many TV series before and since, the title character of *Quincy,
M.E.*, Dr Quincy, was apparently inspired by a real person, in this
case a Los Angeles coroner, Thomas Noguchi, who had earlier been
the inspiration for a Canadian television series called *Wojeck* (CBC,
1966–8) (Anonymous n.d.s). *Quincy, M.E.* began its television career
in a ninety-minute telefilm on rotation in the 'NBC Sunday Mystery
Movie' slot with such other future successful crime series as *McCloud,
Columbo*, and *McMillan and Wife* (Snauffer 2007: 72). After a few
months in this position, the decision was made to cut *Quincy, M.E.*
back to a length of just one hour but produce it as a weekly series.

Produced by Glen A. Larson and starring Jack Klugman as Dr Jack
Quincy, a medical examiner working for the Los Angeles County
Coroner's Office, the opening title sequence established the up-beat,
jazzy energy of the show. We see Quincy in his laboratory, at his
microscope, the lens of which becomes the aperture through which we
view Quincy in a number of more exotic settings, including the sailing
boat where he resides when not staying with his girlfriend or hanging
out at his favourite restaurant by the marina (thus anticipating undercover cop Sonny Crockett's exotic aquatic residence in *Miami Vice* by
some eight years) (see Figure 5.1). (The widowed Quincy's romantic
attachments varied during the course of the seven seasons in which
the show was on air, providing viewers with additional narrative interest while establishing Quincy's attractiveness as a masculine hero.) A

Figure 5.1 Publicity still of *Quincy, M.E.* with microscope. Credit: Photofest

close look at the Emmy Award-winning episode, 'The Thighbone is Connected to the Kneebone', from season two, illuminates the early structure and tone of the show while establishing the now familiar role of the forensic investigator involved.

While excavating a building site on a university campus, the builders unearth a thighbone, but make the decision to throw it away rather than hold up a multi-million dollar construction. A young woman in the graduate class Quincy has been persuaded to teach finds the bone by the roadside and brings it to her lecturer who decides to makes it an object lesson in the revelatory power of forensic science: The class will 'reconstruct' the man to whom this thigh bone once belonged using only the evidence they have to hand. Following a rapid examination, Quincy discovers a nick to the bone. This he immediately decides must have been left by a bullet and concludes without further examination that the victim has died a suspicious death. To the irritation of the university, his immediate boss, and the police, Quincy then holds up the building project and puts the students in danger while exceeding his own duties as a medical examiner in order to bring the murderer to justice using himself as the bait.

The 'body' under investigation in this episode is represented by a thigh bone: There is no blood at the scene or depiction of crime shots to graphically illustrate the trauma suffered by the victim. Instead, we have the reconstruction of a skeleton in a laboratory and a police artist who paints an image of what the man would have looked like, relying not only on the slight physical evidence available, but also on a series of 'logical' inferences made by Quincy. Given the length of the bone, Quincy and his students calculate the victim's height. Given height and the significant wear to the joint, Quincy deduces that the deceased probably played football for the university in the kind of position where such a specific injury as can be deduced may occur. Like the best of the ratiocinative detectives, Quincy solves the puzzle of the thigh bone even in the face of opposition from his immediate superior and the police who want him to butt out of a police investigation that he is neither qualified nor employed to conduct. His girlfriend also warns him of the danger he is courting, but the determined Quincy blunders on, almost getting himself killed in the process. Quincy, like many forensic examiners to follow him, oversteps the line of his responsibility in his quest for justice on the part of his 'silent witness', establishing himself in the process as the hero of the moment.

By an apt coincidence, the night after I had reviewed this early episode of *Quincy*, I was watching a re-run of the Fox network series *Bones* featuring forensic anthropologist Temperance Brennan (*Bones*; Fox, 2005–) in an episode entitled 'The Bones that Weren't' (06: 05), which employed a very similar forensic 'puzzle'. In this case, Brennan and her team are presented with a partial skull buried in concrete, the rest of the body having been eaten away by a fungus. The task, once again, is to reconstruct the entire body for which the skull is merely the synecdoche. This time, however, the technology is considerably more elaborate and includes radar imaging, the reconstruction of the body in a vat of molten plastic in a moment of Frankenstein-like 3D wizardry, and the use of a new fingerprinting technique that miraculously involves 'gold binding with the lipids at an atomic level' to reveal the trace of a handprint on a plastic sheet that has been buried under concrete for several years. This is hi-tech forensic science in which the technology is the star while the forensic anthropologist and her team occupy the role of sci-fi magicians in white coats.

The role of Brennan is also very different from that of Quincy since she is presented as a high-functioning woman, somewhere on the increasingly prevalent Asperger's spectrum that appears to have afflicted many 'brilliant' ratiocinative detectives from Holmes to Saga Norén in the Danish–Swedish co-production, *The Bridge* (DR1, SVT1, 2011–). This is indicated by the fact that Brennan appears to be motivated not by human empathy but by scientific curiosity in a move that could also be read as perversely progressive in feminist terms. Brennan appears to be a woman whose emotions rarely cloud her scientific vision.

The portrayal of the forensic scientist as the empathetic champion of the voiceless victim is a generic trope appearing in other forensic series to follow *Quincy*. For example, Dr (later professor) Sam Ryan (Amanda Burton), the initial protagonist of the British series *Silent Witness* during its first five seasons (BBC One, 1996–), is motivated by her humanitarian concerns. Created by Nigel McCrery, himself a former murder squad detective, who would later go on to create the more light-hearted cold case crime series *New Tricks* (BBC One, 2003–), the character of Ryan was based on the career of a real-life female pathologist with whom McCrery had himself worked as a police officer (Oliver 2008). In the first two-part, ninety-minute-long, episode of this series, Sam arrives in the university town of Cambridge where, like Quincy in the episode discussed above, her role is to lecture to students as well as to 'help' the police. Once again the device of the university classroom is used to 'educate' not only potential students but also the viewer about the value of forensic science. This time we witness only the conclusion of Sam's lecture, which is accompanied by the projection of gruesome crime-scene photographs on the screen behind her. These, she tells students, are precisely the kind of scenes that they must examine minutely if they are ever going to be able to understand how the victim died. This direction to look closely serves not only the enquiring gaze of the students but also that of the viewer who is made privy to the kinds of crime-scene photographs that are usually concealed from public scrutiny.

Like Quincy, Ryan is at odds with the police as she holds up the inquest into the death of a six-year-old girl because she has last minute 'doubts' that the verdict of accidental drowning is correct. Once again, her suppositions are based on the evidence of previous injuries that her close examination of the body has revealed. Like Quincy, Ryan is driven by the desire to secure justice for the victim and as a consequence is portrayed as a moral crusader determined to track down the perpetrator while putting herself (and her family) in danger. Undeterred by the opposition of her superiors and the police, Sam demands the exhumation of another body, that of a baby who may be connected to the current case. This request outrages not only the police but also the local community and the media. The episode ends on a dark note. The killer is identified but not before he has destroyed the lives of another woman and her children. It's a hollow victory.

Unlike the ebullient Quincy, Sam Ryan is more muted and reserved. This is not forensics as light entertainment, but forensics British-style, featuring grey-faced people in gloomy settings who would rather not be dealing with the gruesome crime scenes that they are about to encounter. The aesthetic here is that of the well-established tradition of social realism in British drama. *Silent Witness* thus belongs in its early years to that league of 'gritty' British crime that does not shy away from the blood, gore, and decay with which the forensic patholo-gists have to deal. With its strong, no-nonsense female lead whose short hair and brusque manner make no concessions to feminine 'niceness', the immediate reference here is to the earlier British crime drama, *Prime Suspect* (1991–2006), in which forensics also featured prominently. There is even an interesting visual parallel between the first appearance of Sam Ryan at the podium, lecturing her students while horrific crime scene images are projected behind her and a telling moment in the first episode of *Prime Suspect* (1991). In the latter, we see Tennison addressing her team of detectives in front of a board that is covered with similarly distressing crime-scene images of the dead women whose deaths they are investigating. Tennison, however, is eating a bag of crisps.

In her detailed examination of *Prime Suspect*, Deborah Jermyn has drawn attention to the ways in which writer Lynda La Plante, CBE embraced developments in forensic science such as deoxyribonucleic acid (DNA) analysis that were to change the face of criminal investi-gation, and inevitably also the television crime drama (Jermyn 2010: 82). While the deployment of white-coated scientists discussing blood types in the cool space of the laboratory is one example of *Prime Suspect*'s attention to science, other evidence of this includes the scru-tiny of the corpse when it is discovered in situ and then again in the lab as it is subjected to the inquiring gaze of the forensic examiner (and the audience) under unforgiving fluorescent lights. In this way, Jermyn argues, 'the corpse comes to act as a vivid signifier of the text's realism' even as such displays raise the spectre of voyeurism and ghoulishness (83).

Thus, while the image of Tennison consuming a bag of crisps in the presence of these 'ghoulish' images may be disconcerting since it implies callousness, in Jermyn's reading of the scene, Tennison's crisp munching is indicative of her desire to be seen as a tough, strong woman in control of her emotions, rather than indicating any indifference to the victims about whom she is shown to care a great deal (85). Like Quincy before her and Sam Ryan to follow, it is the evidence of suffering written onto these bodies that motivates and sustains Tennison in her quest to bring the perpetrator to justice. That quest, and her ambition, renders Tennison a rather more complex character in the process. There is, however, as Jermyn points out, a significant difference in the presentation of the victims' bodies in this first episode of *Prime Suspect* and that which we encounter in season six of the intermittent series.

In 'The Last Witness' (*Prime Suspect* 6) first screened in 2003 (written by Tom Hooper), the visual style of *Prime Suspect* is no longer that of 'gritty social realism', but has 'opened up to incorporate a "glossier" look and more "hi-tech" finish' (87). As a result, the autopsy sequence now involves the technically ambitious shot of a body on a table with the flesh peeled back to reveal the inner organs. This invasive move, Jermyn suggests, indicates a desire to present to the gaze of the camera that which has been hidden from view in a move that mimics more recent forensic series such as *CSI*, which had already embarked on this endeavour (89).

While Jermyn raises the uncomfortable possibility that such images are voyeuristic she seeks to allay this accusation by calling attention to the ways in which the penetrating gaze of the camera contributes to the characterisation of Tennison as a woman determined to 'see' the victim and thus find her killer. For Karen Lury, however, the use of such visual strategies, as in the American series *CSI*, is not only obscene but also stylistically pornographic (Lury 2005: 56). Whatever the moral and/or aesthetic intention of this *Prime Suspect* moment, it serves to reveal the stylistic influence of *CSI* that had already begun to change the 'look' of many television crime shows, especially in their portrayal of the body.

CSI and after

As a television series focusing on the work of a group of forensic specialists, *CSI* not only drew upon the history of the television crime drama as a genre, but also made inspired use of new digital technologies and computer-generated imagery to create a TV series that looked and sounded very different from what had gone before (Turnbull 2007). As such, *CSI* adopted the format of an investigative crime drama like *Dragnet* with only limited attention to the emotional lives of the investigators. At the same time it drew on the 'excessive style' of series such as *Miami Vice* as created by Michael Mann, whom original *CSI* director Danny Cannon acknowledged had been an influence on the look of the show. *CSI*, however, took *Miami Vice*'s attention to style and the use of a limited colour palette to new extremes. Shot on Super 35mm film, the resultant images were subjected to a high degree of colour manipulation, resulting in what Lury considers to be an excessively expressionistic aesthetic (Lury 2005: 46), underlining the point once again that some styles appear to be more acceptable than others in the television crime drama.

In terms of its representation of the body, *CSI* invited the viewer to 'see' what the specialist was seeing, and more, as the television screen mimicked the interface of a computer, opening up new 'pages' as the camera 'clicked' on some point of entry or wound. Following a rapid 'snap-zoom' (an accelerated zoom), a prosthetic camera would take the viewer deep into the body on a fantastic voyage of inner space involving computer-generated sequences. This particular device, as Jermyn has pointed out (1997: 86) echoed both the sci-fi cinema classic *The Fantastic Voyage* (1966) and the later sci-fi comedy film that it inspired, *Innerspace*, (1987) both of which involved a tour of the body's inner workings. While it is possible to argue that these penetrative shots mimic a virtual theme-park ride, Karen Lury makes a connection between the *CSI* snap-zoom and what has been identified as 'the money shot' in pornography (Lury 2005: 56).

Setting aside the vexed question of effects, the purpose of this gaze within the context of the show is the solving of the crime through the application of science. Like Joe Friday before him, Gil Grissom just wanted 'the facts' in order to bring the perpetrator(s) to justice, which he and his team usually did while offering some form of moral judgement. Like *Dragnet* in the 1950s, *CSI* embraces certainty (both moral and scientific) in an uncertain world: a certainty that as Michael Allen suggests, may have been one of the reasons that the show was so successful following the 9/11 terrorist attacks on America that shook the confidence of a nation (Allen 2007: 8).

CSI also adopted the canny move of offering the viewer episodic closure with only limited attention to the ongoing stories of its continuing characters. This strategy ensured that any episode of *CSI* could be enjoyed without necessarily needing to know what had gone before – although for the many avid fans of the show, such knowledge would be a reward for their loyal viewing (Pearson 2007). As Matt Hills and Amy Luther discovered in their investigation of the fan postings on a range of *CSI* unofficial message boards, fan assessments of the series had very little to do with its visual aesthetic and much more to do with the characters and the ways in which the style of the show emerged as one that was 'witty, quirky and out of the ordinary' (Hills and Luther 2007: 220).

Whatever the reasons for its success with viewers, CBS rapidly moved to capitalise on the unanticipated ratings of the show and its transnational popularity by creating two spin-off series, *CSI: Miami* and *CSI: New York*, each of which employed a different colour palette in order to distinguish themselves from the parent show while remaining consistent in terms of the format of the series as a whole. For example, in the original series set in Las Vegas the 'hot' neon lights of the city were in vivid contrast to the cool 'blue' of the laboratory with its many glass walls and reflective surfaces. *CSI: Miami*, on the other hand, bathed everything in citrus and white light to evoke the sunlit state of Florida. Meanwhile, *CSI: NY* opted for graphite and blue in a mournful colour scheme that failed to attract and hold viewers in quite the same way as the earlier series (McCabe 2007: 178). As Janet McCabe notes, more than either of the other two CSI franchises, *CSI: NY* was imbued with post 9/11 melancholia written into the series through the character of detective Mac Taylor who lost his wife in the fall of the World Trade Center's Twin Towers (169). However, Mac's mourning proved to be just too depressing for prime time and following a prompt from CBS executives anxious about falling ratings, the second season saw the team moving out of their subterranean gloom. A more upbeat tone was established, including Mac going out on a date and there being no more talk of 9/11, 'and ratings started to stabilise' (179).

The phenomenal success of the *CSI* franchise inspired other television producers in both Britain and the United States not only to introduce more crime drama series 'starring' forensic science, but also to pay more attention to the potential use of colour filters and new digital techniques in the process of depicting this on-screen. Indeed, the British series *Silent Witness*, which had begun its televisual existence as a 'gritty social realist drama', began to look more and more like the glossy and high-tech *CSI*, while never, it may be added, quite losing sight of its dedication to realism. This claim to authenticity was reinforced when an episode from season twelve was pulled from the television schedule on a Bank Holiday weekend in May 2012 because the BBC determined that the storyline was too similar to a case currently going through the courts. The episode in question, 'And Then I Fell in Love', bore reflection to a case that had come to be known in the British press as the 'Rochdale Sex Crimes', which had involved a group of Asian men grooming young girls for sex in and around the town of Rochdale in 2008. However, rather than being impressed by this demonstration of 'torn-from-the-headlines authenticity', fans and followers of the show were quick to let the BBC know that they were far from happy, especially when the episode in question had to be re-edited in order for the ongoing plot line involving two of the central characters to make any sense when the episode was aired (Oliver 2008).

Cold cases

The use of techniques such as DNA fingerprinting to solve much older crimes, or 'cold cases', instigated another type of crime drama during the 1990s, although there had been some earlier instances of 'cold case' series, including *The Enigma Files*, which aired on British TV in 1980 (Anonymous n.d.t). This series featured a detective who is 'punished' for some minor transgression by being relegated to a desk job in charge of prisoners' property. This assignment he turns into an opportunity to right old wrongs. Although the series made adventurous use of the new computer technology, it was by no means a 'forensic' series in terms of the science on display.

Another more recent British series that echoes this 'forensic-lite' approach to cold cases is the 'comedy crime drama' series *New Tricks* (BBC One, 2003–) created by Nigel McCrery and featuring detective superintendent Sandra Pullman (Amanda Redman) who has also been sidelined for a fatal indiscretion, in this case, the accidental shooting of a dog. Her unit, the Unsolved Crime and Open Case Squad (UCOS), is located in an unglamorous and ill-equipped set of offices and is staffed by a group of superannuated detectives whose interplay between themselves and their superiors provides the series with its sitcom overtones.

The presence of Dennis Waterman as one of these elderly policemen, ex-detective sergeant George Lestade, brought to the series a connection with the much earlier series *The Sweeney*, in which Waterman starred as George Carter alongside actor John Thaw as

Jack Regan. Indeed the writers of the show slyly wrote into the back story of Lestade a career that could well have been that of Carter. The fact that Lestrade (with an r) was also the name of the Scotland Yard detective in the Sherlock Holmes short stories indicates the playfulness with which this series acknowledged the history of British television crime and crime fiction in general. The nostalgic appeal of *New Tricks* was apparent in many other ways since far from celebrating advances in forensic science, the members of the UCOS team regularly extol and demonstrate the virtues of dogged, old-fashioned police work with one of the ongoing characters, Brian Lane (Alan Armstrong), who also manifested Asperger-like symptoms, doing most of his sleuthing on a bicycle.

Another series on the BBC, *Waking the Dead* (BBC One, 2000–11), took its cold cases rather more seriously. This time the team included a range of specialists led by detective superintendent Peter Boyd (Trevor Eve), but also included a pair of capable women: the significantly older psychological profiler, Dr Grace Foley (Sue Johnston) and forensic scientist, Frankie Wharton (Holly Aird). At the start of Series 6, the latter was replaced by Dr Eve Lockhart (Tara Fitzgerald) and her research involving the decomposition of bodies became the basis for a spin-off series, *The Body Farm* (BBC One, 2011–), featuring Lockhart in the lead. While the first few episodes of *Waking the Dead* are very much in the 'gritty' British social-realist style (the pilot episode opens on a dump in East London), as the series progressed, like *Silent Witness*, it became increasingly more stylised in its use of both colour and lighting, once again suggesting the influence of *CSI*.

Not surprisingly given that it too was produced by Jerry Bruckheimer for CBS, the cold case series that was most like *CSI* was *Cold Case* (2003–10). Like *Quincy, M.E.*, this show was also accused of 'borrowing' a little too literally from an earlier Canadian series, *Cold Squad* (CTV, 1998–2005).[2] While *Cold Case* may have made strategic use of new techniques in forensic science to solve old crimes, the stylistic flourishes in this series were not around hi-tech science and the penetration of the victim's body, but the historical flashback. In the process, *Cold Case*, constituted what John Thornton Caldwell described as a:

> far more challenging exercise in cinematography, editing, dramatic structure and narrative form than the endless big-budget blockbuster and flat comic book features that are mindlessly cranked out by the major studios. (Caldwell 2005: 91).

While this is a tendentious point, *Cold Case* won three Emmy Awards for art direction in 2005 for the episode 'Factory Girls' before being cancelled in 2010 after seven seasons. Like *CSI* and indeed *Miami Vice*, *Cold Case* also made strategic use of the soundtrack, including music particular to the era to which it had returned while a soundtrack CD of the 'near-ambient background' music by Michael A. Levine, described by one reviewer as both 'moody and atmospheric', was released in 2008 (Ruhlman n.d.).[3]

While part of the attraction of *Cold Case* was certainly its look and its sound, the other was its revisionist approach to history, exploring such twentieth-century issues as racism, homophobia, abortion, and police brutality. Each episode would conclude with the arrest of the killer as the spirit of the victim looked on in appreciation, finally able to rest now that justice had been achieved. What *Cold Case* offered was the promise of closure on an uncomfortable past through the redemptive power of forensic science in the present. As a result, this was the kind of crime drama that routinely offered reassurance.

The profilers

While the practice of forensic science on-screen invited television viewers to participate in the empirical investigation of crime scenes and bodies, the increasing prevalence of psychological profiling encouraged audiences to ponder the mysteries of the criminal mind. Histories of criminal profiling trace the origins of this approach to instances such as the Spanish Inquisition when the profile of a witch was established in order to aid in her apprehension: For example, it was assumed that a witch would be a woman living alone, who had no children, kept pets, and grew medicinal herbs – a description that may encompass many single people today (Turvey 2012: 9).

However, it is not until the twentieth century that the Federal Bureau of Investigation (FBI) began to explore the possibilities of criminal profiling that, despite its pretensions to science, is hardly exact. As FBI profiler Brent Turvey argues, this is a science that sits at the confluence of a number of other fields of inquiry, making selective use of each as it proceeds. Thus the profiler may borrow from the study of crime and criminals (criminology) and from the study of minds and illnesses (psychology and psychiatry) but also make strategic use of the physical evidence (forensic science) in order to arrive at 'the inference of criminal characteristics for investigative and judicial purposes' (38). How those inferences are arrived at is, therefore, hardly a predictable matter since the profiler's reasoning may involve statistical probabilities, their knowledge of criminal behaviours, and own subjective opinion based on personal belief and experience. In a foreword to

Turvey's overview of the field, former FBI profiler W. Jerry Chisum acknowledges the role played by popular culture in disseminating knowledge about the work of the criminal profiler through the films based on the books of crime writer Thomas Harris, *Manhunter* (directed by Michael Mann and starring William Pedersen as profiler Will Graham; 1986) and *The Silence of the Lambs* (dir. Jonathan Demme; 1991) in which fledgling profiler Clarice Starling (Jodie Foster) consulted serial killer Hannibal Lecter (Anthony Hopkins) for some insight into the mind of a serial killer.

It was the success of these films, Chisum argues, which inspired a subsequent wave of American television shows such as *UNSUB* ('Unknown Subject') (NBC, 1989–), *Millenium* (Fox, 1996–9), *Profiler* (NBC, 1996–2000), and *Criminal Minds* (CBS, 2005–), which have in turn inspired 'more than a few criminal justice students' to become profilers (Chisum 2012: xiii). Chisum is, however, critical of those shows that have taken a turn to the 'supernatural': 'Profiles do not come in a flash or a vision', he tells us; 'they require long, hard work examining physical and behavioural evidence' (xiii). While this advice is well taken, the 'long, hard work [of] examining physical and behavioural evidence' does not necessarily make for good television. On the other hand, 'flashes or visions' offer far more opportunities for the kinds of stylistic flourishes that will capture the attention of an audience within the relatively short space of a television timeslot. Furthermore, the addition of supernatural elements introduces an element of genre hybridity that viewers appear to have enjoyed, especially during the 1990s when the creator Chris Carter blurred the lines between sci-fi, mystery, thriller, and horror in *The X-Files* (Fox, 1993–2002).

One of the more interesting aspects of the history of the criminal profiler in Chisum's account is the trajectory it reveals through crime fiction, in this case Thomas Harris's *Red Dragon* (1981) and *Silence of the Lambs* (1988). However, it is the film version of *Silence of the Lambs* (dir. Jonathan Demme; 1991) that Linda Mizejewski identifies as the key influence on such 1990s' television series as *The X-Files* (Fox 1993–2002) and *Profiler* in their style, content, and portrayal of female protagonists (Mizejewski 2004: 89). Given that both shows were produced by Chris Carter, the fact that they share a similar 'gothic tone' and horror movie aesthetic is hardly surprising.

The film of *Silence of the Lambs* (as in the book) presents the character of FBI profiler, Clarice Starling, as a tough but vulnerable heroine up against not only a sadistic serial killer but also the misogynistic and dysfunctional bureaucracy of the FBI. Clarice, therefore, has something in common with detective Jane Tennison who appeared on British screens in *Prime Suspect* in the same year (1991). Whether or not La Plante had read *Silence of the Lambs* or even Patricia Cornwell's first crime novel, *Postmortem*, which also featured a woman (forensic examiner Dr Kay Scarpetta) on the track of a serial killer in a similarly fraught working environment, 1991 was a year in which women as investigators and as victims plus the hostility they encountered in the workplace and the menacing figure of the serial killer were indisputably on the radar. Indeed, the serial killer proved to be an extremely popular offender in many crime novels, films, and shows during the course of the 1990s, leading to the serial killer as hero in the form of *Dexter.*

While Clarice Starling, Jane Tennison, and Kay Scarpetta 'got their man' through dogged detective work, the heroine of the television crime drama *Profiler* (NBC 1996–2000), forensic psychologist Dr Samantha Walker, usually got hers through an ability to 'visualize crime scenes in graphic detail', a psychic gift that was also a gift to the viewers in terms of what they may have revealed to them on-screen (Mizejewski 2004: 108). Meanwhile, the character of police consultant Allison DuBois (Patricia Arquette) based on the experiences of real-life medium Allison DuBois, took the viewer deep into the territory of dreams as well as cryptic visions in the series *Medium* (NBC, 2005–9; CBS, 2009–11). Furthermore, by the time that the series ended after season seven, it had been revealed that all three of Allison's daughters had inherited her 'gift' thus ensuring a possible sequel in the future. Yet another profiler with a 'psychic gift' appeared in *The Mentalist* (CBS, 2008–). This time the profiler was a man, Patrick Jane (Simon Baker), whose 'psychic' powers were revealed to be more Sherlockian than other-wordly. A former 'fake' psychic medium, Jane was presented as an astute interpreter of human behaviour and motive, thus avoiding the more mystic elements of this particular sub-genre of crime.

In each of the profiler series above, episodic narratives were wedded to seasonal and cross-seasonal arcs in the development of the ongoing characters. Thus Sam Waters (*Profiler*) was on a quest to capture the serial killer who murdered her husband, which she manages by the end of season three. Having completed her narrative arc, Sam was replaced by a new forensic psychologist in season four. Patrick Jane is also on a personal quest to apprehend a serial killer – the man who killed his wife and daughter. Allison DuBois's ongoing story arcs, on the other hand, are arguably even more 'soapratic' (that is, soap-opera-like), involving as they do members of her family, her relationship with her husband, Joe, and her relationship with her daughters, as well as her health. The latter became a significant issue in season five when it was revealed that she was suffering from a brain tumour, just as it looked as though NBC may axe the series. Fortunately, Allison woke up from her coma in season six when the show transferred to CBS, only to have Joe killed in a plane crash when CBS finally pulled the plug in 2011. Fortunately, as a medium, Allison is able to 'cross over' and join Joe when she too dies some forty-one years later: a future reunification to which the viewer is witness in the interests of narrative closure, although there always remains the promise of a spin-off involving the three psychic daughters.

In all of the series described above the practice of criminal profiling is wedded to the form of the television crime drama as a weekly episodic entertainment with ongoing story arcs. In each of the cases above, the profiler is also a 'good' person, one whom we are invited to like and even admire. This makes *Cracker* (ITV, 1993–5, 1996, 2006), the British series created by producer Gub Neal and fleshed out by writer Jimmy McGovern something of a novelty since it presented the viewer with an overweight, alcoholic, self-destructive man who makes no attempt to endear himself to anyone, even the viewer.

Cracker

We first meet Dr Edward 'Fitz' Fitzgerald as he listens on the phone, in some agitation, to a horse race. The atmospheric and prophetic blues number 'Stormy Weather' is playing in the background.[4] We are in a corridor of what we soon learn is a university and Dr Fitzgerald is about to lecture to a group of students on the art of criminal profiling. His pedagogical approach, however, is very different from either that of Quincy or Dr Sam Ryan and would probably not go down too well with the FBI profiling unit. For a start it involves hurling an odd assemblage of books, one by one, at his student audience while reading out the names of their authors: Spinoza, Descartes, Hobbes, Locke, Freud, Adler, Jung, and so forth. Having demolished the pile, Fitz announces that it is now the 'end of [the] lecture' and walks out of the frame, leaving the viewer, and the students, staring at a white screen. After a pause, Fitz walks back into the frame to ask the students and the audience at home, 'Moral? What's the moral?' Cut to a shot of a train in motion as the camera tracks backwards, following the progress of a guard as he moves down a corridor into a compartment where a dead young woman lies in a bloody mess on the floor. Back to Fitz who is confronting the students with a bleak analysis of the human condition before advising them to:

go and lock yourselves in a room for a couple of days and study what is here [he punches his heart] the things that you really feel, not all that crap that you are supposed to feel, and when you have shed a little light on the dark recesses of your soul, that is the time to pick up a book.

The final shot of this opening sequence follows the train as it pulls into a siding and a 'cavalry' of police, detectives, and assorted vehicles arrive to begin the task of investigating a crime that they will inevitably need Fitz's help in order to solve.

Fitz's rejection of academic authority is indicative of the fact that he rejects all authority while subjecting himself, his family, and his work colleagues to constant and caustic scrutiny. The answers to the problem of crime, he suggests, are only to be found by looking inward rather than outward, and the skill of the criminal profiler lies in being able to identify with the dark motives of the offender. Cracker's specialist skill, therefore, involves knowing people better than they know themselves. However, in his rejection of authority and in his ability to empathise with the criminal mind, Fitz himself walks a very fine line between law and order, bringing both into question. Nothing is sacred to Fitz, not even his rocky marriage, although he professes to love his wife when she leaves him at the end of the first episode. Later he embarks on an affair with his female colleague detective chief inspector Jane Penhaligon who is subsequently raped by a fellow detective who eventually commits suicide. Indeed, *Cracker* is as much a story about family life and its intersection with work as it is a crime series. As Duguid notes (2009: 22), *Cracker*'s eleven stories 'contain three funerals, three weddings, two births and a christening', these 'big events' echoing the strategies of the melodramatic soap opera in its efforts to 'boost audience excitement'. As a crime drama, Cracker thus sits firmly within the tradition of the episodic crime series such as *Hill Street Blues* that marries a serial narrative concerned with the personal relationships of the ongoing characters to episodic storylines.

In terms of format, however, *Cracker* has more in common with the British crime series such as *Morse* and *Prime Suspect* in their mini-series structure, constituting an intermittent and irregular sequence of television 'events'. *Cracker* comprises of three series, each of two or three episodes, shown in two- and three-part blocks on the British commercial network ITV from 1993 to 1995, with two 'specials' appearing in 1996 and 2006. Watching them again on DVD, the discrete episodes work well within the format of a 100- to 150-minute telemovie to be viewed in one sitting, rather than how they were originally shown – a one-hour format, interrupted by commercial breaks. Of the nine episodes, Jimmy McGovern was the writer of six, Paul Abbott wrote two, and Ted Whitehead one. It is, however, McGovern who is most readily associated with the creation of *Cracker* into which, Mark Duguid has argued, he poured a great deal of himself (his gambling, his drinking, and his grievances against Catholicism) and his politics (Duguid 2009: 20).

A former writer on the British soap opera *Brookside*, McGovern is credited with bringing to the series a preoccupation with the fate of the white, working-class male in post-industrial England as well as an ongoing 'soapratic' attention to the domestic lives and relationships of the central characters, especially Fitz. The result is a tension between the preoccupations of the soap opera as family melodrama and the concerns of the crime drama, with Fitz himself caught somewhere between hard-nosed, tough guy of the past and the sensitive new age man of the future. For Glen Creeber, Fitz is a 'complex anti-hero who seemed to both encapsulate and explore many of the ambiguities and contradictions inherent in contemporary British masculinity' (Creeber 2002: 169). It is no coincidence that Fitz has in the hallway of his home a poster of Clint Eastwood in character as the 'man with no name' from the spaghetti western *The Good, The Bad and The Ugly* or that he affects an American accent at times. Fitz wants to be the hard-boiled hero, the Bogart-esque detective (he affects Bogart's American drawl at times) who bucks authority and does it his way. Unfortunately, he has a wife and two, eventually three, children to support.

Glen Creeber has described Fitz as a transitional figure, hearkening back to the tough guy heroes of earlier cop dramas such as Regan and Carter in *The Sweeney* while trying to come to terms with changing gender roles in contemporary society. This reference to the past of the TV crime drama underestimates the complexity of the relationships between men and women apparent in series like *The Sweeney*. Setting this quibble aside, Creeber is justified in his assessment that *Cracker* is largely about issues of gender and power, as indeed was *Prime Suspect* that appeared two years earlier. *Prime Suspect* and *Cracker* also share a similar aesthetic – a moody noirish palette with artistic and clever framing of grim faces, British landscapes, and interiors. This is British social realism meets film noir to produce the 'gritty' look and feel of the British crime series in the 1990s in their preoccupation with serial killers, rapists, and the abuse of children.

As far as McGovern was concerned, the shift from his work on the regional, Liverpool-based soap opera *Brookside* to a crime series like *Cracker* provided him with an opportunity to say something 'meaningful':

A crime drama is the easiest thing in the world to write . . . You've got your in-built structure: motivation, perpetration, discovery of crime, investigation, interrogation. It is so easy. And therefore . . . in the midst of that crime story, you are duty-bound . . . to say something meaningful about life. (McGovern cited in Duguid 2009: 19)

McGovern's episodes for *Cracker* are, therefore, not only concerned with the darkness within the hearts of their criminals, but also the darkness without.

As Mark Duguid has suggested, Cracker appeared (as did *The Sweeney* and G. F. Newman's *Law and Order* in the 1970s) at a time when the accountability of the British police was being repeatedly called into question (Duguid 2009: 49). The episode that highlights this most clearly is 'To Be a Somebody' (02: 01) starring Robert Carlyle as Albie Kinsella, a working-class man whose anger and frustration with the police and related authorities over the handling of the Hillsborough disaster comes to a head after the death of his father. The background to this episode is important. On 15 April 1989, ninety-six Liverpool supporters lost their lives at Sheffield's Hillsborough Football Stadium when the police mismanaged the crowd. Rather than accept culpability, the police denied responsibility and a subsequent coronial inquest returned a verdict of 'accidental death', a verdict found to be profoundly misleading by an independent panel in 2012 (Bradbury 2012). According to Duguid, at the time this disaster marked the final extinguishing of McGovern's faith in the ideologies of the left (13).

The character of Albie, who transforms himself into a skinhead in a skull-shaving scene reminiscent of Robert De Niro's similar transformation as Travis Bickle in *Taxi Driver* (dir. Martin Scorsese; 1976), is given the following speech just before he stabs to death a Pakistani shopkeeper who earlier failed to give him credit for the paltry sum of four pence.

Treat people like scum, they start acting like scum, you know what I mean . . . I've been a socialist, trade unionist, voted Labour all me life. I marched for the likes of you. But you see me in me clobber, you assume things, you assume the right to treat me like scum.

It's a furious rant, interspersed with racist slurs, in a series in which many characters fulminate about a wide variety of social issues, making *Cracker* one of the most politically charged British crime series of the 1990s.

Consequent of this political engagement, or perhaps because of the power of the performances, in particular that of Robbie Coltrane as Fitz, *Cracker* struck a resounding chord with both audiences and critics; while the first series scored only respectable ratings, by the end of its second season *Cracker* was in the top three TV shows for the year (Duguid 2009: 28), and it went on to receive fourteen British Academy of Film and Television Arts (BAFTA) Award nominations and eventually won seven BAFTAs, including the British Academy Television Award for Best Drama Series in both 1995 and 1996. In recognition of his work, Coltrane won three consecutive British Academy of Film and Television Arts' (BAFTA) Awards in the category of Best Actor while McGovern won the first BAFTA Dennis Potter Award for best television dramatist in 1995. The series was also well received in the United States, receiving strong reviews when it appeared on the cable network Arts and Entertainment (A&E) where it acquired a 'modest but dedicated audience' (130).

In 1996 the decision was made to 'remake' *Cracker* for a bigger audience when Granada received an offer from the ABC network in the United States (130). However, with the inevitable 'toning down' of Fitz for a network audience and the substitution of a slimmer Robert Pastorelli for the man-mountain Robbie Coltrane, the revisioned *Cracker* failed to hit the mark. Given that *Cracker*, as Duguid suggests, was as much concerned with interrogating the practice of modern policing in contemporary Britain as it was about the work of a 'specialist', this is hardly surprising (49). With its setting in the regional city of Manchester and its political ambition, *Cracker* was as impossible to translate to a different cultural context as would be David Simon's *The Wire*.

New directions

While Charlotte Brunsdon has suggested that *Cracker* marked a point of generic change in the TV crime series from the police procedural to crime dramas more concerned with the role of the medical/scientific specialist (Brunsdon 1998), the arrival of *Luther*, starring British actor Idris Elba (who was earlier cast as Stringer Bell in *The Wire*) signalled a merger of the two in yet another example of inspired genre hybridity. Detective chief inspector John Luther is a black policeman, notably the first leading black male character in a British crime series, although black detectives had routinely featured as cops in American crime series, including *Miami Vice*, which frequently addressed issues of race.[5] Like Fitz, Luther has the ability to empathise with the criminal mind, but he also his own demons with which he has to contend (see Figure 5.2).

Figure 5.2 Luther (Idris Elba) wrestles with the police who are attempting to restrain him; 2010. Credit: Photofest

In a compelling 'cold open' to the first episode, lasting 4 minutes and 35 seconds, we witness a terrified white man in a suit and smart coat running through a deserted industrial building at night pursued by a black man wearing a 'hoodie', a garment that has become a powerful signifier of British anxieties about class and race. The music is tense, and the use of shadows is noir-inflected. After scrambling up ladders, the two men confront each other on a narrow walkway high above the ground. As he edges forward to attack the black man with a piece of piping, the white man falls through the rungs. It is then revealed that it is the black man (Luther) who is the detective and the white man (Masden) who is the paedophile who has abducted children. This opening thus subverts possible preconceptions about the connections between criminality and race.

Through cutaways to the police cars descending on a suburban house, we also learn that a child is about to die unless Luther can force Masden to tell him where the girl is. As Masden clings desperately to the platform by his fingertips, he tells Luther where she is concealed in the expectation that Luther will save him in exchange for that information. Instead, Luther simply watches and waits until Masden falls. Yet another preconception is shattered – this time one about police conduct. Seriously injured from the fall and in a coma, Masden is suspended between life and death while Luther is also in suspension, pending an inquiry to determine whether or not he is guilty of attempted manslaughter. It's an impressive opening, which sets up the premise that far from being a law-abiding representative of the law, Luther is a maverick cop prepared to cross the line in the pursuit of his own version of justice.

Creator and writer of *Luther*, Neil Cross, has suggested that the inspiration for his intuitive character lies not in a series like *Cracker*, but rather in Sherlock Holmes and the 1970s' American TV series *Columbo* (Cross 2010). From Holmes, Luther derives what Cross describes as his 'disinterested analytical genius' and from *Columbo*, the 'inverted formula' of a show in which the viewer knows who the criminal is right from the start, but watches to see how the detective is going to catch him or her out (Cross 2010). Thus, every episode pits Luther against a criminal mind while the ongoing narrative arcs follow Luther's relationships with his wife and his colleagues. As in *Cracker*, when Fitz's own family is threatened by an obsessed serial killer ('True Romance'; 03: 03), Luther's wife is targeted by serial killer Alice Morgan, who is fascinated by Luther. Alice doesn't want to kill Zoe but wants rather to help Luther repair his marriage, efforts that come to a resounding halt when Zoe is murdered, not by a serial killer but by Luther's close friend. Alice and Luther subsequently establish an uneasy alliance in a move that arguably humanises the character of serial killer Alice while rendering Luther even stranger.

In their ability to empathise with the mind of the killer, both Fitz and Luther bring their work too close to home and put their families in danger. Both men also appear to teeter on the brink of sanity, confused by the blurred lines between right and wrong, the inadequacy of the law, and the lure of vigilante justice. *Cracker* and *Luther* are also crime dramas in which the crises faced by their central characters are symptomatic of the crises facing society in general. Thus, far from being crime series that reassert the status quo, both *Cracker* and *Luther* raise questions about the desirability of the status quo in the first place.

Dexter as 'promiscuous hybrid'

Dexter is a particularly apposite series with which to conclude this chapter because it marks the culmination of so many different generic impulses of the television crime drama series to date, as well as suggesting how the crime series may take advantage of a diversified production context. The character of Dexter Morgan first appeared in a series of dark and witty crime novels by script writer and playwright Jeff Lyndsay. While the first TV season of *Dexter* followed the first book *Darkly Dreaming Dexter* fairly closely, subsequent seasons have developed their own storylines in ways that have considerably toned down the more horrific moments in the original, despite the fact that *Dexter* was originally created for a cable audience. Like HBO, the cable network Showtime on which *Dexter* first screened in 2006, operates under a different set of regulatory structures from network television in America. With niche audiences prepared to embrace more 'mature' content, cable networks are therefore willing and able to go much further in the portrayal of both sex and violence (Mittell 2010: 33). Other Showtime series included *The L-Word* (2004) and the American adaptation of *Queer as Folk* (2000), both of which portrayed gay sexual relationships in confronting ways that would be unlikely to 'pass' on network TV.

This last point is best illustrated by the fact that when CBS, the parent company of Showtime, announced in December 2007 that it was planning to show a full season of *Dexter* on CBS network television, the first time that this had been done, the decision was greeted with a protest from the Parents Television Council (Howard 2010: xix). CBS, however, stood their ground and the series was shown without cuts. Meanwhile *Dexter* continued to garner a number of Primetime Emmy Nominations and other awards, signalling a positive reception from the television industry. The series also rated extremely well for Showtime, the third season finale in December 2008 giving the cable network its highest ratings for any of its original series since 2005 (Reynolds 2008).

With its portrayal of a 'violent, bloody and ritualistic serial killer' who is also a police officer specialising in blood-spatter analysis, a (sort of) loving brother, a boyfriend, a husband, and, eventually, a truly loving father, according to Douglas Howard *Dexter* taps into a 'provocative line' of contemporary drama that asks the viewer to accept as 'hero' a central character with significant 'personality' issues (Howard 2010: xiv). This 'line', Howard suggests, begins with Tony Soprano in the HBO series *The Sopranos* (1999–2007), although it should be noted that the dysfunctional hero in crime is hardly an original American invention, as the previous discussion of *Cracker* would suggest. As noted earlier, *Dexter* also taps into the ongoing preoccupation of the television crime series with the figure of the serial killer, a preoccupation that can be traced through the trajectory of the character of Hannibal Lecter who first appeared in the 'serial killer thriller' *Red Dragon* (1981) written by Thomas Harris and later adapted by Michael Mann in the film *Manhunter* (1986) in which Lecter was portrayed by actor Brian Cox. However, it was not until Jonathan Demme's *The*

Silence of the Lambs (1991) that Lecter rose to pop culture stardom as portrayed by Anthony Hopkins. Interestingly, Lecter himself made it onto television in 2013 in the series *Hannibal* on the NBC network in an adaptation that followed the original *Red Dragon* even as the eighth and final season of *Dexter* aired.[6]

In terms of structure, *Dexter* followed the now well-established trend of what Robin Nelson has described as the 'flexi-narrative', a hybrid mix of the serial and episodic series form (Nelson 2006: 82). While each seasonal story arc involved Dexter's pursuit/relationship of what was described as the seasonal 'Big Bad',[7] including such nasties as the Ice Truck Killer in Season 1, and Trinity in Season 4, for the casual viewer who only 'drops in' there was also the satisfaction of episodic storylines.

In terms of genre, *Dexter* was a mix of many different elements, including comedy, film noir, and horror. Furthermore, as Stan Beeler has suggested, as a self-styled 'Dark Defender' wearing a mask of normalcy, Dexter may even have qualified as a type of vigilante superhero (Beeler 2010: 228). In arguing for *Dexter's* comedy credentials, James Francis makes the case that like a stand-up comic, Dexter 'takes the stage' from the start through his voice-over narration and through frequent direct address to the camera in the much celebrated title sequence. This begins with a mosquito, a creature attracted to blood, landing on Dexter's arm, the comic irony being that Dexter is a 'fellow blood tracker' (Francis 2010: 176). We then witness a remarkable montage of flesh and blood as we follow Dexter's morning routine of shaving, flossing, dressing, and preparing breakfast in an award-winning title sequence that consists of a series of visual double entendres: The floss is like a garrotte; the slicing of a blood orange suggests the slicing of human flesh; the tomato sauce on the fried egg looks like blood, and so on. As Francis notes, the framing of this quotidian event for the camera knowingly (and ironically) also borrows from the conventions of the horror film while the soundtrack amplified the effects of cutting, slicing, and squishing.

However, as Simon Brown and Stacey Abbott observe in 'The Art of Sp(l)atter', while *Dexter* acknowledged the conventions of horror, it also undermined them, thereby making them more acceptable to an audience that would not normally choose to watch a horror film (Brown and Abbott 2010: 205). 'Horror proper' they argue is 'cinematic', and it is able to go well beyond the restrictions of television in terms of its depictions of sex and violence (Brown and Abbott 2010: 206). At which point it should be remembered that Dexter is both a serial killer *and* a blood-spatter expert working for the police. The depictions of grotesque bodies and blood are therefore framed within the conventions of other TV series like *CSI* and *Bones* in which these disturbing scenes are the focus of what is supposed to be an investigative and scientific gaze.

Dexter also considers himself to be an artist. 'I'm a very neat monster,' he confesses in the pilot episode, which showcases how Dexter stages his murders as performance art, carefully arranging his 'kill room' to confront, mesmerise, and legitimise the murder of the killer he has brought there to punish. The murder itself, on the other hand, is hidden from view since all we see in this episode is the naked body of the 'deserving' victim wrapped to the table as Dexter approaches with a power tool, his head blocking our view. We see the victim's body twitching but nothing more of the dismemberment, and the fact that it has occurred we are likely to deduce only from the neat collection of garbage bags that a now happy and contented Dexter throws overboard from his boat.

While Dexter's murders usually take place at night in dark places, captured by low-key lighting and oblique angles, much of the series takes place in the brightly lit world of daytime Miami that, as in the case of *Miami Vice* and *CSI Miami*, potentially undercuts attempts to frame the series within the conventions of film noir. As Dexter himself suggests in the pilot episode:

> There's something strange and disarming about looking at a homicide scene in the daylight of Miami. It makes the most grotesque killings look staged – like you're in a new and daring section of Disney World: Dahmer [a notorious real-life American serial killer] Land. (*Dexter* 01: 01)

Despite this grotesque staginess, Peirse argues, *Dexter* also plays with many of the tropes of film noir, including that of the male anti-hero with his hard-boiled narrative voice-over (the kind of voice Jeff Lyndsay's books deliberately echo), as well as the use of flashbacks, and even the appearance of a potential femme fatale in the second season (Peirse 2010: 189).

Ultimately, Dexter represents a point of 'knowingness' in the television crime drama. As a series it rewarded the audience's familiarity with a variety of different story-telling modes and genres while featuring a forensic 'specialist' who is also an expert serial killer: Dexter is both a servant of the forces of law and order and a criminal whose actions we are invited to understand if not condone. Dexter is also a vigilante hero, a self-styled 'Dark Avenger', who metes out his own form of justice irrespective of the law.

Conclusion

The 'specialist' has enjoyed a long and honourable career in the television crime drama. As an investigator, he – and occasionally she – has often been portrayed in a tetchy relationship to the police who tend to come off rather badly in the encounter given that the specialist is either perceived to be 'smarter' than the police or more prepared to go out on a limb in the interests of the victim. Meanwhile, the increasing prevalence of forensic techniques in the detection of crime enabled the crime drama series to portray graphic images of the body legitimated by the 'scientific' gaze of the specialist, although such images have also been accused of being 'pornographic'. The growing sophistication of DNA profiling triggered yet another wave of crime dramas featuring cold case specialists and the artful use of the flashback to recreate the original scenes of crime. Employing another kind of criminal profiling altogether are those dramas in which the psychology of the criminal is put under close scrutiny in intense and dramatic confrontations between specialist and killer.

It is tempting to suggest that in those series that deal with the specialists in the human condition, there has been a move away from the demonisation of the offender to a desire to understand them: a move that reaches its culmination in the series *Dexter* where the hero with whom we are invited to empathise is both a serial killer and a forensic specialist. However, as any student of television genre will know, there is no such thing as an end point since the next 'new' development, which may well involve a return to the past (as in the case of the NBC TV series *Hannibal*), is probably already sitting in some television executive's in-tray waiting for the green light.

Finally, while it is tempting to suggest that the work of the specialist has been treated with more seriousness in British crime series that have taken a social-realist approach to the subject of crime, it should be noted that from the forensic endeavours of Sherlock Holmes to the 'cold case' capers of the UCOS team in *New Tricks*, the work of the specialist has figured in British crime dramas that have also been conceived as 'popular' entertainment. Whatever the perceived intention of such shows, there is no doubt that much of their appeal lies in the presentation of various kinds of specialist knowledge. These are the crime dramas in which education and entertainment – the lecture delivered by the specialist to his or her students or colleagues and the enactment of that specialism in the conduct of their investigation – are complimentary rather than competing features.

Finally, it is important to note the relative absence of the female forensic examiner or profiler from the genre before 1990. While Inspector Morse had the assistance of Dr Grayling Russell (Clare Holman) in series three (1989), it was not until Dr Sam Ryan appeared in *Silent Witness* in 1996 that a female pathologist was placed front and centre in a British television show that did not, as it happens, bear her character's name. And this despite the fact that 'specialist' women had been solving crime in crime fiction for some time, an observation that is taken up in more detail in the following chapter that engages with the gender issues involved in the representation of crime on television.

Notes

1. While the Chinese probably got there first, a eugenicist called Sir Francis Gallon apparently established the first system for classifying fingerprints in 1892. However, it was the Henry Classification System that became the standard (Anonymous n.d.r).
2. See discussion thread on the TV fan site *Television Without Pity*: http://forums.televisionwithoutpity.com/index. php?showtopic=3128022 [accessed 16 August 2012].
3. Levine, Michael (2008) *Cold Case [Original Television Soundtrack]* Lakeshore Records, Los Angeles, California.
4. 'Stormy Weather' (1933) written by Harold Arlen and Ted Kohler. Performed on the soundtrack by Carol Kidd.
5. Including a female black detective in the short-lived American series *Get Christie Love!* (NBC, 1974–5) to be discussed in more detail in Chapter 6.
6. See the entry for *Hannibal* at IMDbPro, http://pro.imdb.com/title/ tt2243973 [accessed 31 March 2013].
7. The concept of the 'Big Bad' emerged in relation to the seasonal story arcs in Joss Whedon's TV series, *Buffy the Vampire Slayer*, the term being used both by characters in the show and by commentators, both popular and academic, in their discussion of the show. See the discussion at Spoilerslayer.com: www.spoilerslayer.com/ buffyformula.php [accessed 14 March 2013].

6 Women and Crime

Despite a perception that the television crime drama may be an inherently 'masculine' genre, as this chapter will reveal, women have played a key role in television crime drama right from the start, not just as the helpless victim or the untrustworthy femme fatale, but increasingly as a major player in the unfolding investigation and always as a potential member of the television audience at home from the 1950s to the present day. The approach taken here is, therefore, once again genealogical, with the goal of demonstrating how the portrayal of women in the crime drama series has served both as an index of women's changing role in society while providing a catalyst for debate, both in the popular press and in the field of feminist media studies. Indeed, it is possible to argue that debate about the portrayal of women in the crime drama has mirrored the trajectory of feminist theory, particularly in relation to the representation of women on-screen, as it has evolved over the decades.

While it may be considered a controversial move to devote an entire chapter to the topic of 'women and crime' given that one of the key points to be made is that women have always played an integral role in the television crime drama, it is salutary to consider the various issues raised that constitute a particular canon of feminist television critique. These include issues of representation and the roles accorded to women in the drama. A concern with representation gained momentum in academic contexts with the publication of Laura Mulvey's classic article 'Visual Pleasure and Narrative Cinema' (1975), which used a psychoanalytic argument to suggest that women were constructed as the 'object' of a controlling masculine gaze. While Mulvey qualified her argument in a subsequent article, pointing out that she had only been talking about a specific group of films (Mulvey 1981), concern about the 'objectification' of women in the media has remained a constant theme in academic and popular debates, a concern that eventually conceded the possibility that men too may be the object of a female gaze, or indeed a queer gaze (Cohen and Hark 1993). By the first decade of the new millennium, anxiety about the representation of women had arguably been transferred to a concern about the representation of children imagined as the object of a paedophilic gaze (Duschinsky 2013: 1).

Another issue that has played out in relation to the crime drama has been that of gender equality, in particular the visibility of women in the workforce and the kinds of work that men and women are required to perform. This debate reached something of a crescendo in the analysis of 1980s' television series such as *The Gentle Touch*, *Juliet Bravo*, and *Cagney and Lacey*, which will be discussed in relation to the portrayal of women as authority figures in the police procedural during the 1980s. This was also one of the issues foregrounded in the discussion of *Prime Suspect*, created by actress turned screenwriter and producer, Lynda La Plante, which intermittently appeared over a period from 1991 to 2006 – a period that, as Charlotte Brunsdon suggests, also marked a change in focus from a concern with women as the victims of violent crime to a concern with child abuse and paedophilia (Brunsdon 2012).

The debate about women as victims of crime was also particularly energetic in Australia during the 1980s in the extensive media and academic commentary devoted to the Australian prison-based soap-opera *Prisoner*, aka *Prisoner: Cell Block H* as it was billed in the United Kingdom and in the United States (Grundy productions 1979–86). This show achieved cult status in both the United Kingdom and in the United States. According to Zalcock and Robinson (cited in McKee 2001: 168), *Prisoner* rated only second to *Charlie's Angels* at the time. This is an intriguing suggestion given how very different these two shows were in terms of production quality (one a low-budget soap opera of indeterminate origins and the other a 'glossy' American TV series produced by Aaron Spelling).[1] As Alan McKee points out, *Prisoner* was revolutionary television when it appeared in 1979, not only because the cast for this show was almost entirely female and the characters portrayed encompassed a wide range of types and it focused on the relationships between women to the exclusion (almost) of men (McKee 2001: 166) but because (as many commentators pointed out) the women depicted were decidedly unglamorous, not to say 'homely', at a moment when a quick flick of the TV dial would present the viewer with the blow-waved glamour of the glossy-lipped *Charlie's Angels*.[2]

Another significant aspect of the commentary about gender has included the role of women as creators, writers, and producers of crime drama. Women have been central to the production of crime narratives from the nineteenth century onwards and crime fiction has been, and continues to be, a 'suitable' job for women of literary leanings, many of whose creations have been translated to the small screen. This would include the many adaptations of Agatha Christie's Miss Marple and Hercule Poirot, as well as series such as *Dalgliesh* featuring P. D. (Phyllis Dorothy) James's inspector/poet hero Adam Dalgliesh, and *An Unsuitable Job for a Woman* (1997, 1999), which was 'loosely' based on James's crime novel (1972) of the same name, featuring a female private detective. More recent examples would include the series of telemovies with the overall title *Wire in the Blood* (2002–9), following the cases of British crime writer Val McDermid's forensic psychiatrist Dr Tony Hill. This series, produced by Coastal Productions in the United Kingdom with the approval of McDermid, proved what crime fiction readers already knew – that women crime writers are not averse to depicting graphic sexual violence. Indeed, the on-screen versions of McDermid's books were significantly *less* graphic in their depiction of violence than the literary versions. However, while women crime writers may be as numerous and successful as men, their prominence in the literary field does not always translate into their inclusion in the television industry.

Although women have long played a role in the writing of screenplays and in the production of television crime dramas, they have usually been in a minority. Some of the more prominent figures in this regard would include Verity Lambert in the United Kingdom who was not only a founding producer of the legendary sci-fi TV series *Doctor Who* but who was also a key player in the production of a number of other crime drama series, including the comedy caper series *Minder* (ITV, 1979–84) and the comedy, mystery, and magic series *Jonathan Creek* (BBC One, 1998–2004), as well as the ground-breaking miniseries *Widows* (1983) written by Lynda La Plante. In her own version of a genesis myth, La Plante has often told interviewers that having tired of playing bit roles in crime dramas such as *The Sweeney*, she finally decided to write her own TV series with women in a central role.

As producers and writers of television crime, Lambert and La Plante were exceptional precisely because they were in a minority: a minority that still exists according to John Thornton Caldwell in his study of the Hollywood TV production cultures (2008: 215). Caldwell's suggestion is confirmed by Sara Fain, executive producer of the American ABC network series *Women's Murder Club* (ABC, 2007–8). In an interview about the trials of being a female writer in the TV business, Fain told her interviewer that according to the writer's guild membership figures women only constituted 27 per cent of television writers in Hollywood, coming to the inevitable conclusion that it was still (in

2007) much harder for a woman to make it in the American television industry than a man (Silverstein 2007). The relative absence of
women in the business of making television thus raises issues about
the relationship between the role of women behind the scenes and the
portrayal of women on-screen. While this debate may only be resolved
by another kind of industry study altogether, this chapter will focus
on the ways in which women have been represented in the television
crime drama, and the issues that have been raised in the popular press
and academic literature as a consequence.

Object of the gaze or female action hero?

But where to begin? With PC Willoughby's shapely leg as she poses
in front of the mirror before heading off into darkest Soho in *Fabian of
the Yard* in 1954? Or with the not-to-be-underestimated Miss Marple
who 'first' appeared on American television in 1956? At that time she
was played by then world famous British singer and entertainer, Gracie
Fields, in an episode of the anthology series *Goodyear TV Playhouse*
based on the book *A Murder Is Announced* (1950). It was, however, not
until the 1960s that a woman would star in a television crime series that
bore the name of her character, and the 'first' to do so was Honey West.

In her study of primetime women investigators, Linda Mizejewski
traces the origins of private investigator Honey West to a 1964 James
Bond movie, *Goldfinger* (dir. Guy Hamilton). *Goldfinger* featured British
actress Honor Blackman as a sexually ambiguous character with the
suggestive moniker Pussy Galore. While Pussy's sexual orientation was
initially unclear, she inevitably succumbs to the suave masculine charms
of Bond (Sean Connery). According to Mizejewski, Honey West was
created with Blackman in mind. However, when Blackman turned the
part down, the role was offered to a Blackman lookalike, Anne Francis
(Mizejewski 2004: 55). What Mizejewski's American-based account of
Honey West's origins omits to mention is that even before her appearance in *Goldfinger*, actress Honor Blackman had embodied a character
who could be regarded as the prototype for both Pussy Galore and
Honey West in the iconic 1960s' British television spy-series, *The
Avengers* (1961–9), a series that inspired much debate at the time about
the representation of women (Buxton 1990; Miller 1997; O'Day 2001).

While *The Avengers* may have begun as a tough spy thriller featuring
two male protagonists as played by Patrick McNee and Ian Hendry, in
season two Hendry was replaced by Honor Blackman as Mrs Catherine
Gale, 'a sophisticated, but not upper class, ex-pat widow possessing a
Ph.D in anthroplogy' (O'Day 2001: 223). Note Mrs. Gale was not

known as Dr Gale, the 'Mrs' signalling the prevalent ideology that saw women defined by their marital status. Dressed in a pair of black, leather, tight-fitting trousers, a matching leather jerkin, and a pair of 'kinky' boots, Cathy Gale was an action heroine with sado-masochistic overtones whose hand-to-hand combat skills routinely excelled those of her rather less athletic sidekick, John Steed (Patrick McNee). Mrs Gale's successor, Emma Peel (played by Diana Rigg), was another 'glamorous twenty-something widow with academic credentials and independent means' (O'Day 2001: 223) who also had a penchant for pant suits, fetish gear, and throwing men over her shoulder. Her often flirtatious relationship with Steed operated on a continuum that O'Day describes as encompassing 'mutual respect, professionalism, humour and not a little innuendo' (ibid.). According to Anna Gough-Yates, America's ABC network executives were so impressed by *The Avengers*'s 'sexy, yet active and challenging heroines' that they wanted to create one of their own such heroines (Gough-Yates 2001: 84).

The result was *Honey West*, a series produced by Aaron Spelling and based on a series of pulp crime novels published from 1957 to 1965 by a husband and wife team who wrote under the pseudonym G. G. Fickling.[3] Like Mrs Gale and Mrs Peel, Honey West wore trousers with confidence and, as is evident in the first scene of the first episode, could also flip a hefty bloke over her shoulder in the blink of an expertly made-up eye. Honey was also not averse to 'playing the blonde bombshell', making strategic use of her feminine assets on the job – Honey by name, 'honey-trap' by profession, apparently. Her other accoutrements included a pet ocelot called Bruce and a wardrobe replete with animal prints. In sync with the 1960s' vogue for spy thrillers such as *The Man From U.N.C.L.E.* (NBC, 1964–8), Honey was also equipped with an attractive male sidekick called Sam with whom she communicated via a wide range of technological devices embedded in such fashion accessories as lipsticks and sunglasses.

In Mizejewski's opinion, the character of Honey West merely constitutes a male fantasy of the action heroine, even if she appeared to be 'a woman doing a man's job'. The fact that her assignments frequently required her to go undercover in situations requiring either bikinis or flimsy evening wear arguably defused any potential threat that she may have posed to television's more macho male detectives. While this may well be true, the inspiration of Mrs Gale, Mrs Peel, and Honey West as prototypical action heroines should not be under-estimated. While some commentators have treated these series harshly, it is important to consider the context in which they appeared. As a teenager growing up in the North of England, to offer another personal narrative as a corrective to retrospective criticism, I well remember being inspired by these women who gave as good as they got in relationships where they 'appeared' to be equal without subservience. They also got to wear great clothes in an era of increased attention to fashion known as the 'swinging sixties'.

Despite its novelty, and an Emmy Award Best Actress nomination for Francis, *Honey West* lasted only one season (ABC, 1965–6) and it was not until the mid-1970s that another woman would front a crime show on American television, even though women were becoming increasingly visible in the 'real life forces of law and order' (Mizejewski 2004: 61). While the role of the female hero in the television police procedural will be discussed later, the most obvious successors to Mrs Gale, Mrs Peel, and Honey West were the three private investigators known as Charlie's Angels in another television series produced by Aaron Spelling. *Charlie's Angels* (ABC, 1976–81) carried on the *Honey West* tradition of camp, tongue-in-cheek, teasing knowingness coupled with the keen fashion sense of its 1960s' predecessor.

Charlie's Angels
In her level-headed essay on a series that has been hotly debated by feminist critics both then and since (Schwichtenberg 1981), Gough-Yates (2001) argues that the emergence of a series like *Charlie's Angels* should be considered both in relation to the American television industry during the 1970s when the networks were in a constant battle for ratings, as well as in the context of the 'action series' as a genre featuring women as spectacle. Gough-Yates, therefore, traces the genealogy of *Charlie's Angels* back to *Honey West* as well as the spin-off spy thriller series *The Girl from U.N.C.L.E.* (NBC, 1966–7) and *The Bionic Woman* (ABC, 1975–7), the latter starring Lindsay Wagner as a 'beautiful cyborg secret agent' (Gough-Yates 2001: 85). Not to be forgotten in this account of the female action figure on the small screen is the character of *Wonder Woman* who migrated from her graphic origins in a comic book series originally created by William Moulton Marston in 1942 onto the ABC network in 1976. It is clear that the American television industry at this time was attempting to deal with what may be described as a 'feminist push', although what this genealogy suggests is that shows like *Honey West* and *Charlie's Angels* were perceived by their feminist critics to belong to the realm of male sexual fantasy rather than to the realm of the television crime drama with aspirations to any form of serious social commentary. And yet, as Gough-Yates goes on to suggest, *Charlie's Angels* did manage to say some important things about women's role in society.

As evidence of this, Gough-Yates discusses *Charlie's Angels* within the context of 1970s' America and changing attitudes to women, particularly single women, spurred on by the second wave of feminism, the introduction of the contraceptive pill, and the public pronouncements of significant female media figures such as Gloria Steinem (editor of the feminist *Ms* magazine) and Helen Gurley Brown. In 1962 Gurley Brown wrote *Sex and the Single Girl* before going on to edit the magazine *Cosmopolitan*, which is widely assumed to have played an important role in the evolution of women's thinking about their lives and sexuality. As Gough-Yates has suggested, in the pages of *Cosmopolitan*, 'the power of the single woman' was to be found 'in her sexual confidence and her ability to deploy her sexuality as a weapon in a quest for material reward and personal fulfilment' (88). The original Angels – Jill (Farrah Fawcett), Kelly (Jaclyn Smith), and Sabrina (Kate Jackson) – fitted rather neatly within *Cosmopolitan*'s construction of the glamorous, heterosexual, and autonomous 'single girl', whose dedication to her work and her working colleagues was a more than adequate substitute for marriage and a monogamous relationship. Indeed, the world of the working girl was a continuing theme, as evident in the opening title sequence of the first episode, which began with a voice-over account from the always invisible Charlie (voiced by actor John Forsythe) of how the Angels came to be.

'Once upon a time,' Charlie tells us in an infantalising fairy tale with a 'happy' ending, 'there were three little girls who went to the police academy.' As visual testimony we see first the gates of the police academy and then Sabrina at the shooting range, Jill swinging cheerfully on the monkey bars, and Kelly, in true Mrs Gale/Mrs Peel-style, chucking yet another hefty bloke over her shoulder on the judo mat. Charlie continues in an ironic vein: 'And they were assigned very hazardous duties.' At this point the screen splits into three and we see Jill at a typewriter, Sabrina pinning a parking infringement under a windscreen, and Kelly as a lollipop lady assigned to a school crossing. 'But I took them away from all that,' says Charlie, adding somewhat smugly, 'and now they work for me.' The three Angels walk towards the camera, smiling and chatting, dressed casually in stylish flared trousers with perfectly coiffed hair. 'And my name is Charlie,' Charlie informs the viewer, as we see each of the three Angels happily engaged in some form of sport – Sabrina is show-jumping, Jill is playing tennis, and Kelly is swimming – before each of these activities is interrupted by a telephone call. The message, received with identical high-wattage smiles, is the same, 'It's Charlie, Angel. Time to go to work.' These are women who *love* their work.

For feminist commentators, the proprietary voice-over of Charlie, an unreconstructed patriarchal male figure with complete control over his 'little girls', immediately disqualified the show as being in any way 'feminist'. However, as Gough-Yates points out, many of the cases to which the Angels were assigned had serious overtones, including workplace crime in fields 'renowned for their sexism, exploitation, and/or objectification of women' (89). Said assignments routinely required the Angels to go undercover as 'high fashion models, show girls, car racers, gamblers, soldiers and playmate centrefolds, call girls, masseuses and even actresses in the "adult" film business', thereby ensuring a degree of sexual display on the part of the Angels (Gough-Yates 2001: 96). Nevertheless, the storyline would implicitly challenge this form of sexual objectification and overtly 'resist' the sexism of the context in ways that ensured that the series had it both ways.

Gough-Yates concludes that *Charlie's Angels* is an extremely 'contradictory text', endeavouring at some level to reconcile the 'feminist' with the 'feminine': a strategy which she identifies in the subsequent film revivals of the series (91). In the end, she argues, the series should be judged favourably in terms of its fledgling feminist politics, since while it was an extremely popular show (at least in the first few years) it also offered 'pleasurable glimpses of female solidarity and strength' that had resonance for the many women who watched it at the time (96). What is missing from this analysis, however, is how 'other' kinds of audience may have watched and received the show. This would include its many homosexual viewers, who may even have been watching the Australian soap opera *Prisoner: Cell Block H* at the same time.

While *Prisoner* made no attempt to disguise the centrality of lesbianism to its narratives, both Gough-Yates (90) and Mizejewski (2004: 70) point to the fact that any spectre of lesbianism in *Charlie's Angels* was allayed by routinely depicting lesbian women as villains. This ensured that the Angels themselves were perceived as firmly heterosexual, even if they lacked long-term partners and appeared to constitute their own self-sufficient 'family'. Despite this determinedly heterosexual orientation, *Charlie's Angels* did indeed attract a strong gay following, suggesting the audience's capacity to 'read against the grain' of the text, a possibility which should not be underestimated in any analysis of the reception of a television crime drama.

Equality at work

In turning to the portrayal of women in the police procedural during this period, it is important to note that there is an immediate point of

connection between the fairy-tale world of *Charlie's Angels* as undervalued policewomen assigned to menial tasks before being rescued from
terminal boredom by Charlie, and the more 'serious' NBC series *Police
Woman* (1974–8). *Police Woman* began life in the Joseph Wambaugh
anthology series *Police Story*. In an episode entitled 'The Gamble'
(01: 21), Angie Dickinson's policewoman character (here called Lisa
Beaumont) tells the head of the vice squad that she wants more challenging work. For the last two and a half years, she complains, she has
been assigned to desk duties and runaway kids. Warned as to what
to expect if she makes the move to the vice squad, she asserts, 'I can
handle it.' And handle 'it' she does. Thus despite being rather different
kinds of crime drama series, *Charlie's Angels* and *Police Woman* both
reference the changing role of women inspired by a demand for equality of opportunity in the workforce during the 1970s.

Launched in 1974, *Police Woman* was one of three television series
that appeared in that year to feature women as lead characters. This
new prominence, Mizejewski argues, reflects the 'real-life' gender
politics of the time. While in 1971 there were only a dozen policewomen in the entire United States, by 1974 this had risen 2 to 3
per cent in certain states and it had risen to 6 per cent of the police
in Washington, D.C. (Mizejewski 2004: 60). In recognition of the
increasing prominence of women on the force, and no doubt with an
eye on the female viewer at home, NBC gave its audience *Amy Prentiss*:
a series based on the premise that when the chief of the San Francisco
Police Chief suddenly dies, his widow is (improbably) the next in line
for the job. *Amy Prentiss*, however, lasted less than a season.

In the same year, NBC also launched *Get Christie Love*, featuring
black actress Teresa Graves as 'a hip, black L.A. undercover cop
with advanced karate skills' and the catchphrase 'You're under arrest,
sugah!' (61). While *Get Christie Love* fared only marginally better than
Amy Prentiss in the ratings, lasting only one season, she clearly made
a lasting impression. In a recent review of a new ABC television series
entitled *Scandal* in 2012, the television critic for *The New Yorker*, Emily
Nussbaum, noted that *Scandal* 'is the first network drama with a black
female lead character since *Get Christie Love*' (Nussbaum 2012: 68).
Nussbaum went on to describe the earlier show as a 'blaxploitation-
inflected crime series', advising her readers to check out the confronting racial and gender politics of *Get Christie Love* in a recently posted
YouTube clip.

As Mizejewski notes, the character of Christie Love was based on a
real person, in this case veteran New York police detective Olga Ford.
However, in the interests of entertainment rather than realism, *Get*

Christie Love capitalized on the physical attributes of Graves who was best known as the bikini-wearing comedian from the then current TV sketch comedy show *Rowan and Martin's Laugh-In* (NBC 1968–73). As a result, although the producers of *Get Christie Love* may have made some high-minded pronouncements about their desire to portray black women in positions of power, in reality, like *Charlie's Angels*, the series clearly wanted to have it both ways, frequently veering towards what Nussbaum identifies as the 'blaxplotitation' end of the spectrum (68).

The politics of representation in the more commercially successful *Police Woman* were equally problematic. In the original episode from the *Police Story* series, police woman Lisa Beaumont is sent undercover as a hooker with the primary goal of getting as close as she can to the bosses of a chain of illegal gambling casinos. Her job, the bosses tell her, is to 'just look pretty' while pulling in the high-stake punters. Her assignment involves dressing seductively and flirting while managing to stave off the advances of her casino bosses. At one point in her undercover assignment, Lisa leaves a poker game in the company of a good-looking young millionaire who has just lost disastrously. To the outrage of her male colleagues eavesdropping in the surveillance van, she takes off her wire in order (it is implied) to have consensual sex in a liaison that has nothing to do with advancing the investigation. This incident does, however, establish her as a sexually active and liberated woman of the 1970s.

The theme of the episode, ironically, is all about women and trust in the workplace. 'Men trust broads,' the casino boss tells her, as she asks why he needs her services. Meanwhile, the head of the vice unit is unsure whether he can trust a female police officer to not crack under pressure. Lisa, on the other hand, is not sure that she can trust her fellow male police officers to back her up if she gets into trouble. When trouble inevitably arrives, and her male colleagues fail to respond to her calls for help, Lisa manages remarkably well until they arrive, whereupon she insists on 'cuffing her collar' herself. Police officer Beaumont thus proves her trustworthiness to her masculine counterparts on the front line of crime, with only a dodgy wireless connection and her own wits to protect her. In the final scene, however, when her superior officer tells her that he will take her for a congratulatory drink only *after* she has finished her paperwork, he adds the cheeky comment that if he does end up taking her out, he is likely to be arrested as a pimp, given how she is dressed. The camera freezes on Lisa's comically (?) outraged face. Like *Charlie's Angels*, the subsequent spin-off series *Police Woman* continued to negotiate some tricky gender territory while frequently producing some jarring moments.

A close analysis of the title sequence to the subsequent spin-off series *Police Woman* serves to illustrate the ongoing ambivalence in the depiction of Angie Dickinson's character, now re-conceived as sergeant Pepper Anderson, caught somewhere between her role as a serving police officer and her feminine masquerade as a hooker. The sequence begins with the white-on-black title *Police Woman*, the letters of which are dynamically reduced to appear on the barrel of a gun held by Dickinson who is looking out of the frame and camera left. Filmed in black and white, this initial shot is vaguely reminiscent of the iconic opening of James Bond films with Bond in silhouette held in the lens of a gun scope. This is Pepper Anderson as a female action hero. However, as the camera pulls back and the gun is fired, the screen explodes into colour with the now brilliantly blonde Anderson clad in fetching peach with the title 'starring Angie Dickinson' in bright yellow. The next six shots all feature Dickinson in close-up. Shot two and we see her head in a crowd – she tosses her hair and laughs at the camera before looking back over her shoulder. Shot three comprises another head-shot of Dickinson screaming, as she is grabbed by a man dressed in denim. Shot four and we see only a pair of shapely slim legs in high-heeled white sandals walking down a white staircase. Shot five comprises yet another close-up of Dickinson, wearing a flowered denim cap and a pink shirt and looking anxiously camera right before she is suddenly grabbed by the head and pushed backwards by a pair of male hands on to a car. Shot six features yet another head-shot of Dickinson looking camera right in what appears to be a nightclub. She stands up to reveal clunky earrings and a low-cut, pink, halter-neck dress. As she rises, the camera lingers on her cleavage, which is now centre frame. In the last shot Dickinson appears as an air-hostess, wearing a white hat, an orange uniform, and a check pattern scarf. The rest of the title sequence depicts a number of action sequences, most of them involving her male colleagues, including her immediate superior, sergeant William Crowley (Earl Holliman) and the two undercover cops, Royster (Charlies Dierkop) and Styles (Ed Bernard), one white and small and the other black, bearded, and big, with whom she is regularly partnered.

In her assessment of the gender politics of this show, Mizejewski is scathing, arguing that its only feminist claim to fame is the fact that Dickinson was forty-three years old when she became the lead character in a television series for which she would become arguably become more famous than for her previous film work (Mizejewski

2004: 65). The aspect of the series that troubles Mizejewski the most, however, is the frequent depiction of rape, suggesting that at the very moment when feminists were addressing this issue in the legal system, *Police Woman* perpetuated all the very worst stereotypes, including the myth about women 'asking for it'. The depiction of a rape victim in the first episode of the series is, however, entirely sympathetic. The young woman concerned is unwilling to admit to having been raped precisely because of the social opprobrium and blame that frequently attaches itself to the victim of this crime. This episode raises questions about the stigma of rape and seeks to elicit the sympathy of the audience through both the portrayal of the victim and through Anderson's concerned response.

While both *Police Woman* and *Charlie's Angels* have been dealt with somewhat harshly by feminist media critics, they clearly proved to the American television networks in the 1970s that a TV crime drama series starring women could attract and hold a large audience. Although some of that audience may well have been compelled by what was crudely described by the industry as the 'T&A' ('tits and ass') component (D'Acci 1994: 15), as Anna Gough-Yates has argued in the case of *Charlie's Angels*, for female viewers there were other possible pleasures to be had in watching women confront the clearly sexist mores of the time (2001: 97), and I personally know of many women my own age who have confessed over the years to their having been 'inspired' by *Charlie's Angels* when they first encountered it, as they were by *Cagney and Lacey*, an American police procedural that has also prompted much commentary and inspired a recent British reinvention, *Scott and Bailey*.[4]

Women's work

The story of how *Cagney and Lacey* arrived on television constitutes the kind of production narrative that John Thornton Caldwell has described as both a 'war story' and a 'genesis myth' (Caldwell 2008: 38). As recounted by Julie D'Acci in her landmark book *Defining Women: Television and the Case of Cagney and Lacey* (1994) it is also a story about women's role in television production as well as television's role in the cultural construction of gender during an era of energetic feminist debate.

In 1974 Barbara Avedon and Barbara Corday, who had earlier written for such television shows featuring women as the sitcom *Maude* (CBS 1972–8) and the action series *Wonder Woman* (Snauffer 2006: 123), collaborated on a film script inspired by their reading of *From*

Reverence to Rape: The Treatment of Women in the Movies by film critic Molly Haskell (1974) (D'Acci 1994: 16). According to D'Acci, determined to create a crime film starring women, their research involved ten days following the working lives of New York City policewomen who took their jobs 'very seriously'(D'Acci 1994: 17). However, being seasoned television writers with a good working knowledge of the industry, Avedon and Corday appreciated that they had to make their film 'entertaining' if they were to get their feminist message across. The script they subsequently created entitled 'Freeze' involved a 'spoof' role reversal of the more usual male buddy cop drama in which policewomen Christine Cagney and Mary Beth Lacey discover the existence of a brothel run by a character called the Godmother in which men are the prostitutes and women the clients (19).

The job of selling this script to the studios fell to producer Barney Rozenzweig who had also been politicised by his reading of Haskell's book and was on side with the role reversal strategy. While the male heads of the major studios couldn't see the point, Sherry Lansing at MGM did, persuading the studio to finance the movie. The problem here was that those in charge would only agree to green light the project if the already established and distinctly glamorous film actresses Raquel Welch and Ann-Margaret starred as the crime-fighting duo. In a deliberately self-defeating move, the finance allocated to the project was woefully inadequate to secure such headline stars at the time (D'Acci 1994: 19). Thus began what has been narrativised as the long and tortuous battle over casting that would ensue before *Cagney and Lacey* appeared on-screen. This they eventually did in a made-for-TV movie airing on the CBS network at 8 p.m. on Thursday, 8 October 1981. The stars were Loretta Swit as Christine Cagney (who was then co-starring in the network's hit comedy drama series *M*A*S*H*) and Tyne Daly as Mary-Beth Lacey.

As Julie D'Acci describes it, the pre-publicity for the show demonstrated a struggle over competing definitions of 'woman, women and femininity' and the telemovie was launched on a wave of feminist approval and support (D'Acci 1994). Prominent feminist Gloria Steinem featured Swit and Daly in character on the cover of the October issue of her *Ms* magazine, which also contained in its pages a supportive essay by feminist film critic Marjorie Rosen. Meanwhile, CBS publicity was keen to play down the feminist aspect and determined to play up Cagney's physical attractiveness and sexual desirability (D'Acci 1994: 21). *Cagney and Lacey*'s future, however, was decided by the ratings. To the surprise of everyone, but especially the network, the telemovie attracted a 42 per cent share of the television audience in a timeslot where CBS had only been achieving 28 or 29 per cent (D'Acci 1994: 25). Less than two days after the premiere, the network heads had contacted Rosenzweig and invited him to create a weekly series to launch in spring 1982.

The six-episode series that eventuated starred Meg Foster as Christine Cagney (Swit was too busy with *M*A*S*H* to devote time to another television series), but failed to attract and hold its Tuesday night audience, although it did much better in the summer re-runs (Snauffer 2006: 123). In a controversial move that D'Acci attributes to the fact that Meg Forster was perceived by prominent critics and commentators as too tough, too threatening, and not feminine enough, the decision was made to replace Forster as Cagney (D'Acci 1994: 30). The sub-text here was Forster's earlier portrayal of a lesbian character in the film *A Different Story* (dir. Paul Aaron; 1978), which she had declared to be her favourite role – a declaration that as far as the network executives were concerned meant that Foster was 'a dyke' and was therefore unsuitable for a mainstream television show that featured two women as ongoing characters. As D'Acci points out, when lesbianism was depicted in television at the time, this was usually as a 'social' issue dealt with in a single-episode storyline (D'Acci 1994: 31). In terms of the possibility of an ongoing gay television character, homophobia clearly ruled, and the network demanded Foster's removal if the show was to continue.[5]

Cagney and Lacey was subsequently relaunched in the autumn of 1982 with an actress considered by the network to be much more 'feminine' in the role of Christine Cagney (Snauffer 2006: 124; D'Acci 1994: 35). The substitution of Sharon Gless, who had in fact been Corday and Avedon's initial choice for the part, clearly went some way to appease the network homophobes while ironically garnering a strong lesbian fan following, despite the fact that her character was coded as heterosexual and single (D'Acci 1994: 20). But the ratings were not inspiring, and following a relatively low-rating initial season, *Cagney and Lacey* was once again threatened with cancellation. According to D'Acci, in an effort to save the series and in a move that prefigured the kinds of 'crowd-sourcing' strategies more common today, Barney Rosenzweig launched a massive letter-writing campaign that deluged the network and major newspapers throughout the country with letters from fans of the show who stressed its importance in terms of the representation of strong female characters (D'Acci 1994: 44). Even more persuasive was the fact that the show received four Emmy nominations in its first year with Tyne Daly winning what would be the first of four Emmy Awards in the category of Outstanding Lead Actress in A Drama series. *Cagney and Lacey* was renewed once again, to continue for seven seasons, garnering thirty-six Emmy Award nominations and fourteen wins until its cancellation in 1988. In the process, it became what Caldwell identifies as an 'against all odds' allegory of triumph over adversity (Caldwell 2008: 38).

Like their predecessors in *Police Woman* and *Charlie's Angels*, Cagney and Lacey were portrayed in the original telemovie as two women stuck on hooker detail begging for a chance to tackle a 'real investigation' (Snauffer 2006: 123). This they were given in episodes that tackled a wide variety of crimes drawing attention to such issues as 'wife beating, abortion, breast-cancer, sexual harassment, date rape and alcoholism', routinely personalised in terms of the main characters (D'Acci 1994: 55). In Snauffer's opinion the show thus walked a fine line between genres, 'often focusing more on the characters' personal lives than their professional careers' (Snauffer 2006: 124). D'Acci goes even further, suggesting that as the show evolved its generic balance altered, making it less of a police genre and more of a 'feminine form' as identified (somewhat erroneously) by John Fiske in his influential book *Television Culture* (D'Acci 1994: 105).

What Fiske (wrongly) assumes in his distinction between 'masculine' and 'feminine' forms is that television shows can be 'gendered' in terms of their narrative structure (Fiske 1987). In this analysis, a 'masculine' form is assumed to be episodic with a single climax while a 'feminine' form is more multi-layered, complex, and ongoing. To be fair to Fiske, this was an argument that had been proposed by a number of feminist commentators on television, including Marsha Kinder (cited in Modleski 1997: 45) who had argued that there was an inherent affiliation between the multi-climaxed narrative form of the soap opera and women's sexuality. While this latter suggestion is debatable, Modleski's argument that soap opera narratives appealed to women because they underlined the importance of family and relationships and regularly featured women in key roles is more plausible, and this was certainly the case in *Cagney and Lacey*.

To further undermine the problematic gendering of narrative form, in embracing a melodramatic turn and a focus on the emotional lives of the detectives or police concerned, *Cagney and Lacey* was hardly unusual in the history of the television crime drama series in either the United Kingdom or the United States. Indeed, it was part of a trend that had become increasingly evident from the mid-1970s onwards in America, first in *Police Story* and subsequently in *Hill Street Blues*. In fact, there were more than a few similarities in structure, tone, and style between *Hill Street Blues* and *Cagney and Lacey*; both combined comedy with melodrama and ongoing storylines with episodic narratives set in realistically 'messy' police headquarters and downbeat urban settings. As Snauffer notes, the director of photography for the *Cagney and Lacey* telemovie, Ted Post, deliberately shot the series in what he describes as the 'dark gritty style' of *Hill Street Blues*, an aesthetic choice that went some way to mitigating any suspicion that this was simply a soap opera masquerading as a crime drama (Snauffer 2006: 123).

As a result of this and other moves, the 'feminist' credentials of *Cagney and Lacey* were much debated as producers and writers attempted to negotiate the network's desire to tone down the feminist politics as against a desire on the part of the producers, writers, and, indeed cast, to grapple with these head on. Underpinning the portrayal of two strong women in a working relationship was the real-life working relationship of the show's creators Barbara Avedon and Barbara Corday who described themselves both as 'partners' in their business of writing scripts and as best friends (D'Acci 1994: 17). Thus one of the most significant achievements of *Cagney and Lacey* was the creative role it accorded to women in production. A total of seventy-five of the series' 125 scripts were written or co-written by women (D'Acci 1994: 207). Furthermore, 104 episodes were credited to one or more women as producer or supervising producer and twenty-nine of its 125 episodes were directed by women, including the episode 'Heat' (04: 02), which garnered a Best Director Emmy for Karen Arthur (D'Acci 1994: 207).

In terms of the development of the television crime genre, *Cagney and Lacey* not only drew attention to the significant role of women in the production of a TV crime drama, but also to the ways in which the popular male 'buddy' series of the previous decade, such as *Starsky and Hutch* (ABC 1975–9) and *CHiPS* (NBC 1977–83) might be inverted. In the portrayal of two strong women – one single and one married – as close friends, both at and outside of work, *Cagney and Lacey* thus provided a model for female buddy series such as *Scott and Bailey* in the United Kingdom (ITV, 2011 –). At the time of their emergence, however, Christine Cagney and Mary-Beth Lacey were something of an 'odd couple' in a television landscape featuring a great many male/ female crime duos during the 1980s.

Mixed doubles

While there was always Sherlock Holmes and Watson, the coupling of a male and female crime fighter has another genealogy altogether that can be traced through both crime fiction and film. For example,

in the early twentieth-century *Strong Poison* (1930) author Dorothy
L. Sayers first introduced her aristocratic detective hero Lord Peter
Wimsey to the Oxford-educated advertising executive Harriet Vane
who would become his partner in crime and in life.[6] Tommy and
Tuppence Beresford, creations of Agatha Christie, were a pair of
upper-middle-class young things in the 1920s who first appeared in
The Secret Adversary (incidentally the 'first' Christie book to be adapted
for the screen as a German silent film in 1928 entitled *Abenteuer
G.m.b.H*, which translates as *Adventures Inc*).[7] Both Tommy and
Tuppence, as well as Lord Peter Wimsey and Harriet Vane, made
it on to television in the 1980s during what may be described as the
era of the mixed doubles in crime: the former in a series for London
Weekend Television in 1984 entitled *Partners in Crime* and the latter
in three telemovies starring Edwin Petherbridge and Harriet Walter
made for the BBC in 1987.[8] Meanwhile, over in America, Dashiell
Hammett's series of crime novels featuring private detectives Nick and
Nora Charles had been successfully adapted as a series of films during
the 1930s and 1940s starring William Powell and Myrna Loy, and
then as television series entitled *The Thin Man*, starring Peter Lawford
and Phyllis Kirk (1957–8) (Mizejewski 2004: 73).

While the 1960s' penchant for spies and gadgetry had earlier resulted
in such television pairings as Mrs Gale/Mrs Peel with John Steed in
The Avengers in the United Kingdom and the bumbling Maxwell Smart
and the much smarter Agent 99 in the Mel Brooks-created sitcom *Get
Smart* in the United States (NBC, 1965–9; CBS, 1969–70), in tracing
the emergence of the heterosexual couple in crime in the 1970s and
1980s, Linda Mizejewski invokes the film genre of screwball comedy.
Screwball, she argues, may have its roots in Shakespearian comedy,
but its movie tradition begins with Claudette Colbert and Clark Gable
as 'bickering road companions in *It Happened One Night*' (dir. Frank
Capra; 1934) (Mizejewski 2004: 72). 'In screwball,' Mizejewski suggests, 'the feisty woman demands equality, kicks up a fuss, but ends in
the arms of the guy who's all the better for having duked it out with
her' (Mizejewski 2004: 72). The legacy of screwball comedy with its
fiercely independent and frequently warring couples who may or may
not fall into bed together is then traced through such crime series as
McMillan and Wife (NBC, 1971–7) starring Rock Hudson and Susan
St James, *Hart to Hart* (ABC, 1979–84), starring Robert Wagner and
Stefanie Powers, and *Scarecrow and Mrs King* (CBS, 1983–7), pairing
Bruce Boxleitner with *Charlie's Angels*' alumnus Kate Jackson as a
housewife turned federal agent.

One of the most notable of these series to blend romance, Unresolved

Sexual Tension (URST), screwball comedy, allusions to film noir, and the private eye genre of crime drama was *Remington Steele* (NBC, 1982–7), starring Stephanie Zimbalist as Laura Holt, a private investigator who in recognition of the conflicted gender politics of the day, needs a 'man' to front her agency in order to inspire consumer confidence. The astute Laura, therefore, hires a former thief and conman (played by then unknown newcomer Pierce Brosnan) as the handsome face for a business over which she herself has complete control. With its playful intertextual allusions to crime films and detective fiction of the past, *Remington Steele* exhibited what has been described as a postmodern awareness of genre conventions even as it acknowledged the yet to be fully achieved equality of women in the workplace. As such, this series speaks to 'uncomfortableness' with the conventions of the genre and the role of men and women in it. No series illustrates this better than *Moonlighting* (ABC, 1985–9), a series that took postmodern playfulness with the genre conventions of the television crime drama to a whole new level during the 1980s.

Complicitous critique

In her book *Seeing through the Eighties: Television and Reaganism*, Jane Feuer (1995) discusses a number of television series that she considers characteristic of an era defined by the presidential career of Ronald Reagan in terms of its neo-conservative politics and aggressive foreign policy. While the cinema may have been obsessed with the 'hard bodies' of the male action hero, television, Feuer suggests, was 'both more feminized and more ideologically complex' (Feuer 1995: 2). Given that television has always been self-reflexive in terms of drawing attention to its own construction, particularly in the endless comedy shows that parody various television forms from advertisements to crime dramas, Feuer argues that this self-reflexivity reached another level altogether in the 1980s in a move that she identifies as a form of 'complicitous critique' (7). Shows such as the comedy crime series *Moonlighting* thus constituted a new form of 'art television' by consistently drawing attention to their own artfulness. In the process, as I will argue here, they also self-reflexively drew attention to current expectations and indeed anxieties about changing gender roles. As such, *Moonlighting* is a series that merits close analysis since it marks a significant moment in the evolution of the TV crime drama series, the moment when the genre appeared to have entered a phase of baroque experimentation that effectively undermined its own rationale while also drawing attention to the politics of gender.

Moonlighting was based on the premise that after losing her entire fortune to an embezzling business manager, former high fashion model Maddie Hayes (played by Cybill Shepherd) is left with nothing but a dubious detective agency intended to be run at a tax-dodging loss. The wise-cracking detective in charge, David Addison (played by Bruce Willis), has been working hard at doing nothing until Maddie moves in to make a go of it. As *Newsweek* described the set-up at the time, it was the 'punk versus the prom queen with "a sexual chemistry potent enough to curl plexiglass"' (cited in Mizejewski 2004: 79). While this may seem like a good premise for a conventional romantic-comedy type crime show à la *Remington Steele* or *Hart to Hart*, creator and producer Glen Gordon Caron was reportedly determined to push the genre envelope even further with fanciful plots that provided endless opportunities for the characters to engage in rapid-fire banter with scripts that were almost double the length of a usual one-hour show (Snauffer 2006: 146).[9] This Snauffer attributes to one of those production narratives in circulation at the time that suggests that Caron (who earlier had been instrumental in establishing the gender politics of *Remington Steele*), apparently made the entire cast and crew watch the Howard Hawks' screwball comedy *His Girl Friday* (starring a fast-talking Cary Grant and Rosalind Russell) before they started work on the series (Snauffer 2006: 144).

In endeavouring to assess the significance of *Moonlighting*, and in particular its self-conscious engagement with gender politics, the third series episode 'Atomic Shakespeare' (03: 07), in which Maddie and David appear as Katerina and Petruchio in a period costume rework-ing of Shakespeare's *Taming of the Shrew* has been discussed and found largely wanting (Radner 1995; Mizejewski 2004). While this episode belonged to the screwball comedy end of *Moonlighting*'s genre spec-trum, it is an earlier episode from season two, 'The Dream Sequence Always Rings Twice' (02: 04), which will be analysed in more detail here. What is of particular significance about this episode is that it explicitly addresses the gender politics of women on-screen and women's relationship to crime as this had been portrayed in a variety of crime fiction, film, and television series to date.

The first, and most obvious, reference is to the remarkable novel *The Postman Always Rings Twice* by James M. Cain published in 1934 and subsequently adapted for the screen at least six times. However, while *The Postman Always Rings* twice is a bleak book, *Moonlighting* was intended as a relatively light-hearted series. Significantly, the episode opens with an announcement recorded shortly before his death by revered film director Orson Welles (his patrician presence signalling the artful aspirations of the series to the canon of 'quality' television), who warns the family viewers at home that fifteen minutes into the episode the TV screen will fade to black to white. Following this prologue, 'The Dream Sequence Always Rings Twice' opens with private investigators Maddie and David arriving at the Flamingo Cove, which the owner wants to sell as part of a scheme to rid himself of his wife (whom he misogynistically describes as Godzilla). Dismayed to find that private detectives David and Maddie have been unable to 'dig up any dirt' on his unfortunate spouse, the owner abandons his renovation plans and walks out on the assembled group of interested parties, including the architect. It is the latter who tells David and Maddie the story of the Flamingo Cove murder involving a band-leader apparently murdered by his wife and her lover, the cornet player. In the car on the way back to the office David and Maddie argue ferociously (as they usually did in typical screwball mode) with David taking the side of the cornet player and Maddie taking the side of the wife. After both accuses the other of being 'sexist', David adds insult to injury by describing Maddie as 'the sexiest sexist' that it has even been his pleasure to meet.

Once home, an enraged Maddie kicks off her shoes, pours a drink, and falls asleep to dream a black-and-white scenario in which the innocent wife (Maddie) is seduced by the scheming cornet player (David) whose idea it is to kill the husband (played by the architect). This is achieved with a single blow to the husband's head, delivered by the cornet player, who lets the wife take the rap for the murder. Maddie's dream sequence ends with a dejected and rain-sodden Maddie being taken into custody by the police as David watches with one of his smuggest smiles. In keeping with its aesthetic aspirations, the style and tone of this sequence is reminiscent of such noir 'women's films' of the 1940s as *Mildred Pierce* (dir. Michael Curtiz; 1945) also based on a James M. Cain novel. This is apposite since in Maddie's version of the story the wife is portrayed as a flawed, and yet sympathetic, woman whose fate is an effect of poor judgement rather than criminal intent.

David's dream sequence, which also mimics and effectively parodies the noir film, portrays the wife as the prime mover and a full-blown femme fatale, as in the original Cain novel. David's version of Maddie vamps it up with a seductive hair-do and low-cut outfits that make the most of her cleavage and curves. The song she sings with the band is not the yearning and innocent 'Blue Moon'[10] of Maddie's dream but the upbeat and decidedly more sassy 'I Told Ya I Loved Ya, Now Get Out!'.[11] Other significant differences include the return of the original Cain first-person narrative voice in David's voice-over, constituting a playful parody of the original. His character's name, he tells us, is 'Chance, Lucky, Whatever', and he plays his cornet in his underwear while seated in the window of his room with flashing neon signs in the background, because 'I look good that way' in a move that also pokes fun at narcissistic masculinity. David's dream sequence thus plays it for laughs while implying that he is the innocent fall guy. Not surprisingly, in David's version it is the wife who strikes the fatal blow and the sequence ends with an 'innocent' man on his way to the electric chair, not unlike the ending of the original Cain novel.

The coda to this episode brings us back to the present. David and Maddie start their new day in the office pretending that all is forgotten about their disagreement, while their voice-over thoughts tell us that each is still firmly of the opinion that 'the other' is to blame. As in the formula of the classic situation comedy, the status quo has been reasserted and nothing has changed, either in the nature of their relationship or in the deeply entrenched gender positions that they have both assumed. This episode in particular, but also the series as a whole, thus exhibited not only the genre hybridity that was a constant feature of *Moonlighting* (romantic, screwball, situation comedy combined with traces of noir) but also the complexity with which the series dealt with the politics of gender. It may be argued that in dramatising both Maddie's dream and David's dream, the series had it both ways, reinforcing masculine prejudices while at the same time confirming feminist suspicions about deluded and narcissistic masculinity. Complicitous critique indeed.

Prime Suspect

If *Moonlighting* marks a particular highpoint in the 1980s' play with gender and genre the British police procedural *Prime Suspect* that aired only two years later was firmly located within the tradition of British social-realist crime dramas. While *Prime Suspect* has been usefully compared to earlier British police procedurals featuring women in lead roles such as *Juliet Bravo* (BBC One, 1980–5) and *The Gentle Touch* (ITV, 1980–4), Gillian Dyer has argued that neither of these earlier series did much to challenge the conventions of the television crime drama or to question 'women's relationship to the law and consensus morality' (Dyer 1987: 11). What they offered instead, as Deborah Jermyn suggests, was a 'benevolent' image of policing at a time when the reality was very different (Jermyn 2010: 34). As Jermyn points out, in April 1981, 300 police officers were injured during three days of anti-police rioting in Brixton, scenes that were repeated some three months later in Liverpool (Jermyn 2010: 35–6). With Prime Minister Margaret Thatcher in charge, the 1980s was a decade of struggle and strikes in the United Kingdom with the police frequently called upon to suppress what was often cast as various forms of civil disobedience.

Largely because of *The Gentle Touch*'s limitations as a 'feminist' television crime drama, it was during an episode of this series that an actress named Lynda Marchal found herself unable to utter what was in the context a completely inane line, causing herself and star Jill Gascoigne to 'corpse' repeatedly. Convinced that she herself could write a better script, Marchal (whose maiden name was Titchmarsh and whose married name was La Plante) proceeded to do so. Sadly, all of La Plante's submitted scripts were rejected, although one did come back with the written comment, 'This is brilliant' (Jermyn 2010: 15). Spurred on by this encouragement, La Plante took her script to Euston Films, which she knew to have already produced a series entitled *Out* (1978) that was about a career criminal trying to go straight. Written by Trevor Preston (one of the primary writers for *The Sweeney*), and starring Tom Bell (who would go on to play the memorable DCI Otley in *Prime Suspect*), in its sympathetic portrayal of a criminal out to settle the score with a corrupt senior police officer, *Out* established a dramatic precedent for La Plante's *Widows*.

Crucial to La Plante's success in getting her script for *Widows* approved was producer Verity Lambert, who, while head of drama for Thames Television from 1974 to 1983, had commissioned a number of TV series that specifically featured and addressed women (Hallam 2007: 20). These included *Shoulder to Shoulder* (1974) about the suffragette movement and *Rock Follies* (1976) following the fortunes of a female rock band (20). Described by Jermyn as both 'ambitious' and 'provocative' (Jermyn 2010: 16), *Widows* opened with the depiction of a botched armed robbery in which three men are killed. Their widows, led by the redoubtable Dolly Rawlins (Ann Mitchell), subsequently pick up where their late husbands have left off in the execution of a bank raid. The critical and ratings success of *Widows* resulted in two sequels (*Widows 2* in 1985 and *She's Out* in 1995). However, despite La Plante's best efforts, it was not until 1991 that she was given the go ahead for her next major project, *Prime Suspect*, with a woman in the lead role as a senior police officer (Jermyn 2010: 16).

While the backdrop to *The Sweeney*, *Law & Order*, and *Out* had been corruption in the metropolitan police force during the 1970s, the backdrop to *Prime Suspect* was the 'very public real-life tribunal' of Merseyside's assistant chief constable Alison Halford, which drew attention to the extent of sexual discrimination within the force at the time (Jermyn 2010: 4). In the very first instalment of *Prime Suspect* in 1991, such sexual discrimination is front and centre, as Jane Tennison encounters the reluctance of her male superiors to give her control of a murder case for which she is eminently qualified. The detailed attention that this series then paid to the procedures and processes of a homicide investigation was largely consequent of the assistance of real-life homicide detective chief inspector Jackie Malton; it was after shadowing Malton through the incident rooms and police laboratories that La Plante apparently felt confident enough to proceed with the development of her script (18).

Although *Prime Suspect* was perceived as a ground-breaking show, it was also very much of its time in terms of the particular crime that it depicted in its first instalment (a serial killer preying on women) and in its attention to forensics and the practice of criminal profiling: two themes that would come to dominate 1990s' crime fiction and the television crime drama. In 1991 American author Patricia Cornwell's first crime novel, *Postmortem*, was published in which the central character, dedicated medical examiner Dr Kay Scarpetta, has to deal with many of the same issues and problems as Tennison. These include not only institutional misogyny but also a serial killer who rapes and tortures his female victims. Coincidentally, these are also the problems faced by yet another dedicated female investigator and would-be criminal profiler, Clarice Starling (Jodie Foster), in the film adaptation of Thomas Harris's serial-killer-thriller, *Silence of the Lambs*, which also appeared in 1991.The serial killer with whom Jane Tennison has to deal, George Marlow (John Bowe), is, however, very different from the grotesque monsters created by Harris and Demme and all the more scary as a result.

Marlow is a man who in his mundane ordinariness bears more resemblance to one of Britain's more famous real-life serial killers, Peter Sullivan, aka The Yorkshire Ripper, than to the larger-than-life Hannibal Lecter and 'Buffalo Bill' (although the latter characters were also inspired by such real-life notorious American serial killers as Ed Gein, Ted Bundy, and Jeffery Dahmer). Sullivan, who was eventually arrested in 1981 as a result of a random number plate check after being interviewed and released on nine prior occasions, was found guilty of murdering thirteen women, most of them prostitutes, whom he had picked up while travelling around Northern England (Jermyn 2010: 78). Unlike Lecter and Buffalo Bill, and very like Marlow, Sullivan was an 'unassuming married man living in a semi-detached house in a respectable Yorkshire suburb' (ibid.).

With all of these cultural resonances, the first *Prime Suspect*, featuring already respected theatre and film actress Helen Mirren who brought with her a cachet of 'quality' as a result, was a television event that immediately captured the attention of the British viewing public, thereby ensuring a sequel the following year. *Prime Suspect 2* (December 1992) for which La Plante supplied the storyline but did not write the script, addressed the issue of racism within the force and society at large. *Prime Suspect 3* (1993), which La Plante both researched and wrote, dealt with the abuse of children in care and the prevalence of paedophilia within the upper echelons of society.

While Tennison's first case has been much discussed (Mizejewski 2004: 89–96; Jermyn 2010), *Prime Suspect 3*, the last to be written by La Plante before she relinquished control of both her character and the series after 'irresolvable creative differences with Granada emerged during the third series' (Jermyn 2010: 13), has attracted rather less commentary.[12] In this episode, Tennison once again deals effectively with a male hierarchy determined to protect their own and frustrate her investigation and manages against the odds to win promotion to superintendent. On the personal front, she achieves this by choosing to pursue her career rather than a relationship, not an entirely difficult choice given that the lover – who wants to take her back to the States – is a married man with four children. Having sent him packing and in the midst of her investigation, Jane discovers that she is pregnant. With her usual efficiency and composure, she arranges an abortion over the telephone. And then she breaks down in tears, in her office, alone. The final moments of this scene are played with Tennison's back to the camera. We watch Jane's shoulders heave and we hear her sobbing, but we do not see her face: It is hidden even from the audience who has been a witness to other moments in Jane's private life. It's a telling moment, marking a watershed for the series as a whole, inviting the viewer to wonder what may have developed if La Plante had kept some control over the direction of the series.

Indeed, it is on this last point that much debate has subsequently hinged, particularly that which occurred around the last instalment. In 2007 'The Final Act' portrayed an alcoholic Tennison losing her edge and facing a lonely retirement. La Plante was extremely upset by this conclusion for her character – a choice made by the writers in consultation with actor Helen Mirren. In an interview with BBC Breakfast to discuss her latest crime novel, La Plante said, 'I just find it very sad that for the end of a great character, female, somebody has to say "make her a drunk". Why'? (Anonymous 2006). Meanwhile, Mirren, who had become closely identified with Tennison, continued to garner numerous accolades in both the United Kingdom and the

United States, winning three BAFTA Awards in succession for *Prime Suspect 1–3* , and Emmy Awards for the fifth and seventh 'seasons' in a series that, in terms of format, varied considerably. While the first three *Prime Suspects* were each a case of two-part, two-hour episodes, *Prime Suspect 4*, which appeared in the United Kingdom in 1995, was divided into three self-contained narratives of 102 minutes' duration each ('The Lost Child', 'Inner Circles', and 'Scent of Darkness'). *Prime Suspect 5* 'Errors of Judgement' (1996), and *Prime Suspect 6* 'The Last Witness' (2003), returned to the original format of two-part, two-hour episodes, as did the controversial *Prime Suspect 7* 'The Final Act' (2007). Given the occasional and intermittent nature of this series over such an extended period of time, the resonance of Tennison reveals that the impact of a character or indeed a TV series may have little relationship to the amount of screen time accorded.[13]

After Jane

In her essay entitled 'Television Crime Series, Women Police, and Fuddy-Duddy Feminism', Charlotte Brunsdon considers the legacy of *Prime Suspect* and how we may approach the 'daughters of Jane Tennison' in such British series as *Ghost Squad* (Channel 4 2005) and *Murder in Suburbia* (ITV 2004–5). Brunsdon is primarily interested in how these latter shows may relate to the concept of post-feminism that she acknowledges has become a highly contested term, encompassing as it does a wide range of positions and arguments. Brunsdon's major point is that while each of these series assumes a world in which feminism 'has been taken into account' (everyone is aware of the discourses of equal opportunity and antidiscrimination) they nevertheless continue to pose some tricky questions about the representation and role of women in the television crime drama and how this relates to women's 'actual' position in the field of contemporary policing (Brunsdon 2012: 15).

When it comes to what we now see on the screen, my own review of the television crime dramas on offer on free-to-air television in Australia during the first week of October 2013 produced a tally of twenty different crime dramas, fourteen being from the United States, four being British, and typically only two were produced in Australia. Although women may play a key role in dramas that included *Waking the Dead*, *CSI*, and *Law & Order: Special Victims Unit*, only four of these series were named after their female characters. This included the frequently dark police procedural, *Scott and Bailey*, a Manchester-based re-imaging of *Cagney and Lacey*, as well as *Rizzoli and Isles* (TNT, 2010), another American police procedural based on the crime novels of American author Tess Gerritsen, featuring a police detective and a medical examiner who work closely together. This latter series was, however, hidden away on one of the network multi-channels with little promotion from its parent network. Much more prominent in the well-established ABC Friday night crime slot was the second series of *Miss Fisher's Murder Mysteries*. This gentle period crime drama based on the crime fiction series of Australian author and barrister, Kerry Greenwood, features the beautiful flapper heiress Phryne Fisher. Clad in fabulous hats and frocks, the dauntless Phryne moonlights in 1920s' Melbourne as a private investigator. While Greenwood's feminist politics are clearly expressed in the books, on-screen these are mitigated by Phryne's glamour and the frisson of an ongoing romantic relationship with detective Jack Robinson, a relationship that is underplayed in the books where Phryne's sexual adventures with many different partners are much more risqué.

The strategy of pairing a male and female investigator is also apparent in the crime series *Bones*, which takes its title from the nickname of forensic anthropologist Dr Temperance Brennan (Emily Duschamel). In this series, based on the crime fiction of real-life forensic anthropologist Kathy Reichs, the independence of the female central character in the novels is once again modified on-screen by the proximity of her male offsider (special agent Seeley Booth) whose role has been augmented in such a way as to recall the comedy crime 'mixed doubles' of the 1980s. While in the books Brennan is an older women and a recovering alcoholic, in the TV series (that author Kathy Reichs has suggested may be considered a lighter prequel to the novels), Brennan is cast as a dedicated scientist with poor interpersonal skills: a characteristic that locates her within another more recent trend in television crime drama, that of the dysfunctional detective located somewhere on the spectrum of Asperger's syndrome. Although *Bones* has its share of gruesome scenes featuring decomposing bodies, these have taken on a decidedly ghoulish and even comic aspect, while attention has shifted to the increasingly screwball relationship between the ongoing characters.

The 'true' daughters of Jane Tennison are therefore to be found elsewhere in the network schedule. In Australia, they are to be found on the Special Broadcasting Service (SBS) with its multicultural remit. Here, season three of the Danish drama *The Killing* (*Forbrytelesen*; DR1, 2007–) was drawing to its climax while the second series of the Swedish/Danish co-production *The Bridge* (Danish: *Broen*/Swedish: *Bron*) was foreshadowed later in the year. Although neither of these series bears the name of their female protagonist, both series paid particular attention to the two female detectives leading the case. Detective Sara Lund (Sophie Gråbøl) has much in common with Jane Tennison. In the first season of *The Killing* she is job-focused to the detriment of her relationship with her partner, her son, and her mother. Like Tennison, Lund is a brilliant detective who makes the connections that others (especially her male colleagues) do not see. As in the first *Prime Suspect*, the first case on which we see Lund at work involves the rape and murder of a young woman. This time, however, it would seem that we are not dealing with a suspected serial killer, but with a crime that may have been committed by anyone within the girl's social ambit. Suspects include her boyfriend, her school teacher, her father, and even a local politician with whom she has been having an affair. What women should fear most, this narrative suggests, is not an unknown serial killer, but someone close to them.

Unlike Tennison, Lund is not in charge of the investigation but she is partnered with a male colleague who finds her lack of warmth and her uncommunicativeness to be both irritating and alienating. Unlike Tennison who took great care to arrange her appearance in order to present herself as a professional women, Sara Lund's unkempt ponytail and ubiquitous Faroese sweater and jeans signify her complete lack of personal vanity, her sweater achieving iconic status in the process (see Figure 6.1). In a 2011 Christmas special episode of the British BBC sitcom *Absolutely Fabulous*, character Edina Monsoon (Jennifer Saunders) dreams that Lund, in her iconic sweater, is searching her bedroom with a flashlight, the cameo role by Gråbøl underlining the currency and popularity of the character of Sarah Lund outside her country of origin.

According to an article by Gerard Gilbert in *The Independent* newspaper, like Helen Mirren, Gråbøl came to the part of Lund after a career encompassing both stage and Emmy Award-winning television work (Gilbert 2011). Like Mirren, she also took an interventionist role in the construction of her character, declaring at one point her opposition to a romantic sub-plot with the odd statement, 'I am Clint Eastwood! He doesn't have a girlfriend!' As Gilbert goes on, in Gråbøl's refusal to compromise her character's loner status, Lund may well be Clint (the hard-boiled Clint of the police procedural *Dirty Harry* rather than romantic Clint of *Bridge over Madison County* one assumes), but is she a feminist role model? According to Gråbøl, DCI Jane Tennison was defined by the antagonism of her male colleagues and as a result the decision was made by the writers of *The Killing* 'not to make Lund's sex an issue' (ibid.). While this may be true in so far

Figure 6.1 Sara Lund (Sophie Gråbøl) in one of her iconic Faroese sweaters; 2007. Credit: Picture Desk

as Lund's status as a *female* police detective is never questioned in a post-feminist equal-opportunity workplace, 'sex' or rather 'gender' is nonetheless still an issue. As Gilbert himself reveals when he concludes that in her refusal to assume many of the usual feminine characteristics such as care of the self and family, Lund has effectively 'redefined the female police detective' (ibid.). Before considering what this redefinition may involve, it is salutary to compare Sarah Lund with another Scandinavian homicide detective, Saga Norén (Sofia Helin) in the Danish–Swedish co-production *The Bridge* (*Broen/Bron* DR1, SVT1,

Figure 6.2 *The Bridge*: detective Saga Norén (Sofia Helin) and detective Martin Rhode (Kim Bodnia) examine the body on the Øresund Bridge; 2011. Credit: Photofest

2011–), which also achieved a global audience, and like *The Killing*, an American remake (FX, 2103–).

Following the format of *The Killing*, *The Bridge* is constructed as a serial crime drama involving the investigation of a particular murder. In the case of the latter, this comprises a series of related crimes beginning with the death of a high-profile Swedish female politician whose body is found lying in the middle of the Øresund Bridge connecting Denmark and Sweden and the cities of Copenhagen and Malmo. Detective Saga Norén of the Swedish police and detective Martin Rhode (Kim Bodnia) of the Danish police both attend the scene, the imperative to collaborate becoming apparent when it is revealed that the body has been cut in two and lain quite precisely across the border line (see Figure 6.2). While the torso may be Swedish, the lower half is that of a Danish prostitute who disappeared a year earlier.

Like Sara Lund, Saga is a woman who takes her post-feminist equal-opportunity workplace for granted. Like Sara, she has no personal vanity, dressing for most of the ten episodes in the same leather trousers, what looks like an army surplus overcoat, and a sweater. Her only costume change involves the removal of her T-shirt in order to put on a clean one. This she does in front of her male colleagues, in an act that demonstrates her complete oblivion to their obvious discomfiture when she strips down to her bra. Again, like Sara, Saga is entirely focused on her job and is even more isolated given that there is no partner, child, or mother in the background to be ignored. When Saga wants sex she goes to a bar and asks an attractive man if he would like it too, taking her somewhat astonished pick-up back to her flat where he wakes in the morning to find Saga viewing the gruesome autopsy images of the dismembered women on the bridge. Not surprisingly, he beats a hasty exit. As a coda to this anti-romantic encounter, in the final episode Saga rings him to suggest that they have dinner. This is not, however, a move that comes easily to her, since, as one of Saga's colleagues tell her hapless Danish offsider Martin, she is 'special'.

What 'special' appears to mean is that Saga is not like other people and that she is a high-functioning woman somewhere on the continuum of the increasingly prevalent Asperger's syndrome. Therefore, while Saga may well be a brilliant detective, she has problems reading other people's emotions or understanding irony and humour. Saga is not, however, completely devoid of emotion, as the last episode reveals when Saga has to tell Martin that his son has been killed. It is on the way home from this encounter that Saga rings her former sex-partner in what may be read as an intention to establish a more profound relationship, although how successful this endeavour may be is left to the viewer's imagination.

In attempting to locate exactly where these two characters may sit in relation to some version of feminism and the genre of the television crime drama, it is possible to argue that Sara and Saga are cast as feminised versions of the traditional 'noir' detective, as described by Raymond Chandler in his much-quoted essay 'The Simple Art of Murder' written in the 1940s, when the gender of the (male) detective was taken for granted.

> Down these mean streets a [woman] must go who is [herself] not mean, who is neither tarnished nor afraid. The detective in such a story must be such a [woman]. [She] is the hero, [she] is everything. [She] must be a complete [woman] and a common [woman] and yet an unusual [woman]. (Chandler 1946: 237)

Sara and Saga are indeed 'unusual' women and there is little doubt that they do indeed inhabit a 'mean world' scenario, situated as they are in a bleak present in which society itself appears to be the crime. This bleakness, evoked in moody lighting and grim urban landscapes has been described as 'Scandinavian noir' or even 'Scandinoir', a term that encompasses a recent wave of film and television series as well as crime fiction from the Scandinavian countries that have achieved international popularity (Wilder 2012).

It is also possible to position Sara and Saga in relation to that broad spectrum of brilliant but socially dysfunctional detectives that includes Sherlock Holmes in many of his on-screen representations, most recently as performed by Benedict Cumberbatch in *Sherlock* and Johnny-Lee Miller in *Elementary*. That the socially inept and driven detective has largely been coded as male, while the female detective has often been coded as skilled in the reading and valuing of interpersonal relationships, only serves to underline the departure that these two women represent.

While Sara Lund and Saga Norén may indeed be the Scandinavian daughters of Jane Tennison, in their absence of personal vanity, their lack of interest in clothes, and in their lack of care of the self, these women are also markedly different from Jane in her ambition to 'get on' in a masculinist culture. In fact, Lund and Norén have more in common with the isolated and beleaguered male detectives of such recent series as *Rebus* and *Wallander*, than they do either with Tennison or the self-conscious post-feminist heroines of recent British crime series as identified by Charlotte Brunsdon (2012). Like Rebus and Wallander, Lund and Norén are representatives of the familiar trope of the gifted and isolated detective whose dedication to the job alienates them from others and frequently puts them into conflict with their superiors, with Norén's 'specialness' setting her even more apart from the norm.

Are we there yet?

It would be gratifying to conclude this chapter with the suggestion that gender equality has been achieved in the television crime drama and that gender issues are no longer of great significance in the debate about the representation of crime; however, this is hardly the case. The welter of commentary on another Scandinavian crime series that has achieved global renown and an American remake clearly suggests otherwise (Bronsons 2012). In its portrayal of the complex character of computer hacker and rape victim, Lisbeth Salander, the international success of *The Girl With the Dragon Tattoo* (initially released as the first of three films and later as a six-part television series based on the Millennium trilogy of the late Swedish author Stieg Larsson) demonstrates the ongoing interest in the representation of both men and women in crime. The fact that the original Swedish title of the Larsson's first book published in 2005 was *Men Who Hate Women* (*Man som hatar kvinnor*) and that there is now a collection of critical essays entitled *Men Who Hate Women and Women Who Kick their Asses*

(King and Smith 2012), highlights the ongoing centrality of gender relationships to the contemporary cultural context in which these crime texts are received. As this chapter has hopefully demonstrated, while times and the television landscape may change, gender continues to matter in the case of crime, both on- and off-screen.

Notes

1. While teaching in a high school in the state of New Jersey in the United States in the 1980s, I was informed by my then students that their favourite daytime soap was *Cell Block H* – a show, they cheerfully informed me, came from 'England'.
2. As evidence of the legacy and ongoing popularity of *Prisoner*, in 2012 a re-imagined version of the series, *Wentworth*, was commissioned by Foxtel (Dallas, 2012).
3. With titles such as *This Girl for Hire* – clearly a play on the hard-boiled film title *This Gun for Hire*, which was based on a novel by British author Graham Greene that was entitled *A Gun for Sale*.
4. 'It's the *Cagney and Lacey* of Manchester' said actress Suranne Jones who told the TV listings' magazine *What's on TV* how she and another actress came up with the idea for a show based on *Cagney and Lacey* (Anonymous 2011b).
5. The successful Australian soap opera *Number 96* (1972–7) featured a sympathetic gay character, lawyer Don Finlayson (Joe Hasham), some ten years earlier, with considerable rating success.
6. Sayers herself worked in the advertising industry in London until the success of her crime fiction enabled her to give up her day job.
7. As described on the 'official' Agatha Christie website (Anonymous n.d.u).
8. Bohm (n.d.).
9. By the end of its second season, *Moonlighting* was at number twenty-four in the Nielsen ratings, scoring sixteen Emmy nominations. Following the Writers' Guild of America strike in 1988, the show was cancelled in 1989, concluding with an episode that true to the show's artful tradition of 'breaking the fourth wall', featured Maddie and David returning to their office to discover the set of *Moonlighting* being dismantled.
10. The song '*Blue Moon*' (1934) was written by Richard Rogers and Lorenz Hart.
11. The song 'I Told Ya I Loved Ya, Now Get Out!' was written by Lou Carter, Herb Ellis, and Johnny Frigo.
12. La Plante subsequently set up her own production company that

went on to produce fifteen series for British television and a number of successful series for the American networks, including *The Prosecutors* (NBC, 1996) and *Bella Mafia* (CBS, 1997). La Plante thus became one of the very few British women to break into the lucrative American television market (Hallam 2007: 27).

13. In 2012, there was an 'official' American remake of *Prime Suspect*, created by Alexandra Cunningham for NBC. Launched with a fanfare, the site for the show included a photographic history of the role of women in the New York Police Department (NYPD) from 1888 onwards. The show was cancelled after only one season.

Conclusion:
Coming up Next . . .

In the final stages of completing this project, I acquired a DVD copy of the second season of the Danish crime drama *The Killing* (DRI, 2009). Rationing myself to one episode a night – apart from giving in on the twelfth night and watching the last two of the thirteen episodes back to back – I was vividly and viscerally reminded of why I love television crime. Hunkered down in front of the television, as physically close as I could get in order to cut out all other distractions, I was completely caught up in a serial narrative that encompassed a family melodrama, a killer who may or may not have been a terrorist with a link to covert military activities in Afghanistan, a political struggle constituting a kind of Danish *West Wing* set in the corridors of power in Copenhagen, and a police procedural featuring the return of detective Sarah Lund (Sophie Gråbøl) from her enforced exile as a border security guard after the shooting of her offsider last season. And it was beautiful to look at, shot in a style best described as 'nordic noir': a combination of deeply shadowed interiors and washed-out daylight exteriors in urban and rural Denmark. Like the viewers of the melodrama *Dallas* in Ien Ang's landmark audience study (1985), I was caught up in the 'tragic structure of feeling' mobilised by the character and the action but was also fascinated by lifestyle issues, that is, the spaces and places in which these people lived and worked in a cultural and political environment that was so different, and yet so similar, to my own (Ang 1985: 46).

Given that I was watching this Danish series with English subtitles, in Australia, on DVD, my engagement with *The Killing*, in terms of both its form and its content, serves to revisit some of the key questions that this book has sought to address. These include the changing contexts of production and reception, modifications in the format and narrative construction of the crime drama, questions of style and aesthetics, as well as attitudes to crime, criminality, and policing, and the nature of the audience experience.

Changing production practices and reception contexts

In his book *Television and American Culture*, Jason Mittell identifies three stages in the development of American television: first, the classic network era lasting from the mid-1940s to the mid-1980s in which the television was dominated by the three major national networks, ABC, CBS, and NBC; second, the multi-channel era of the 1990s when satellite and cable television as well as new technologies such as the remote control and the video cassette recorder (VCR) changed the ways in which people experienced the medium; and, finally, the current era of convergence in which the television is but one of many screens in the home and elsewhere on which programmes may be watched (Mittell 2010: 11). These shifts parallel the experience of television in the United Kingdom and Australia, as the 'era of scarcity' as John Ellis identifies it, has, over the years, given way to an 'era of plenty' (Ellis 2000: 39).

What is common to both the British and Australia experience in the 'era of scarcity' is just how much American crime drama was shown on free-to-air television, with the United Kingdom traditionally faring somewhat better in the production of its own home-grown product. While the BBC was quick to start making television crime drama in the early1950s, albeit in the documentary unit, it was not until 1964 that Australia managed to produce its own indigenous crime series, *Homicide* (Crawford productions for Channel Seven, 1964–77), a show that in its strategic use of cars and hats owed more to the iconography of American crime drama than the British series of the same era. This was hardly surprising given that in 1960 up to 70 per cent of Australian television was imported and 80 per cent of the imported programming was American (McKee 2001: 52).

The influence of the American crime drama series on the development of both the British and Australian crime drama has been considerable and to some extent elusive, although stories of origin such as Troy Kennedy Martin's about the inspiration for *Z-Cars*, emanating from the American series *Highway Patrol*, signal the tip of a very large subtextual iceberg. More recently in Australia the commercial network Channel 9 commissioned the development of the first of what has become an ongoing series of true crime drama series, *Underbelly*, based on Melbourne's recent gangland wars after the surprise ratings success of *The Sopranos* in a late night slot. In the spirit of cross-fertilisation and hybrid invention, *Underbelly* was Australia's wannabe *Sopranos* with the CBS cable drama network in the United Kingdom touting the series as 'the Australian *Sopranos*' in its promotion (Anonymous n.d.v).

Meanwhile America continues to 'remake' successful crime dramas produced elsewhere, such as *The Killing* and *The Bridge*, as it did earlier successful British crime dramas such as *Cracker* and *Prime Suspect*. In the case of *The Killing*, the remake was produced by the Fox Television Studios, shot in Vancouver, British Columbia and shown on the cable station AMC where the pilot episode rated extremely well and the first season of thirteen episodes was greeted with critical acclaim. AMC, which boasts on its website that it is 'the most Emmy nominated basic cable network', is home to a range of other hit series, including *Mad Men* and *Breaking Bad*.[1] Formerly known as American Movie Classics, since 2002 AMC has adopted the format of the long-form television drama series in a move that signals that the audience for classic movies is now also embracing the television drama series in an era when 'quality' television, as defined by its niche audience, is clearly an attractive commodity for both older and younger audiences (Anonymous n.d.w). As the AMC example illustrates, cable TV networks are now also in the business of making TV and selling DVDs.

In the United Kingdom, the Danish version of *The Killing* was shown on BBC Four in the spring of 2011, where it attracted more viewers than AMC's other hit series, *Mad Men*, before going on to win a BAFTA Award, beating three other American series, *Mad Men*, *Boardwalk Empire*, and *Glee* in the same category of International TV. The British television industry and audiences would appear to be receptive to a subtitled crime drama series (Anonymous n.d.x). As were the Australian critics and audiences when the series was shown on the first of the Special Broadcasting Service channels, SBS1 in the company of other Scandinavian crime drama series such as *The Eagle* and *Unit One* on repeat (Craven n.d.). Writing in March 2010 on the Australian public broadcaster's online blog, *The Drum*, well-known Australian literary critic Peter Craven related the arrival of *The Killing* on television to the release one week earlier in Australia of the Swedish (subtitled) film version of *The Girl with the Dragon Tattoo* (dir. Niels Arden Oplev; 2009). For Craven, *The Girl with the Dragon Tattoo* and *The Killing* were part of a tide of a Scandinavian wave of crime fiction and television crime dramas, which he admired for their 'compositional brilliance, all that winter light and thin fading sun, and the uniform excellence of the scriptwriting and the acting' (ibid.). For Craven, as for many others, Scandinavian television would appear to be the new 'quality TV'. Not all crime dramas, however, circulate equally well. While the Scandinavian crime drama may have enjoyed recent success, the global trade in the crime has long been dominated by the British and the American product with *CSI* still the most watched television crime drama series in the world (Bibel 2012).

Questions of form

CSI is a very different kind of crime drama series to *The Killing*. In its episodic structure *CSI* hearkens back to the early days of the television crime drama, such as *Dragnet*, while in its long-form narrative format *The Killing* follows the more recent trend for serialisation that has generic roots in fiction as well as radio long before it arrives on television in the form of the literary adaptation or daytime soap opera. By the 1980s, as Mittell suggests, the serial narrative had entered 'prime-time' television with the success of such family melodramas as *Dallas* and *Dynasty* (Mittell 2012: 230). In his discussion of the 'millennial wave of revolutionary dramas', television critic Alan Sepinwall identifies *Hill Street Blues* as the television drama that marks an 'evolutionary leap' in its blurred moral landscape and its complex narrative form, involving multiple narrative threads of various lengths (Sepinwall 2012: 8). While the 'flexi-narrative' (Nelson 1997: 30) was to become one of the most popular narrative forms during the 1990s, series such as *Twin Peaks* (ABC, 1990–1) and *The X-Files* (Fox, 1993–2002), both of which sit somewhere on the outer limits of the TV crime drama, were already toying with the possibilities afforded by extended seasonal narrative arcs. With *The Sopranos* (HBO, 1999–2007), *24* (Fox, 2001–10), and *The Wire* (HBO, 2002–8), full-blown seriality became a viable, and increasingly popular, alternative to either the episodic or flexi-narrative structure of the crime drama.

The TV crime drama has continued to vary in format from the half-hour to one-hour episodic narrative with or without ongoing character and relationship development, to the extended telemovie or mini-series format shown over one or more nights, in parallel with the increasingly prevalent use of a serial narrative ranging in length from six to twenty-four episodes, which people may choose to watch in 'binge' mode, enabled by DVD release. As Jacqueline Furby notes of the 'thriller' *24*, 'the audience cannot view casually, but instead enters into a contract of intense involvement that endures over twenty-four weeks if viewed as original broadcast, or for eighteen hours of viewing episodes on DVD' (Furby 2007: 59). Seriality has become a viable ploy on the part of television producers to capture and hold an audience in an era when there are so many competing demands for their attention and 'appointment' television may no longer be the standard practice for viewing in the home. Meanwhile, as the success of *CSI*

demonstrates, television series employing an episodic format that
requires no prior knowledge of either the characters or the narrative
scenario in which they are embedded, may allow for more occasional,
unplanned, and less committed viewing.

Style and aesthetics

Considering the last sixty years of television history, it is clear that the
television crime drama has often been at the forefront of experimentation with style, making innovative use of the technologies to hand.
This would include the use of film during the 1950s when live production was considered one of the hallmarks of quality in television, as
well as the stylistic appropriation of film noir and documentary that
were so oddly juxtaposed in early crime dramas such as *Fabian of the
Yard* and *Dragnet*. Landmark series such as *Hill Street Blues* and *Miami
Vice* in the 1980s demonstrated the competing pull of the neo-realist
documentary style and the 'excessive style' of film noir, re-imagined
in the case of the latter as a kind of 'neon-noir'. The use of colour
coding carried over into *CSI*, which was also ground breaking in its
use of computer-generated imagery (CGI) to reveal the mysteries of
forensic science in a style that may best be described as 'hyper-real'. As
Caldwell suggests, cinematographers and camera operators today are
now 'versatile' and 'hybrid theorisers' able to choose from an extensive
set of competing aesthetic traditions, including film noir and neoreal-
ism and expressionism. Caldwell also identifies what he describes as
an 'MTV style', which he associates with *Miami Vice*, and the use of
'Rembrandt lighting' (that he assumes is self-explanatory) (Caldwell
2008: 19).

   While many aesthetic and stylistic choices are the result of careful
consideration, Caldwell has written compellingly about the need to
consider the 'critical industrial practices' that are operational in the
production of any television crime drama. Richard Paterson's account
of the making of *The Sweeney*, written from the Marxist perspective of
1970s' screen studies, is an exemplary instance of this kind of research.
Here Paterson explores the particular industrial and social base of *The
Sweeney*, the cost constraints, the choice of film (16mm for television,
as opposed to the more expensive 35mm for a film), the freelance
nature of the Euston Film production house employees at the time
and the kinds of creative choices that are contingent on a variety of
production moments. For example, the failure of a particular car to
arrive for the filming of a stunt sequence led to the producer working
with the stunt director to come up with a whole new way of shooting

the scene (Paterson 1976: 8). This is the kind of information that is now often accessible via the 'commentary' or special making-of feature on the DVD boxed set available to the home viewer and the television scholar, who may now be one and the same person. Such commentaries may usefully include (as did the retrospective commentary on *The Sweeney*) a range of 'behind-the-scenes' anecdotes and insights that help to provide a context for what eventually appeared on-screen, the kinds of production decision made, and why. However, as Mayer et al. (2009: 1–2) demonstrates, such stories should be treated with caution since they tend to emerge after the fact and are usually self-serving in some way.

As the entertainment president of the American WB network recently admitted, 'There's no such thing as a master plan in this business' (Sepinwall 2012: 205). As Sepinwall's account of what he identifies as 'a revolution' in television drama reveals, the emergence of these shows appears to be incidental and contingent on any number of different factors that have as much to do with industry personnel, business plans, and the quest to find an audience as they do with the creativity and ideas of the producers. As this book has attempted to illustrate, in seeking to understand why this or that television crime drama appears at any one time, it is useful to consider the production narratives in which it is embedded in order to understand what appears on-screen and how.

For example, in an illuminating paper presented to a conference entitled 'Crime, Cameras, Action!' in 2012, screenwriter Felicity Packard spoke eloquently about her work on the television crime series *Underbelly*, and the kinds of decisions that she was required to make when adapting the 'messy reality' of real-life crime into the aesthetically pleasing format of a series drama for a commercial television network with a mainstream audience. Packard had read up on genre theory, knew the history of the 'true-crime' television drama in Australia, and exactly where *Underbelly* would sit in relation to this sub-genre of crime. She was also well aware of the aesthetic demands of a three-act narrative structure, the need for a cause-and-effect series of actions and consistent characters, when the real-life people were anything but consistent in either character or action. 'In writing *Underbelly*,' she said, 'I was seeking to represent chaos – but I was seeking to do so within the framework of generic forms that resist precisely the sort of chaos *Underbelly* seeks to represent' (Packard 2012). The kind of chaos, one may add, which writer and producer David Simon, working within the niche environment of the HBO cable channel in the United States, was more willing to embrace, although, as Amanda Klein has demonstrated, *The Wire* was not without its melodramatic strategies of engagement and artful structures (Klein 2009: 177).

In terms of what eventually went to air in the first *Underbelly* series, Packard once again demonstrated the contingent nature of television production in her account of how those working on the show were initially informed that they were in the business of creating a post-9.30pm watershed show for a more 'mature' audience (à la *Sopranos*). However, after the network chiefs had viewed the first episodes, and come to the conclusion that they had a potential ratings winner on their hands, they decided to pull the timeslot back to 8.30pm, which subsequently had an affect on the writers' choices about the levels of sex and violence that could be shown. Ironically, such industry self-regulation appears somewhat futile in an era of DVD sales and downloads when those who are determined can easily obtain access to that that they are denied. And indeed there was an extensive interstate trade in DVD copies and illegal downloads of *Underbelly* after the first series was banned in the State of Victoria because of a court injunction relating to a case then current in the courts. The relationship of *Underbelly* to the 'real' world of crime brings us to another key theme in the history of the television crime drama: the representation of law and order issues.

Changing attitudes to police and policing

John Ellis has argued that television in all its multiple modes of story-telling is a medium that enables viewers to 'work through' the major public and private concerns of their society (Ellis 2000: 74). Given that 'crime' was a major feature of television story-telling right from the start, the crime drama is thus a particularly productive site for exploring just what has been worked through and when. Taking the long view, it is then tempting to engage in broad-brush periodisations about what kinds of crime get depicted and how, starting with the post-war period in which home burglary and the problem of juvenile delinquency may be supposed to dominate even as cold-war anxieties are played out in the spy thriller and its spoofs. The 1960s would then be identified as the era of armed robbery and gangs, the 1970s as that of drugs, drop-outs, and rape, the 1980s as an era of white collar crime, and the 1990s as the period dominated by the serial killer and the paedophile with science increasingly coming to the rescue. Post 9/11 it would be possible to argue that crime has gone global in an era of terrorism and people-smuggling at the same time as there is an increasing sympathy and/or fascination with those who find themselves on the wrong side of the law, leading to a spate of crime drama series in which the focus is on the perpetrator and their motivations with *The Sopranos*, *Dexter*, *Breaking Bad* (AMC, 2008–13), and *Sons of Anarchy* (FX, 2008–) as a series of loosely linked sub-generic offshoots.

Such periodisation, however, is wildly impressionistic and even after watching so much television crime for the purpose of this book, it is hard to make general claims about a genre that has developed in such an unpredictable fashion and where the success of one series or character inevitably spawns a copycat in a move that may have more to do with ratings and entertainment values than societal concerns about crime and punishment. Nevertheless, it is clear that the television crime drama has frequently touched on sensitive nerves at particular moments in different contexts. Witness, for example, the preoccupation with police corruption in Britain during the 1970s as evident in *The Sweeney*, which came to a head in G. F. Newman's *Law and Order*, or the issue of institutional misogyny addressed obliquely and then head-on in shows such as *Cagney and Lacey* and *Prime Suspect*; or the fraught relationship between sexuality and crime in *Law & Order: SVU*; or the portrayal of global politics during the second season of *The Killing* in which the role of foreign troops in Afghanistan was brought into sharp focus at a moment in 'real life' when a former commander of the Australian forces in that region suggested that the loss of his soldiers' lives was simply 'not worth it' (Thompson n.d.). The television crime drama, even when it is at its most playful, as in the case of *Moonlighting* or *Dexter*, routinely seeks out the fault lines of a society in order to reveal the fissures through the refracted lens of fiction.

The pleasures of the text

At the other end of the spectrum there are those crime dramas in which the focus is not so much on the social causes of crime as the skills of the sleuth who is conducting the investigation. Sometimes the sleuth will have specialist knowledge, sometimes they will have only their own ingenuity, but they will always be entertaining to watch. Here the viewer delights in the game, the process of deduction, the performance of genius, or its opposite, in the detection of a crime that will inevitably be 'solved'.

In almost all cases, what the crime drama series offers is the satisfaction of an epistemological quest. At the end of this quest for knowledge, the viewer will know not just who, but also how and why events have unfolded as they have and who or what to blame, even if the larger problem they represent (that may well be society itself) cannot be solved. Finally, it's all about knowledge – who has it and who doesn't – with the viewer privy to the kinds of information that those in the midst of the drama so often lack. Resolution, however, even when it does occur, may only be temporary and contingent, since the problem with crime is that it will not go away. And so we return, over and over again, to the scene of our anxiety, our fascination, and our pleasure, in search of the 'new' in a genre that we expect will continue to surprise, divert, confront, and entertain us while telling us something about ourselves and the world in which we live.

Note

1. See: www.amctv.com/newsletter-subscription

Bibliography

Allen, Michael (ed.) (2007), *Reading CSI: Crime TV under the Microscope*, London/New York: I. B. Tauris.

Ang, Ien (1985), *Watching Dallas: Soap Opera and the Melodramatic Imagination*, London/New York: Methuen.

Ang, Ien, Hawkins, Gay, and Dabboussy, Lamia (2008), *The SBS Story: The Challenge of Cultural Diversity*, Sydney: University of New South Wales.

Angelini, Sergio (n.d.), *The Gentle Touch*, London: BFI Screenonline.

Anonymous (n.d.a), The Newgate Calendar, www.exclassics.com/newgate/ngintro.htm [accessed 14 January 2014].

Anonymous (n.d.b), 'Around the World with Barnaby', http://midsomermurders.org/midsomerworld.htm [accessed 6 September 2012].

Anonymous (n.d.c), 'Jack Webb Memorial Page', www.qsl.net/kg6ejj/memorial.htm [accessed 28 September 2012].

Anonymous (n.d.d), *Missing-Episodes.Com: The British TV Missing Episodes Index*, www.btinternet.com/~m.brown1/zcars.htm [accessed 17 November 2011].

Anonymous (n.d.e), *The Works of Troy Kennedy Martin – Screenwriter*, h2g2, 24 September 2009, http://h2g2.com/edited_entry/A17526008 [accessed 6 November 2011].

Anonymous (n.d.f.), http://unrealityshout.com/blogs/ashes-ashes-series-finale-series-3-episode-8-episode-review [accessed 8 December 2011].

Anonymous (n.d.g.), www.businessdictionary.com/definition/branding.html [accessed 5 March 2013].

(Anonymous n.d.h), *The Case-Book of Sherlock Holmes*, Imdb, www.imdb.com/title/tt0098765 [accessed 20 July 2012].

(Anonymous n.d.i), *The Original Illustrated 'Strand' Sherlock Holmes*, http://books.google.co.uk/books/about/The_Original_Illustrated_Strand_Sherlock.html?id=Fq1uKmT02aMC [accessed 20 July 2012].

(Anonymous n.d.j), *'Dalgliesh'*, *TV Rage*, www.tvrage.com/shows/id-3210/episode_list/1 [accessed 24 July 2012].

(Anonymous n.d.k), *Radio Times*, 30 August–5 September 2008.

(Anonymous n.d.k), *Inspector Morse*, BFI Film and TV Database, http://ftvdb.bfi.org.uk/sift/series/9084 [accessed 25 July 2012].

(Anonymous n.d.l), *Inspector Morse*, BFI Film and TV Database, http://ftvdb. bfi.org.uk/sift/series/9084 [accessed 25 July 2012].

(Anonymous n.d.m), http://en.wikipedia.org/wiki/Yellow_Bird_%28company %29 [accessed 25 July 2012].

(Anonymous n.d.n), www.barb.co.uk/report/weeklyTopProgrammes/? [accessed 25 July 2012].

(Anonymous n.d.o), www.bafta.org/awards-database.html?sq=Wallander [accessed 26 July 2012].

(Anonymous n.d.p), www.guardian.co.uk/tv-and-radio/tvandradioblog/2012/ jul/23/wallander-cant-get-enough?newsfeed=true [accessed 25 July 2012].

Anonymous (n.d.q), www.ianrankin.net.

Anonymous (n.d.r), *How Stuff Works*, http://science.howstuffworks.com/ forensic-lab-technique1.htm [accessed 6 August 2012].

Anonymous (n.d.s), *Wojeck*, *The Classic TV Archive*, http://ctva.biz/Canada/ Wojeck.htm [accessed 17 January 2014].

Anonymous (n.d.t), *The Enigma Files*, www.imdb.com/title/tt0147763 [accessed 10 August 2012].

Anonymous (n.d.u), 'official' Agatha Christie website, *The Secret Adversary*, http://uk.agathachristie.com/christies-work/detectives-and-sidekicks/tom my-and-tuppence [accessed 12 June 2012].

Anonymous (n.d.v), 'Australian Sopranos *Underbelly* to Air on CBS Drama in the UK', http://article.wn.com/view/2012/08/31/Australian_Sopranos_ Underbelly_to_air_on_CBS_Drama_in_UK [accessed 26 September 2012].

Anonymous (n.d.w), 'When TV Network Changes Name, Look Close', CNN.com/Entertainment, http://web.archive.org/web/20080417043745/ http://www.cnn.com/2003/SHOWBIZ/TV/03/03/networkacronyms.ap [accessed 26 September 2012].

Anonymous (n.d.x), www.bafta.org/television/awards/winners-2011,2394,BA. html#jump7 [accessed 26 September 2012].

Anonymous (2006), 'Lynda La Plante's Fury over Alcoholic Final Act for *Prime Suspect*', *Mail Online*, www.dailymail.co.uk/tvshowbiz/article-411694/ Lynda-La-Plantes-fury-alcoholic-final-act-Prime-Suspect.html [accessed 20 January 2014].

Anonymous (2009), 'The Wire: Arguably the Greatest Television Programme Ever Made', *The Telegraph*, 2 April, www.telegraph.co.uk/news/uknews/50 95500/The-Wire-arguably-the-greatest-television-programme-ever-made. html [accessed 17 January 2014].

Anonymous (2011a), '*Midsomer Murders* Producer Suspended Over Race Row', *BBC News*, *Entertainment and Arts*, 15 March, www.bbc.co.uk/news/ uk-12741847 [accessed 6 September 2012].

Anonymous (2011b), 'Suranne: "It's the Cagney and Lacey of Manchester"', *What's on TV*, 23 May, www.whatsontv.co.uk/scott-and-bailey/news/ suranne-its-the-cagney-lacey-of-manchester [accessed 20 January 2014].

Armstrong, Stephen (2008), 'Making Mischief is a Good Thing', *The Guardian*,

27 October, www.guardian.co.uk/media/2008/oct/27/bbc [accessed 25 July 2012].

Bradbury, Sean (2012) 'Hillsborough Independent Panel Report', *Liverpool Echo*, 18 September, www.liverpoolecho.co.uk/2012/09/18/hillsborough-independent-panel-report-liverpool-echo-readers-give-their-verdict-1002 52-31860576 [accessed 20 September].

Barnes, Alan (2011), *Sherlock Holmes on Screen: The Complete Film and TV History*, London: Titan Books.

Battles, Kathleen (2010), *Calling All Cars: Radio Dragnets and the Technology of Policing*, Minneapolis: University of Minnesota Press.

Beeler, Stan (2010), 'From Silver Bullets to Duct Tape: Dexter versus the Traditional Vigilante Hero', in F. Douglas Howard (ed.), *Dexter: Investigating Cutting Edge Television*, London/New York: I. B. Tauris, pp. 221–30.

BFI Screen Online (n.d.), 'Verity Lambert', www.screenonline.org.uk/people/id/550923/index.html [accessed 11 May 2012].

Bianco, Robert (2008), 'Too Few Were Plugged In, but HBO's *The Wire* was Electric', *USA Today*, 3 March, http://usatoday30.usatoday.com/life/television/news/2008-03-05-the-wire_N.htm [accessed 23 February 2013].

Bibel, Sara (2012), '*CSI: Crime Scene Investigation* is the Most-Watched Show in the world', *TV by the Numbers*, 14 June, http://tvbythenumbers.zap2it.com/2012/06/14/csi-crime-scene-investigation-is-the-most-watched-show-in-the-world-2/138212 [accessed 17 January 2014].

Bignell, Jonathan (2007), 'Seeing and Knowing: Reflexivity and Quality', in Kim Akass and Janet McCabe (eds), *Quality TV: Contemporary American Television and Beyond*, London: I. B. Tauris, pp. 158–70.

Bohm, Ulrike (n.d.), 'Dorothy La Sayers's Lord Peter Whimsey and Harriet Vane Features (BBC)', *Themis-Athena Review*, www.themisathena.info/movies/wimseyvane.html [accessed 20 January 2014].

Bonner, Frances (2003), *Ordinary Television: Analysing Popular TV*, London: Sage.

Bonner, Frances (2011), *Personality Presenters: Televisions Intermediaries with Viewers*, Farnham: Ashgate Publishing.

Brew, Simon (n.d.), www.denofgeek.com/tv/ashes-to-ashes/20452/the-significance-of-the-final-shot-of-ashes-to-ashes [accessed 12 February 2013].

Brickell, Wendy (2008), 'Is It the *CSI* Effect Or Do We Just Distrust Juries', *Criminal Justice*, 23 (2): 10–17.

Briggs, Asa (1995), *The History of Broadcasting in the United Kingdom: Volume 5: Competition*, Oxford: Oxford University Press.

Bronsons, Eric (2012), *The Girl with the Dragon Tattoo and Philosophy*, Hoboken: John Wiley and Sons.

Brown, Simon and Abbott, Stacey (2010), 'The Art of Sp(l)atter: Body Horror in *Dexter*', in Douglas Howard (ed.), *Dexter: Investigating Cutting Edge Television*, London/New York: I. B. Tauris, pp. 205–20.

Brunsdon, Charlotte (1990a), 'Television Aesthetics and Audiences', in

Patricia Mellencamp (ed.), *Logics of Television: Essays in Cultural Criticism*, Bloomington: Indiana University Press, pp. 59–72.

Brunsdon, Charlotte (1990b), 'Problems with Quality', *Screen*, 31: 67–90.

Brunsdon, Charlotte (1998), 'Structure of Anxiety: Recent British Television Crime Fiction', *Screen*, 39 (3): 223–43.

Brunsdon, Charlotte (2000), 'The Structure of Anxiety: Recent British Television Crime Drama', in Edward Buscombe (ed.), *British Television: A Reader*, Oxford: Oxford University Press, pp. 195–217.

Brunsdon, Charlotte (2010), *Law and Order*, London: British Film Institute/ Palgrave Macmillan.

Brunsdon, Charlotte (2012), 'Television Crime Series: "Women Police and Fuddy-Duddy Feminism"', *Feminist Media Studies* 1 (1): 1–20.

Burns, Rex (1999), 'Hard-boiled Fiction' in Rosemary Herbert (ed.), *The Oxford Companion to Film and Mystery Writing*, New York/Oxford: Oxford University Press, pp. 199-201.

Buscombe, Ed (1976), 'The Sweeney – Better Than Nothing?', *Screen Education* 20: 66–9.

Butler, Jeremy (2012), *Television: Critical Methods and Applications*, New York: Routledge.

Buxton, David (1990), *From the Avengers to Miami Vice: Form and Ideology in the TV Series*, Manchester: Manchester University Press.

Caldwell, John Thornton (1995), *Televisuality: Style, Crisis and Authority in American Television*, New Brunswick, NJ: Rutgers University Press.

Caldwell, John Thornton (2005), 'Welcome to the Viral Future of Cinema (Television)', *Cinema Journal* 45(1): 90–7.

Caldwell, John Thornton (2008), *Production Culture: Industrial Reflexivity and Critical Practice in Film and Television*, Durham/London: Duke University Press.

Carrabine, Eamonn (2008), *Crime Culture and the Media*, Cambridge: Polity Press.

Cawelti, John (1976), *Adventure, Mystery, and Romance: Formula Stories as Art and Popular Culture*, Chicago/London: University of Chicago Press.

Chandler, Raymond (1946), 'The Simple Art of Murder', in Howard Haycraft (ed.), *The Art of the Mystery Story*, New York: Grosse and Dunlap, pp. 222–37.

Chapman, James (2002), *Saints and Avengers: British Adventure Series of the 1960s*, London/New York: I. B. Tauris.

Chisum, Jerry W. (2012), 'Foreword to the Third Edition', in Brent E. Turvey (ed.), *A History of Criminal Profiling: An Introduction to Behavioural Evidence Analysis* (4th edn), Burlington: Academic Press, pp. xi–xv.

Churchill, Carolyn (2008), 'Branagh is Given Lead Role in 6m pound BBC Scotland Adaptation of Hit Crime Novels', *The Herald*, 11 January, www. heraldscotland.com/branagh-is-given-lead-role-in-pound-6m-bbc-scotland-adaptation-of-hit-crime-novels-1.872386 [accessed 6 December 2013].

Christie, Agatha (1950), *A Murder is Announced*, London: Collins Crime Club.

Clarke, A. (1983), 'Holding the Blue Lamp: Television and the Police in Britain', *Crime and Social Justice*, 19: 44–51.

Clarke, A. (1986), 'This is Not the Boy Scouts: Television Police Series and Definitions of Law and Order', in T. Bennett, C. Mercer, and J. Woollacott (eds), *Popular Culture and Social Relations*, Milton Keynes: Open University Press, pp. 291–32.

Cohen, Steven and Hark, Ina Rae (eds) (1993), *Screening the Male: Exploring Masculinities in Hollywood Cinema*, London/New York: Routledge.

Collins, Max Allen and John Javna (1988), *The Best of Crime and Detective TV*, New York: Harmony Books.

Conan Doyle, Arthur (1967a [1883]), 'The Speckled Band', in William Baring-Gould (ed.), *The Annotated Sherlock Holmes*, Volume 1, New York: Clarkson N. Potter, Inc., pp. 243–62.

Conan Doyle, Arthur (1967b [1883]), 'A Study in Scarlet', in William Baring-Gould (ed.), *The Annotated Sherlock Holmes, Volume 1*, New York: Clarkson N. Potter, Inc., pp. 143–234.

Cooke, Lez (2001), 'The Police Series', in Glen Creeber (ed.), *The Television Genre Book*, London: British Film Institute, pp. 19–23.

Cooke, Lez (2003), *British Television Drama: A History*, London: British Film Institute.

Cosmopolitan (1965–), New York: Hearst Corporation.

Coveney, Michael (2010), 'Alan Plater Obituary', *The Guardian*, 25 June, www.theguardian.com/stage/2010/jun/25/alan-plater-obituary [accessed 16 January 2014].

Craven, Peter (n.d.), 'Scandinavia's Crime Goldmine', *The Drum Opinion*, www.abc.net.au/unleashed/34346.html [accessed 26 September 2012].

Creeber, G. (2001), *The Television Genre Book*, London: British Film Institute.

Creeber, Glen (2002), 'Old Sleuth or New Man? Investigations into Rape, Murder and Masculinity in *Cracker* (1993–1996)', *Continuum: Journal of Media & Cultural Studies* 16 (2): 169–83.

Creeber, Glen (2003), 'The Origins of Public Service Broadcasting (British Television before the War)', in Michele Hilmes (ed.), *The Television History Book*, London: British Film Institute, pp. 22–4.

Creeber, Glen (2004), 'Prime Suspect', in Glen Creeber (ed.), *Fifty Key Television Programmes* London: Edward Arnold Publishers Ltd, pp. 159–63.

Creeber, Glen (ed.) (2004), *Fifty Key Television Programs*, London: Edward Arnold Publishers Ltd.

Cross, Neil (2010), 'Introducing *Luther* – with Love to Inspector Columbo', 20 April, www.bbc.co.uk/blogs/tv/2010/04/introducing-luther-with-love-t.shtml [accessed 22 August 2012].

Curtis, Hilary (1999), 'It's a Cop Out', *The Guardian*, 8 October.

D'Acci, Julie (1994), *Defining Women: Television and the Case of Cagney and Lacey*, Chapel Hill/London: University of North Carolina Press.

Dale, David (2011), 'No Bones About It, Got to Love a Good Murder', *The Sydney Morning Herald*, 26–7 February.

Dallas, Sam (2012), 'Foxtel Commissions New Prisoner Series, titled Wentworth', if.com.au, 5 March, http://if.com.au/2012/03/05/article/Foxtel-commissions-new-Prisoner-series-titled-Wentworth/BYJXEEGD WR.html [accessed 20 March 2013].

Davis, Helen (2001), 'Inspector Morse and the Business of Crime', Television and New Media 2(2): 133–48.

De Quincey, Thomas (1949 [1827]), Selected Writings of Thomas De Quincey, New York: The Modern Library.

Den of Geek, (2012), 'Stephen Moffat and Mark Gattis Interview', 21 July, www.denofgeek.com/tv/sherlock/20536/steven-moffat-and-mark-gatiss-int erview-sherlock [last accessed 21 July 2012].

Dennington, John and Tulloch, John (1976), 'Cops, Consensus and Ideology', Screen Education 20 (autumn): 37–46.

Deusch, Sarah and Gray Cavender (2008), 'CSI and Forensic Realism', Journal of Criminal Justice and Popular Culture 15 (1): 34–53.

Diviny, Clare (2007), Performances of Wounded Masculinity in Cracker (MA thesis, University of Melbourne).

Downey, Christine (2007), 'Life on Mars, or How the Breaking of Genre Rules Revitalises the Crime Fiction Tradition', Crimeculture, www.crimeculture. com/Contents/Crimeculture.html [accessed 6 December 2013].

Drummond, Phillip (1976), 'Structural and Narrative Constraints and Strategies in "The Sweeney"', Screen Education 20(autumn): 15–33.

Duguid, Mark (2009), Cracker, London: British Film Institute/Palgrave Macmillan.

Duschinsky, Robbie (2013), 'Childhood, Responsibility and the Liberal Loophole: Replaying the Sex-Wars in Debates on Sexualisation', Sociological Research Online 18 (2): 1–11, www.socresonline.org.uk/18/2/7.html [accessed 6 December 2013].

Dyer, Gillian (1987), 'Women and Television: An Overview', in Helen Baehr and Gillian Dyer (eds), Boxed In: Women and Television, London: Pandora, pp. 6–16.

Ellis, John (2000), Seeing Things: Television in the Age of Uncertainty, London/New York: I. B. Tauris.

Eschholz, Sarah, Mallard, Matthew, and Flynn, Stacey (2004), 'Images of Prime Time Justice: A Content Analysis of "NYPD" and "Law and Order"', Journal of Criminal Justice and Popular Culture 10 (3): 61–180.

Feuer, Jane (1995), Seeing through the Eighties: Television and Reaganism, Durham, NC/London: Duke University Press.

Feuer, Jane (2007), 'HBO and the Concept of Quality TV', in Kim Akass and Janet McCabe (eds), Quality TV: Contemporary American Television and Beyond, London: I. B. Tauris, pp. 145–57.

Fiske, John (1987), Television Culture, London/New York: Methuen.

Flanders, Judith (2011), The Invention of Murder: How the Victorians Revelled in Death and Detection and Created Modern Crime, London: Harper Press.

Flitterman, S. (1985), 'Thighs and Whiskers: The Fascination of *Magnum P.I.*', *Screen* 26 (2): 42–58.

Francis, James Jr (2010), 'The Lighter Side of Death: *Dexter* as Comedy', in Douglas Howard (ed.), *Dexter: Investigating Cutting Edge Television*, London/New York: I. B. Tauris, pp. 175–88.

Furby, Jacqueline (2007), 'Interesting Times: The Demands *24*'s Real-time Format Makes on its Audience', in Steven Peacock (ed), *Reading 24: TV Against the Clock*, London/New York: I. B. Tauris, pp. 59–70.

Gardner, Julie and Parker Claire (2012), 'In Conversation', in Stephen Lacey and Ruth McElroy (eds), *Life on Mars: From Manchester to New York*, Cardiff: University of Wales Press, pp. 169–83.

Gilbert, Gerard (2011), 'Ten People Who Changed the World: Sophie Gråbol, Star of *The Killing*', *The Independent*, 25 March, www.independent.co.uk/arts-entertainment/tv/features/ten-people-who-changed-the-world-sofie-grabol-star-of-the-killing-6282315.html [accessed 29 March 2013].

Gitlin, Todd (1983), *Inside Prime Time*, New York: Pantheon Books.

Glover, David (2003), 'The Thriller', in Martin Priestman (ed.), *The Cambridge Companion to Crime Fiction*, Cambridge: Cambridge University Press, pp. 135–53.

Goode, Ian (2007), 'CSI: Crime Scene Investigation: The Fifth Channel and "America's Fines"', in Kim Akass and Janet McCabe (eds), *Quality TV: Contemporary American Television and Beyond*, London: I. B. Tauris, pp. 118–28.

Gorman, Bill (2010), '*CSI: Crime Scene Investigation* is the Most Watched Show in the World!', *TV By The Numbers*, 11 June, http://tvbythenumbers.zap2it.com/2010/06/11/csi-crime-scene-investigation-is-the-most-watched-show-in-the-world/53833 [accessed 24 April 2012].

Gough-Yates, Anna (2001), 'Angels in Chains? Feminism, Femininity and Consumer Culture in *Charlie's Angels*', in Bill Osgerby and Anna Gough-Yates (eds), *Action TV: Tough Guys, Smooth Operators and Foxy Chicks*, London: Routledge, pp. 83–99.

Gregg, Melissa and Wilson, Jason (2010), '*Underbelly*: True Crime and the Cultural Economy of Infamy', *Continuum: Journal of Media and Cultural Studies*, 24 (3): 411–27.

Gussow, Mel (1995), 'Jeremy Brett, an Unnerving Holmes, is Dead at 59', *The New York Times*, 14 September, www.nytimes.com/1995/09/14/obitu aries/jeremy-brett-an-unnerving-holmes-is-dead-at-59.html [accessed 20 October 2012].

Hallam, Julia, (2007), 'Independent Women: Creating TV Drama in the UK in the 1990s', *Critical Studies in Television* 2 (1): 18–34.

Hammond, Michael and Mazdon, Lucy (eds) (2005), *The Contemporary Television Series*, Edinburgh: Edinburgh University Press.

Harrington, Ellen Burton (2007), 'Nation, Identity and the Fascination with Forensic Science in Sherlock Holmes and *CSI*', *International Journal of Cultural Studies* 10 (3): 365–82.

Hill, Annette (2000), 'Crime and Crisis: British Reality Television in Action', in Ed Buscome (ed.), *British Television: A Reader*, Oxford: Oxford University Press, pp. 218–34.

Hills, Matt and Luther, Amy (2007), 'Investigating *CSI* Television Fandom: Fans' Textual Path Through the Franchise', M. Allen (ed.), *Reading CSI: Crime Television Under the Microscope*, London: I. B. Tauris, pp. 208–21.

Holmes, Su (2008), *Entertaining Television: The BBC and Popular Culture in the 1950s*, Manchester: Manchester University Press.

Horton, Donald and Wohl, Richard (2006 [1956]), 'Mass Communication and Para-Social Interaction: Intimacy at a Distance', *Participations* 3 (1), May, www. participations.org/volume%203/issue%201/3_01_hortonwohl.htm [accessed 17 September 2012].

Howard, Douglas L. (ed.) (2010), *Dexter: Investigating Cutting Edge Television*, London/New York: I. B. Tauris.

Hurd, G. (1976), 'The Sweeney: Contradiction and Coherence', *Screen Education*, 20: 47–53.

James, P. D. (1972), *An Unsuitable Job for a Woman*, London: Faber and Faber.

Jacobs, Jason (2004), '*Charlie's Angels*', in Glen Creeber (ed.), *Fifty Key Television Programs*, London: Edward Arnold Publishers Ltd, pp. 45–9.

Jarossi, Robin (2008), 'Branagh is Swedish Cop Wallander, British/Australian TV@suite 101', http://suite101.com/article/kenneth-branagh-stars-as-swed ish-cop-wallander-a68811 [accessed 25 July 2012].

Jennings, Ros (2004), '*Cagney and Lacey*', in Glen Creeber (ed.), *Fifty Key Television Programs*, London: Edward Arnold Publishers Ltd, pp. 36–9.

Jermyn, Deborah (2003), 'Women with a Mission: Lynda La Plante, DCI Jane Tennison and the Reconfiguration of TV Crime Drama', *International Journal of Cultural Studies* 6 (1): 46–63.

Jermyn, Deborah (1997), 'Body Matters: Realism, Specactle and the Corpse in *CSI*', in M Allen (ed.), *Reading CSI: Crime Television Under the Microscope*, London: I. B. Tauris, pp. 79–89.

Jermyn, Deborah (2007), 'Reasons to Split Up: Interactivity, Realism and the Multiple-image Screen in *24*', in Steven Peacock (ed.), *Reading 24: TV against the Clock*, London/New York: I. B. Tauris, pp. 49–57.

Jermyn, Deborah (2010), *Prime Suspect*, London: British Film Institute/ Palgrave Macmillan.

Johnson, Catherine (2005), 'Quality/Cult Television: *The X-Files* and Television History', in Michael Hammond and Lucy Mazdon (eds), *The Contemporary Television Series*, Edinburgh: Edinburgh University Press, pp. 57–71.

Kaye, Peter (2011) 'Writing Music for Quality TV: An Interview with W.G. 'Snuffy' Walden', in Janet McCabe and Kim Akass (eds), *Quality TV: Contemporary American Television and Beyond*, London and New York: I. B. Tauris, pp. 221–7.

Kennedy Martin, Troy (1964), 'Television Drama – Is This the Way Ahead?', *Screenwriter* 15: 18–25.

Kidd-Hewitt, David and Osborne, Richard (eds) (1995), *Crime and the Media: The Post-modern Spectacle*, London: Pluto.

King, Donna and Smith, Carrie Lee (eds) (2012), *Men Who Hate Women and Women Who Kick Their Asses*, Nashville: Vanderbilt University Press.

Klein, Amanda Ann (2009), '"The Dickensian Aspect": Melodrama, Viewer Engagement, and the Socially Conscious Text', in Tiffany Potter and C. W. Marshall (eds), *The Wire: Urban Decay and American Television*, New York: Continuum, pp. 177–89.

Lacey, Stephen and McElroy, Ruth (eds) (2012), *Life on Mars: From Manchester to New York*, Cardiff: University of Wales Press.

Laing, Stuart (1990), 'Banging in Some Reality: The Original *Z Cars*', in John Corner (ed.), *Popular Television in Britain: Studies in Cultural History*, London: BFI Publishing, pp. 125–44.

Lavery, David (2002), *This Thing of Ours: Investigating the Sopranos*, New York: Columbia Press, 2002.

Lavery, David (2004a), 'The Sopranos', in Glen Creeber (ed.), *Fifty Key Television Programs*, London: Edward Arnold Publishers Ltd, pp. 188–92.

Lavery, David (2004b), 'The X-Files', in Glen Creeber (ed.), *Fifty Key Television Programs*, London: Edward Arnold Publishers Ltd, pp. 242–6.

Lavery, David (2004c), 'Twin Peaks', in Glen Creeber (ed.), *Fifty Key Television Programs*, London: Edward Arnold Publishers Ltd, pp. 222–6.

Lavery, David (2010), '"Serial" Killer: *Dexter*'s Narrative Strategies', in Douglas Howard (ed.), *Dexter: Investigating Cutting Edge Television*, London: I. B. Tauris, pp. 43–8.

Lavery, David (2012), 'The Emigration of *Life on Mars*: Sam and Gene do America', in Stephen Lacey and Ruth McElroy (eds), *Life on Mars: From Manchester to New York*, Cardiff: University of Wales Press, pp. 145–52.

Lavery, David, (ed.) (1995), *Full of Secrets: Critical Approaches to Twin Peaks*, Michigan: Wayne State University.

Leader, Michael (2010), 'Steven Moffat and Mark Gattis Interview: Sherlock', *Den of Geek*, 21 July, www.denofgeek.com/tv/sherlock/20536/steven-mof fat-and-mark-gatiss-interview-sherlock [accessed 22 July 2012].

Lichter, L. and Lichter, S. (1983), *Prime Time Crime*. Washington, D. C.: Media Institute.

Luhr, William (2012), *Film Noir*, Malden/Oxford: Wiley-Blackwell.

Lury, Karen (2005), *Interpreting Television*, London: Hodder Arnold.

McAleer, John (1999), 'Freeman, Richard Austin', in Rosemary Herbert (ed.), *The Oxford Companion to Crime and Mystery Writing*, Oxford: Oxford University Press, pp. 168–9.

McCabe, Janet (2007), '"Mac's Melancholia: Scripting Trauma, 9/11 and Bodily Absence in *CSI: NY*', in M. Allen (ed.), *Reading CSI: Crime Television under the Microscope*, London: I. B. Tauris, pp. 167–80.

McCabe, Janet and Akass, Kim (2011), *Quality TV: Contemporary American Television and Beyond*, London/New York: I. B. Tauris.

McKee, Alan (2001), *Australian Television: A Genealogy of Great Moments*, Oxford: Oxford University Press.

Marc, David (1984), *Demographic Vistas: Television in American Culture*, Philadelphia: University of Philadelphia Press.

Marshall, C. W. and Potter, Tiffany (2009), '"I am the American Dream": Modern Urban Tragedy and the Borders of Fiction', in Tiffany Potter and C. W. Marshall (eds), *The Wire: Urban Decay and American Television*, New York/London: Continuum, pp. 1–14.

Martin, Philip (2008), 'On Location: Wallander', *Broadcast*, 26 November, www.broadcastnow.co.uk/on-location-wallander/1935374.article [accessed 24 July 2012].

Mayer, Vicki, Manks, Miranada J., and Caldwell, John T. (eds) (2009), *Production Studies: Cultural Studies of Media Industries*, New York/London: Routledge.

Medhurst, Jamie (2006), "Case Study: A (Very) Brief History of Television', in Glen Creeber (ed.), *Tele-visions: An Introduction to Studying Television*, London: British Film Institute, pp. 115–23.

Miller, Toby (1997), *The Avengers*, London: British Film Institute.

Miller, Toby (2001), 'The Action Series', in Glenn Creeber (ed.), *The Television Genre Book*, London: British Film Institute, pp. 17–18.

Mills, Brett (2009), *The Sitcom*, Edinburgh: Edinburgh University Press.

Mills, Brett (2012), '"American Remake – Shudder": Online Debates about *Life on Mars* and British-ness', in Stephen Lacey and Ruth McElroy (eds), *Life on Mars: From Manchester to New York*, Cardiff: University of Wales Press, pp. 133–44.

Mittell, Jason (2004), *Genre and Television: From Cop Shows to Cartoons in American Culture*, London/New York: Routledge.

Mittell, Jason (2010), *Television and American Culture*, New York/Oxford: Oxford University Press.

Mittell, Jason (2012), *Complex TV: The Poetics of Contemporary Storytelling*, Media Commons Press, http://mcpress.media-commons.org/complextelevision/about [accessed 20 January 2014].

Mizejewski, Linda (2004), *Hardboiled & High Heeled: The Woman Detective in Popular Culture*, New York: Routledge.

Modleski, Tania (1997), 'The Search for Tomorrow in Today's Soap Operas: Notes on a Feminine Narrative Form', in Charlotte Brunsdon, Julie D'Acci, and Lynn Spiegel (eds), *Feminist Television Criticism: A Reader*, Oxford: Clarendon Press, pp. 36–47.

Ms (1971–), Arlington: Feminist Majority Foundation.

Mulvey, Laura (1975), 'Visual Pleasure and Narrative Cinema', *Screen* 154 (3): 6–8.

Mulvey, Laura (1981), 'Afterthoughts on "Visual Pleasure and Narrative Cinema" Inspired by King Vidor's *Duel in the Sun*', *Framework* 15(17): 12–15.

Musser, Charles (1991), *Before the Nickelodeon: Edwin S. Porter and the Edison Manufacturing Company*, Berkeley: University of California Press.

Nannicelli, Ted (2009), 'It's All Connected: Televisual Narrative Complexity', in Tiffany Potter and C. W. Marshall (eds), *The Wire: Urban Decay and American Television*, New York: Continuum, pp. 177–89.

Neale, Steve (1980), *Genre*, London: British Film Institute.

Neale, Steve (2001), 'Introduction: What is Genre?', in G. Creeber (ed.), *The Television Genre Book*, London: British Film Institute, pp. 1–3.

Negra Diane (2009), *What a Girl Wants: Fantasizing the Reclamation of the Self in Postfeminism*, London/New York: Routledge.

Nelson, Robin (2006), 'Analysing TV Fiction: How to Study Television Drama', in Glen Creeber (ed.), *Tele-visions: An Introduction to Studying Television*, London: British Film Institute, pp. 74–86.

Nelson, Robin (2004), '*Hill Street Blues*', in Glen Creeber (ed.), *Fifty Key Television Programmes*, London: Edward Arnold Publishers Ltd, pp. 100–4.

Nelson, Robin (1997), *TV Drama in Transition: Forms, Values and Cultural Change*, Basingstoke: Macmillan.

Newcomb, Horace and Alley, Robert S. (1983), *The Producer's Medium: Conversations with the Creators of American TV*, New York/Oxford: Oxford University Press.

Norden, Martin F. (1985), 'The Detective Show', in Brian G. Rose (ed.), *TV Genres: A Handbook and Reference Guide*, Westport: Greenwood Press, pp. 33–55.

Nunn, Heather and Biressi, Anita (2003), '*Silent Witness*: How Forensic Anthropology is Used to Save the World's Toughest Crimes', *Feminist Media Studies* 3 (2): 193–206.

Nussbaum, Emily (2013), 'Deep Dive', *The New Yorker*, 25 March, pp. 106–7.

Nussbaum, Emily (2012), 'Primary Colours', *The New Yorker*, 21 May, pp. 68–70.

O'Day, Marc (2001), 'Of Leather Suits and Kinky Boots: *The Avengers*, Style and Popular Culture', in Bill Osgerby and Anna Gough-Yates (eds), *Action TV: Tough Guys, Smooth Operators and Foxy Chicks*, London: Routledge, pp. 221–35.

O'Regan, Tom (1998), *Australian Television Culture*, St Leonards: Allen and Unwin.

Oliver, Sara (2008), 'Revealed: The Rags-to-Riches Life of the Master Stroyteller who is Now TV's Secret Superstar', *Mail Online*, 8 November, www.dailymail.co.uk/tvshowbiz/article-1084088/Revealed-The-rags-riches-life-master-storyteller-TVs-secret-superstar.html [accessed 17 January 2014].

Osgerby, Bill, Gough-Yates, Anna, and Wells, Marianne (2001), 'The Business of Action: Television History and the Development of the Action TV Series', in Bill Osgerby and Anne Gough-Yates (eds), *Action TV: Tough Guys, Smooth Operators and Foxy Chicks*, London/New York: Routledge, pp. 13–31.

Packard, Felicity (2012), 'Is that What Really Happened?: Uncovering New Modes of Practice and Generic Space in the Writing of *Underbelly*', paper presented to the conference 'Crime, Camera, Action', University of Wollongong, New South Wales, November 2012.

Paterson, Richard (1976), 'The Sweeney: A Euston Films Product', Screen Education 20: 5–14.

Pearson, Roberta (2007), 'Anatomising Gilbert Grissom: The Structure and Function of the Televisual Character', in M. Allen (ed.), Reading CSI: Crime Television Under the Microscope, London: I. B. Tauris, pp. 39–56.

Pearson, Jesse and Andrews, Philip (2009), 'David Simon', Vice, December, www.vice.com/read/david-simon-280-v16n12 [accessed 17 January 2014].

Peirse, Alison (2010), 'In a Lonely Place? Dexter and Film Noir', in Douglas Howard (ed.), Dexter: Investigating Cutting Edge Television, London: I. B. Tauris, pp. 189–204.

Pete Kelly's Blues (n.d.), The Digital Deli Too: Preserving the Golden Age of Radio for a Digital Future, www.digitaldeliftp.com/DigitalDeliToo/dd2jb-Pete-Kellys-Blues.html [accessed 17 January 2014].

Plunkett, John (2009), 'The Wire's David Simon', The Guardian, 28 August, www.guardian.co.uk/media/2009/aug/28/david-simon-the-wire [accessed 23 February 2013].

Poniewozik, James (2009) 'Top 10 TV Shows of the 2000s', Time Entertainment, 17 December, http://entertainment.time.com/2009/12/29/10-best-tv-shows-of-the-decade/slide/the-wire [accessed 17 January 2014].

Potter, Tiffany and Marshall, C. W. (eds) (2009), The Wire: Urban Decay and American Television, New York/London: Continuum.

Rachman, Steven (2008), 'Edgar Allen Poe and the Origins of Mystery Fiction', Strand Magazine, www.strandmag.com/poe.htm [accessed 9 September 2012].

Radner, Hilary (1995), Shopping Around: Feminine Culture and the Pursuit of Pleasure, New York/London: Routledge.

Reijnders, Stijn (2009), 'Watching the Detectives: Inside the Guilty Landscapes of Inspector Morse, Baantjer and Wallander', European Journal of Communication 24 (2): 165–81.

Reijnders, Stijn (2010), 'Places of the Imagination: An Ethnography of the TV Detective Tour', Cultural Geographies 17 (1): 37–52.

Reynolds, Mike (2008), 'Dexter Third Season Finale's a Killer', Multichannel, 16 December, www.multichannel.com/article/160932_Dexter_Third_Season_Finale_s_A_Killer.php [accessed 27 August 2012].

Rhineberger-Dunn, Gayle M., and Nicole E. Rader (2008), 'Constructing Juvenile Delinquency through Crime Drama: An Analysis of Law & Order', Journal of Criminal Justice and Popular Culture 15 (1): 94–116.

Robards, Brooks (1985), 'The Police Show', in Brian G. Rose (ed.), TV Genres: A Handbook and Reference Guide, Westport: Greenwood Press, pp. 11–31.

Robertson, Ed (1995), This is Jim Rockford: The Rockford Files, Los Angeles/London: Pomegranate Press.

Rogers, Margaret (2004), Previously on The Bill: Factors in the Longevity of a British Television Police Series (PhD thesis, Central Queensland University).

Rogers, Margaret (2009), 'The Bill 1984–2009, Production, Redefinition', Refractory: A Journal of Entertainment Media 15, June, http://refractory.

unimelb.edu.au/2009/06/25/the-bill-1984-%E2%80%93-2009-genre-pro
duction-redefinition-margaret-rogers [accessed 2 April 2013].

Rose, Brian G. (ed.) (1985), *TV Genres: A Handbook and Reference Guide*, Westport: Greenwood Press.

Ruhlmann, William (n.d.), 'Cold Case [Original Television Soundtrack}: Review', *All Music*, www.allmusic.com/album/cold-case-original-television-soundtrack-mw0000795513 [accessed 17 January 2014].

Schrader, Paul (1972), 'Notes on Film Noir', in Alain Silver and James Ursini (eds), *Film Noir Reader* (Seventh Limelight Edition), New York: Limelight Editions, pp. 53–63.

Schwarzbaum, Lisa (1993), 'The Jailhouse Rock', *Entertainment Weekly* 159, 26 February, www.ew.com/ew/article/0,,305720,00.html [accessed 15 February 2013].

Schwichtenberg, Cathy (1981), 'A Patriarchal Voice in Heaven', *Jump Cut* 24 (25): 13–16.

Scott, Andrew (2010), '*Law and Order* Officially Cancelled', *Huffington Post*, 13 May, www.huffingtonpost.com/2010/05/13/law-order-canceled-by-nbc_n_575657.html [accessed 2 April 2013].

Scott, Wilbur, S. (2002), 'Introduction', in Wilbur S. Scott (ed.), *The Complete Tales and Poems of Edgar Allan Poe*, Edison: Castle Books, pp. I–XIV.

Sepinwall, Alan (2012), *The Revolution Was Televised: The Cops, Crooks, Slingers and Slayers Who Changed TV Drama Forever*, New York: Simon and Schuster.

Sherwin, Adam (2012) 'Johnny Lee Miller to Play Sherlock Holmes in US series', *The Independent*, 15 February, www.independent.co.uk/arts-entertainment/tv/news/jonny-lee-miller-to-play-shcrlock-holmes-in-us-ser ics-6939158.html [accessed 26 March 2013].

Silverstein, Melissa (2007), 'On Being a Female Writer in the TV Business', *Huff Post Entertainment*, 11 December, www.huffingtonpost/com/melissa-silverstein/on-being- [accessed 11 May 2012].

Simkin, John (n.d.), 'Dashiell Hammett', *Spartacus Educational*, www.sparta cus.schoolnet.co.uk/USAhammett.htm [accessed 7 September 2012].

Simon, David (1991), *Homicide: A Year on the Killing Streets*, Boston: Houghton Mifflin.

Simon, David and Burns, Edward (1997), *The Corner: A Year in the Life of an Inner-City Neighbourhood*, New York: Broadway.

Snauffer, Douglas (2006), *Crime Television*, Westport: Praeger Publishers.

Sparks, Richard (1992), *Television and the Drama of Crime: Moral Tales and the Place of Crime in Public Life*, Buckingham/Philadelphia: Open University Press.

Sparks, Richard (1993), 'Inspector Morse: "The Last Enemy"', in George W. Brundt (ed.), *British Television Drama in the 1980s*, Cambridge: Cambridge University Press, pp. 86–102.

Stout, Rex (1946), 'Watson Was a Woman', in Howard Haycraft (ed.), *The Art of the Mystery Story*, New York: Grosse and Dunlap, pp. 311–18.

Surette, Ray (1998), *Media, Crime and Criminal Justice: Images and Realities* (2nd edn), Belmont: Weste/Wadsworth.

Sussex, Lucy (2010), *Women Writers and Detectives in Nineteenth-century Crime Fiction: The Mothers of the Mystery Genre*, Basingstoke: Palgrave Macmillan.

Sydney-Smith, Susan (2002), *Beyond Dixon of Dock Green: Early British Police Series*, London: I. B. Tauris.

Thomas, Liz (2008), 'Branagh to Star in Harries Crime Drama', www.broad castnow.co.uk http://www.broadcastnow.co.uk/news/multi-platform/news/branagh-to-star-in-harries-crime-drama/456889.article [accessed 25 July 2012].

Thomas, Lyn (1997), 'In Love with *Inspector Morse*: Feminist Subculture and Quality Television', in Charlotte Brunsdon, Julie D'Acci and Lynn Spigel (eds), *Feminist Television Criticism: A Reader*, Oxford: Clarendon Press, pp. 184–204.

Thompson, Geoff (n.d.), 'Is It Worth It? Former Commander Wrestles with Afghan War', ABC News, www.abc.net.au/news/2012-04-16/australian-general-says-afghan-war-not-worth-it/3951728 [accessed 27 September 2012].

Thompson, Robert J. (1996), *Television's Second Golden Age: From Hill Street Blues to ER*, New York: Continuum.

Thompson, Robert J. (2011) 'Preface', in Janet McCabe and Kim Akass (eds), *Quality TV: Contemporary American Television and Beyond*, London/New York: I. B. Tauris, pp. xvii–xx.

Todorov, Tzvetan (1977), *The Poetics of Prose*, Oxford: Blackwell.

Turnbull, Sue (1996), 'Too True: The Representations of True Crime', *Australian Feminist Law Journal* 6: 179–84.

Turnbull, Sue (2002a), '"Nice Dress, Take it Off", Crime, Romance and the Pleasure of the Text', *International Journal of Cultural Studies* 5 (1): 67–82.

Turnbull, Sue (2002b), 'The Mystery of the Missing Discourse: Crime Fiction Readerships and Questions of Taste', in Margaret Thornton (ed.), *Romancing the Tomes*, Oxford: Clarendon Press, pp. 241–56.

Turnbull, Sue (2007), 'The Hook and the Look: *CSI* and the Aesthetics of the Television Crime Series', in M. Allen (ed.), *Reading CSI: Crime Television Under the Microscope*, London: I. B. Tauris, pp. 15–32.

Turnbull, Sue (2008), 'Understanding Disappointment: The Australian Book Lovers and Adaptation', in Martin Barker and Ernest Mathijs (eds), *Watching Lord of the Rings: Tolkien's World Audiences*, New York: Peter Lang Publishers, pp. 103–10.

Turner, Graeme (2001), 'Genre, Format and "Live" Television', in Glenn Creeber (ed.), *The Television Genre Book*, London: British Film Institute, pp. 6–7.

Turvey, Brent E. (2012), *A History of Criminal Profiling: An Introduction to Behavioural Evidence Analysis* (4th edn), Burlington: Academic Press.

van Zoonen, Liesbet (1994), *Feminist Media Studies*, London: Sage.

Vinall, Daryl and Robinson, Shelley (2007), 'The View from the Trainee and the Professional' in M. Allen (ed.), *Reading CSI: Crime Television under the Microscope*, London: I. B. Tauris, pp. 201–7.

Wagner, E. J. (2007), *The Science of Sherlock Holmes*, Oxford: John Wiley and Sons.

Walker, Andrew (2004) 'The Sweeney's Proud History', *BBC News*, 17 May, http://news.bbc.co.uk/2/hi/uk_news/3721695.stm [accessed 16 January 2014].

Wambaugh, Joseph (1971), *The New Centurions*, New York: Little, Brown and Company.

Wambaugh, Joseph (1973), *The Blue Knight*, New York: Little, Brown and Company.

Watson, Stephanie (n.d.), 'How Fingerprinting Works', *How Stuff Works*, http://science.howstuffworks.com/fingerprinting3.htm [accessed 17 January 2013].

Watson, Nicola (2006), *The Literary Tourist: Readers and Places in Romantic and Victorian Britain*, Basingstoke: Palgrave Macmillan.

West, Patrick (2007), 'Horatio Caine's Sunglasses: "Looking" and "Being Looked at" in *CSI: Miami*', in M Allen (ed.), *Reading CSI: Crime Television under the Microscope*, London: I. B. Tauris, pp. 140–52.

Wilder, Gabriel (2012), 'Why We Love Scandi-noir', *Sydney Morning Herald*, 1 October, www.smh.com.au/entertainment/box-seat/why-we-love-scandi noir-20120928-26oqs.html [accessed 20 January 2014].

Williams, Linda Ruth (2005), '*Twin Peaks*: David Lynch and the Serial-thriller Soap', in Michael Hammond and Lucy Mazdon (eds), *The Contemporary Television Series*, Edinburgh: Edinburgh University Press, pp. 37–56.

Willis, Andy (2012), 'Memory Banks Failing!: *Life on Mars* and the Politics of Re-imaging the Police in the Seventies', in Stephen Lacey and Ruth McElroy (eds), *Life on Mars: From Manchester to New York*, Cardiff: University of Wales Press, pp. 57–77.

Wise, Jenny (2009), 'Providing the *CSI* Treatment: Criminal Justice Practitioners and the *CSI* Effect', *Current Issues in Criminal Justice* 21 (3): 383–99.

Zuiker Interview, Paley Centre (2001), Paley Centre, www.youtube.com/watch?v=yw05jkfRxWw&feature=relmfu [accessed 13 April 2012].

Index

Note: illustrations are indicated by page numbers in bold